AGRICULTURAL CHANGE
AND PEASANT CHOICE
IN A THAI VILLAGE

Agricultural Change and Peasant Choice in a Thai Village

MICHAEL MOERMAN

UNIVERSITY OF CALIFORNIA PRESS
Berkeley and Los Angeles
1968

University of California Press
Berkeley and Los Angeles, California

Cambridge University Press
London, England

© 1968 by The Regents of the University of California

Library of Congress Catalog Card Number: 68-11893

*This study
is respectfully dedicated
to two wise men who know each other
only through my good fortune in knowing them both:*

CAW KHUN PHYA ANUMAN RAJADHON

and

ACAN LONG THAW MORN NARN THAMACAJ MANKHALAT.

Preface

The data for this study come from about twenty months of anthropological fieldwork in a small Tai-Lue village in northern Thailand. After two months of exploring a number of northern provinces, my wife and I arrived in Chiengkham Town, Chiengrai Province, in September 1959. There we lived in the home of a Tai-Yuan midwife who spoke no English. With time out for acute withdrawal resulting from culture shock, most of our days were spent in learning and practicing the Siamese, Lue, and Yuan dialects of Tai and in getting to know the officials of Chiengkham Town and the Lue villagers of Chiengkham District. As is common in Thailand, but unfortunate for American readers, Chiengkham is the official name of both a district and its administrative center. To avoid confusion, I use "Chiengkham" when the entire district is meant, and "Chiengkham Town" for the capital of the district.

By Christmas of 1959, I had somewhat fortuitously, albeit with excellent rationalizations, chosen Ban Ping as the site for intensive fieldwork. In January 1960 an interpreter and I began to have a thatch-and-bamboo house built in the village headman's compound. During January, I went to the village daily. In February the house was completed and, after appropriate ceremonies, my wife and I and our interpreter began living there. Two weeks later I dismissed our interpreter. From then until the time we left Ban Ping in early April 1961 (with perhaps three months away from Ban Ping for comparative trips to other villages in Thailand and for recreation in Chiengmai and Bangkok), our household consisted of my wife, myself, and A, a servant girl whom villagers called our "daughter." For reasons of preference, convenience, and ideology we lived as much like villagers as our work and the villagers permitted. Our health remained excellent, and our only consistent annoyance (aside from frustration at our initial incompetence in the Lue dialect) was a debilitating lack of privacy. In the summer of 1965 I returned to Ban Ping for a month to inquire into new research problems and correct some small fraction of earlier mistakes. Since 1961, we have been in desultory correspondence with a few villagers.

Although I relate my discussion of farming in Ban Ping to ethnographic science, to the anthropological concepts of technology and peasantry, and to issues of directed economic development, my ethnographic purposes require that this study be concentrated upon a circumscribed area of behavior recognized as a unit by the villagers themselves. This orientation precludes my saying much about Lue economics or about how rice is sold and what is bought with the proceeds of such sales. Even the issue of markets for land, which is clearly related to rice farming, is given short shrift because villagers can farm land without owning it or own land without farming it.

The bases for my narrow range of data and rigid approach to them are elaborated in chapter ii. Here it is sufficient to state that a major part of my purpose is to figure out how the villagers of Ban Ping seemed to make their farming decisions in 1960. This purpose places me, and, I fear, my readers, somewhat at the mercy of my notion of how villagers organize their thoughts about farming. It is my notion of their notions which informs the otherwise gratuitously cumbersome organization of Parts Two and Three of this study. Since I examine the same farming operations from two viewpoints—rational decision making (technology) and "peasantness" (extracommunity relations) —the system entails some unavoidable repetition.

Furthermore, in order to give an honest account of the system of interlocking farming decisions as they were made in 1960, I have restricted the discoveries and surprises of my 1965 field trip to the final chapter. As De Saussure (1959:81) has pointed out, when one wishes to describe a system, "the intervention of history can only falsify his judgement." In order to regard farming as a single systematic domain, I cannot consider things done in 1965 as if they were alternatives known in 1960.

Segregating the 1965 materials also permits the reader to see where my 1960 analysis erred. It matters very little, after all, how some 100 household heads somewhere in Asia went about farming in a particular year. What does matter is the development of techniques for understanding how farmers select among alternative practices. I hope that the basis laid herein will aid ethnographers in studying purposive behavior elsewhere and will also help nations whose survival depends upon the aggregate of millions of farming decisions to study, and so to influence, how those decisions are made.

For the student and practitioner of economic development, this book concerns the " 'technology' or 'state of the arts' " of which Schultz (1964:133 f.) says "the particular factors must be examined

PREFACE ix

and their economic behavior analyzed if growth is to be satisfactorily explained." For those interested in agricultural development, the intrinsic interest of Ban Ping's farming technology is that, by 1960, more than half of the village's rice lands were being plowed with the tractors that had been introduced in 1953.

My own interest in development is real, but untrained. Nevertheless, I have had some experience through serving as a consultant to the Agency for International Development and its United States Operations Mission to Thailand (since 1964), acting as an adviser to the National Statistics Office of Thailand (in 1965), serving on the Executive Committee and participating in the Rural Development Seminar of the Southeast Asia Development Advisory Group (since 1965), and serving as executive secretary of the Academic Advisory Council on Thailand (since 1966). I list these agencies only to establish my credentials and not to imply that their officers share any of my opinions.

This study is a revision and expansion of the doctoral dissertation I presented to Yale University in 1964. For their comments on that and subsequent versions, I am pleased to be able to thank Harold C. Conklin, Sidney W. Mintz, and Karl J. Pelzer of Yale, George Rosen of the Asian Development Bank, and David A. Wilson of the University of California, Los Angeles (UCLA). None of them should be blamed for anything I say or fail to say; their having read successive manuscripts is punishment enough.

The research upon which this study is based was supported by generous grants from the Foreign Area Training Fellowship Program of the Ford Foundation. I am pleased to have this opportunity to record my thanks and to acknowledge support from the Committee on Research of the Academic Senate, UCLA, and the center for Southeast Asia Studies of the Institute of International Studies, University of California, Berkeley, which helped me to return to Ban Ping in 1965.

In Thailand I soon came to depend upon the time, advice, and wisdom offered unstintingly by Caw Khun Phya Anuman Rajadhon, Mr. Kraisri Nimmanhaeminda, Dr. Sala Dasananda, and Achara Thawi Thawiwattana. Our life in Thailand would have been poorer and our research thinner without the aid and comfort of numerous Christian missionaries with whom we may never agree, but whom we shall never cease to admire. We were helped by workers at the Presbyterian Guest House in Bangkok, the United Church of Christ in Thailand at Chiengmai and Chiengrai, and the Overseas Missionary Fellowship at Chiengmai, Chiengrai, and Maehongsorn. In Chiengkham it was our pleasant privilege to know and to lean upon Reverend and Mrs. M. Byers, Reverend and Mrs. C. W. Callaway, Miss D. Uhlig, and Miss I. Williams.

Without the generous cooperation of numerous Thai officials, especially the Chiengkham district officer and assistant district officer, our work could not have been accomplished. Friends and neighbors in Ban Ping gave us acceptance and human warmth as well as information. We can never thank them adequately, but only continue trying to remain members of their community to the extent that they permit.

I wish to thank Carolyn Crawford for drawing the two maps and figure 1, and Mrs. M. Polachek for her editorial assistance.

Marianne, whose share is largest, knows that my debt and my gratitude are not confined to those I have named.

MICHAEL MOERMAN

Contents

PART ONE: BACKGROUND

I. The People and the Place   3
    Contemporary Chiengkham and Ban Ping, 4
    Rice: A Way of Life, 9
    The Lue Past, 12

II. The Problem   17
    Farming and Peasants, 17
    Ethnography, 21

PART TWO: FARMING OPERATIONS

III. Plow Agriculture   33
    The Rice Fields of Ban Ping, 33
    Technology, 36
    Extracommunity Relations, 49
    Summary, 60

IV. Tractor Agriculture   62
    Technology, 62
    Extracommunity Relations, 67
    Summary, 79

PART THREE: RESOURCES IN LAND AND LABOR

V. Land Acquisition   91
    Technology, 91
    Extracommunity Relations, 104
    Summary, 114

VI. Labor Mobilization   116
    Categories of Laborers, 116
    Technology, 128
    Extracommunity Relations, 134
    Summary, 140

PART FOUR: CHOICE AND CHANGE

VII. Choice in Farming ... 147
    The Villagers' Perspective, 147
    Costs and Returns: The Outsider's Perspective, 158
    Net Apparent Advantage, 174

VIII. Change in Farming ... 185
    Change and Economic Development, 185
    Technology, 189
    Ethnography, 190
    Extracommunity Relations, 191

APPENDIXES

A. Glutinous Rice ... 195
B. Obtaining Quantitative Data ... 198
C. Quantitative Comparisons ... 204

EXPLANATORY NOTES

Glossary of Lue Terms ... 209
Units of Measurement ... 210
Key to Genealogical Information ... 210
Orthography ... 210

References Cited ... 213

Index ... 223

PART ONE: *BACKGROUND*

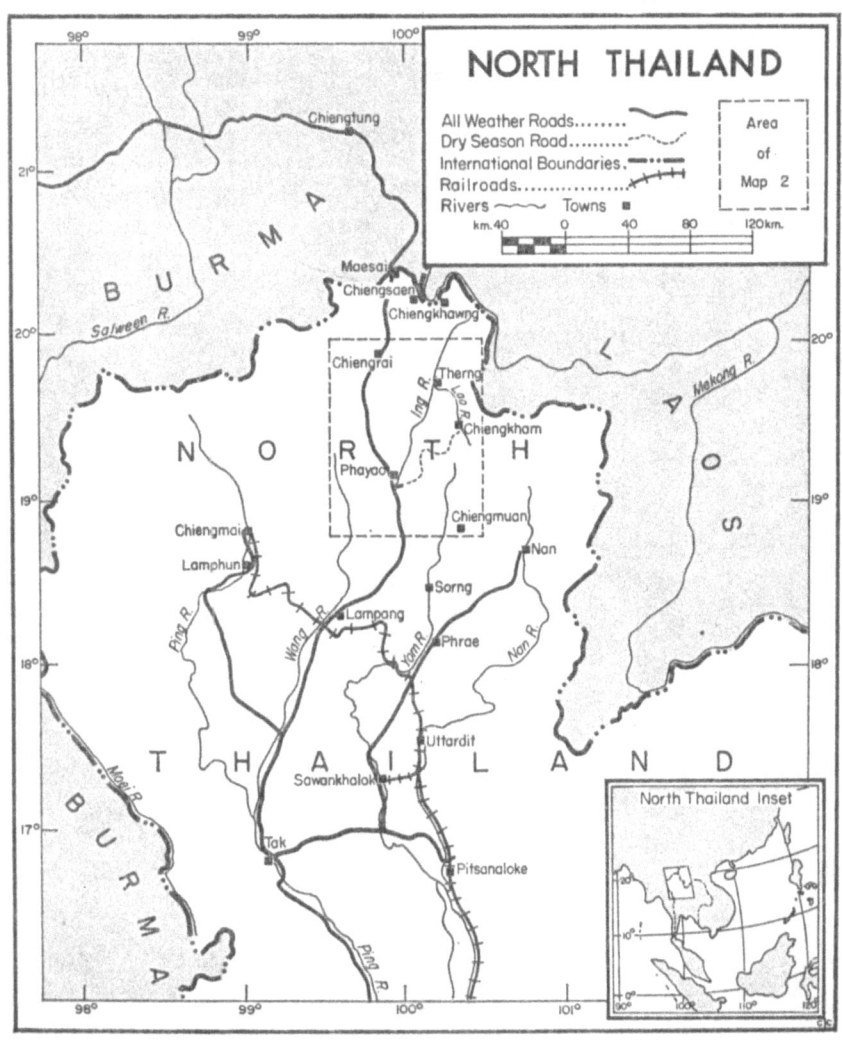

Map 1.

I.
The People and the Place

Although no one knows their number and many dispute their origin, it is safe to say that the Tai [1] are the largest ethnolinguistic group in mainland Southeast Asia. To appreciate their numbers and variety, one must bear in mind that Thailand is not their sole home. The "Tai race," which William Clifton Dodd (1923), a missionary with more enthusiasm than accuracy, called "the elder brother of the Chinese," is found east and north and west of Thailand, extending into Burma, Laos, northern Vietnam, and southern China. To the ethnographer, who is perhaps always an obscurantist and romantic, it seems in a way unfortunate that the Siamese of Thailand have come to stand for all Tai peoples in the minds of most Americans. Modern Thailand, that dynamic, pleasant, and strikingly independent nation, has been the political and cultural center of the Tai since the middle of the nineteenth century. But we should not let its dominance obscure our view of the Khaw and the Khyn, the Lao and the Lai, the Yawng and the Yuan, the Nya and the Nung, the Doi and the Dam, and of the many other subgroups whose variety spices our appreciation and deepens our comprehension of the Tai.

Scholarly Siamese with an interest in their own origins frequently turn to these so-called Tai tribes [2] whose language, customs, and beliefs they think little altered by the Khmer influence, by the Western contact, and by the political power which have transformed the central Thai. Contemporary events in Laos and Vietnam, and the hint of their repetition in northeastern Thailand, emphasize the practical importance of knowing about the variant customs and diverse loyalties of minority Tai subgroups (Kunstadter 1967). Among these Tai subgroups is the Lue.[3]

---

[1] This study follows fairly conventional usage by employing "Tai" for the whole family of closely related peoples and reserving "Thai" for its most prominent member, the Siamese or central Thai of the Chao Phraya plain about Bangkok.

[2] The reasons I think it misleading to call these peoples "tribes" are presented in Moerman 1965; 1967*b*.

[3] Lue is sometimes spelled Lü, and, in Mary Haas's orthography for Siamese (1956:viii–x), is pronounced lýý. The Lue are variously estimated to number be-

3

CONTEMPORARY CHIENGKHAM AND BAN PING

Ban Ping, a Lue village, is in the Chiengkham District of Chiengrai Province [4] in northern Thailand, a region whose dominant city, Chiengmai, is a popular hot-season resort for prosperous Siamese (see map 1). Even a business trip there takes on an air of holiday. The Bangkok official, businessman, or tourist boards the express train in the late afternoon for the 600-mile trip. Sometime early the next morning, perhaps when the train is just dragging itself up the hills that separate Pitsanaloke from Uttardit, he awakens to find the air suddenly much cooler and to see that the wide, manicured plain has given way to steep mountains and narrow gorges. The first appearance of the north contrasts dramatically with the Thailand of uniformly populated plains and ubiquitous canals. Along the rail line, villages are far apart. Instead of occasional knots of fruit trees, there are huge tracts of scrub forest and stands of teak. At each stop passengers are besieged by vendors asking them to sample the pickled tea leaves and the steamed glutinous rice of the north. The holiday mood spreads as the central Thai travelers eat the peasant fare and joke about the peculiar speech, fair skin, and easy manner of the northern girls. Central Thais often express the familiar townsman's image of his country cousin by speaking of the northerners as simpler, more honest, and more pure than they. The non-Tai hill tribes of the north, with their strange customs and colorful dress, are also the objects of condescending curiosity.

The insularity and ethnic heterogeneity of northern Thailand characterize Chiengrai, the northernmost province. The title of the most widely read Tai ethnology, "The Thirty Races of Chiengrai" (Srisiwasdi 1952), speaks for its heterogeneity. The sleepy provincial capital with its three blocks of shops and a few cinemas is far from the cultural center of Bangkok. Even the unsophisticated villagers of Chiengkham recognize that, compared with Chiengmai or Lampang, Chiengrai city is "hardly any fun."

---

tween 72,000 and 400,000 persons, of which perhaps 50,000 are in Thailand. For a concise summary of their history and culture traits, see LeBar *et al.* (1964:206–213).

[4] For administrative purposes, Thailand is divided into seventy-six *changwad*'s (here translated as "provinces"), each under a governor appointed by the minister of the interior. The provinces are divided into *amphur*'s ("districts"), of which the chief administrator is the *nai amphur* ("district officer"), who, like the governor, is a professional civil servant. Chiengkham, like all other rural districts in Thailand, is divided into *tambon*'s ("administrative boroughs") composed of *mu ban*'s ("hamlets"); adult residents elect a headman in each hamlet. One headman is elected by the others to serve as *kamnan* ("borough chief").

Ban Ping is a clearly demarcated natural community which is also an administrative hamlet located in Yuan Borough.

THE PEOPLE AND THE PLACE 5

Like much of northern Thailand, Chiengrai was long held by the Burmese whose memory is guarded by the Burmese-style stone lions that stand at the gates of most northern temples. Chiengsaen, which the Burmese lost in 1804, lies to the north of the province, and even now Chiengrai seems to merge into Burma. The road from Maesai to Chiengtung is indifferently policed; the border is meaningless to the hill peoples who inhabit it.

About halfway along the paved road that connects the Lampang railhead with the provincial capital of Chiengrai lies the old city of Phayao (see map 1). North and east of Phayao are the districts of Chiengkham, Pong (see map 2), Therng, and Chiengkhawng, for-

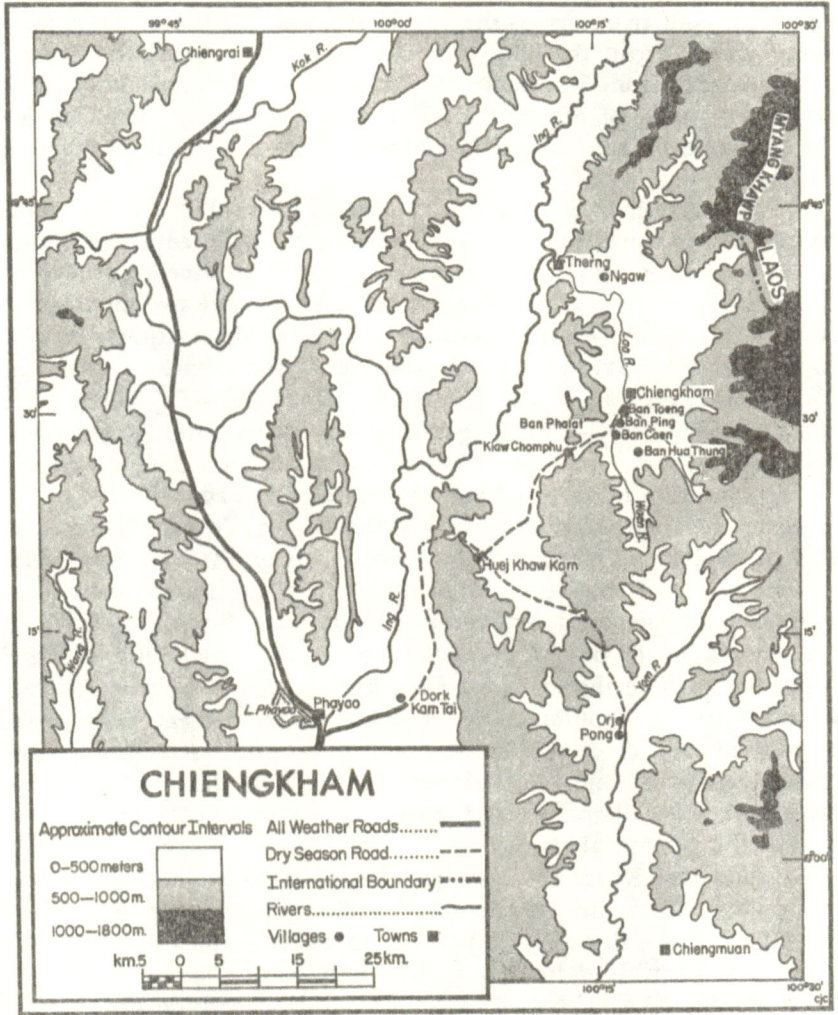

Map 2.

merly dependencies of Chiengsaen. They are connected by one of the worst roads in Thailand (Blofeld 1960:54). No one who travels it can be sure when he will reach his destination. The thick dust of the dry season conceals holes and ridges from the truck driver. In the rainy season, men and animals pull themselves through a knee-deep black porridge of heavy mud. Largely because of the condition of the road, these districts are much less developed than the rest of the province. Many provincial officers would like them to be made into a new province of Phayao in order to leave Chiengrai with only the more accessible districts.

Chiengkham is a large and populous district which borders on the mountains in Myang Khawp in Laos. Hills divide it into two valley networks, both tributary to the Ing River. For Thailand, the climate is temperate. Frost, though quite rare, can occur. Daytime temperatures recorded from September 1959 to April 1961 ranged from 53° F at the beginning of March to 100° F just two months later. During the damp, cold season of November–March, the diurnal range is wide.

From December to May, when the ground is dry, it takes rice trucks eight hours to travel the 45 miles from Phayao to Chiengkham Town. A few nights of rain may increase the traveling time to twelve or fourteen hours, or prevent truck travel entirely. For five months the road is impassable even to four-wheel-drive vehicles equipped with winches. It then takes two full days on foot or horseback to travel the 35 miles between Chiengkham Town and Dork Kam Taj, where there is a stone-filled roadbed leading to Phayao. Rainy-season commerce is by means of oxcarts, which take from three to ten days depending on the condition of the road and the size of the load.

Along the road from Phayao to Chiengkham Town, villages soon become widely separated. The traveler passes through two uninhabited tracts of mountain forest. Even in the valleys, there is unclaimed land suitable for farming. The halfway house for lunch in the dry season, or overnight in the wet, is the tiny center of Huej Khaw Kam where the roads for Chiengkham and Pong part. Chiengkham District is populous and sprawling, so Huej Khaw Kam serves as a secondary center. Officials, merchants, and ecclesiastics often travel between it and Chiengkham Town. Huej Khaw Kam has a large mill, a few shops, a small market, a noisome hotel, and an outpost of the provincial police.

Beyond Huej Khaw Kam are rice fields and then, once again, the mountains. From this range the traveler descends at Ban Kiaw Chomphu into a narrow valley. After an abrupt climb he begins the scarcely perceptible descent onto the high plain that surrounds the town of Chiengkham. Ban Ping and two other roadside Lue villages precede the town. Beyond them the road runs for half a mile through shimmering rice fields, which show Chiengkham as a flat green bowl rimmed by steep blue hills. A turn to the north, and the traveler is in the capital of Chiengkham.

It seems to have changed little since Reginald Le May (1926:188) saw it as "a long straggling village . . . almost completely surrounded by hills." For most of the year, only bare feet, cart wheels, and bicycles cross its dusty streets. There is no cinema, no running water, no town electricity. During the rainy season only a single strand of telephone wire or an unusually strong urge to travel connects the town with the rest of Thailand. Then, the officials say half-seriously, "Chiengkham becomes an independent country," immune from inspection by provincial and national officers. Even during the dry season, access to the provincial capital is unusually difficult for the highly centralized administration of modern Thailand. Each year, district officials prophesy that the road to Chiengrai will be better maintained than the road to the rice entrepôt of Phayao. Each year the enterprising truck owners are more effective than the government's projects, and officials find that in order to attend provincial meetings in Chiengrai, they had best travel via Phayao.[5]

Chiengkham Town is uncomplicated and rather charming. Like many small places, it displays little more than its major institutions. There is no confusion of vendors and buses and tourist foods, of entertainments and tenements. Facing the bridge that leads to the district civil and police offices is a large school building. Near it are the homes of the officials and the licensed distillery. Across the street are the marketplace, some shops, a hotel and restaurants for visiting merchants and officials, and a few small, low houses for artisans and transient civil servants. Buddhist temples and two large rice mills complete the central part of Chiengkham Town. The relative size and decoration of its buildings give the visitor his physical and social bearings in less than an hour. In the government compound, the district officer has the largest house, the chief assistant district officer the second largest. Throughout the town, everything is built of wood except the temples and the ambitious home of the revenue officer. Flowing through Chiengkham Town are the Lao and Waen rivers which enrich the district's farms; all about it are the mountains.

In Chiengkham there is a rather clear ethnic division of labor. The district census records that almost all of its 77,000 people are Tai: Lue and Yuan. There are no reasonable estimates of the numbers of Yao

---

[5] A compacted laterite road, largely supported by United States foreign aid, has been completed from Chiengrai to Chiengkham and Chiengkhawng. It has reduced rainy season travel time between the first two towns from three days to about three hours, and also altered the routes and prices of the rice trade.

and Miao in the mountains. The few Chinese, as in the rest of Thailand, own most of the shops. The peasants are all Tai; they grow rice to eat and to sell to the Chinese millers. The hill tribes avoid other groups, especially the officials. While they maintain trading contacts with a few Tai villagers, they usually deal with the Chinese, with fellow tribals who have become Chinese, or with itinerant Haw (Panthay) opium agents. The higher government officials are members of or pretenders to central Thai culture. Officials, at all levels, are a fairly discrete social group, but the lower ranks associate somewhat with the villagers from whom they came, and the higher ranks, with the Chinese merchants whose interests they share.

At Chiengkham Town are the officials who administer Ban Ping and tax its land, the millers who buy Ban Ping's rice, the sophisticates who may suggest new ways to farm. To the villager of Ban Ping, the outside world begins with Chiengkham Town. It is a world with which his farming activities bring him into frequent contact.

The village of Ban Ping extends for about half a mile along the Phayao–Chiengkham road. West of the village lie its vegetable gardens and bamboo groves, on the banks of the Waen River. To the east are its old rice fields. At the north and south, the "tail" and "head" of Ban Ping, are groves and altars dedicated to its protective spirits. At the four corners of the village are ceremonial gates which enclose the area protected by the spirits. These gates and short, uninhabited tracts separate Ban Ping from its Lue neighbors to the south and north.

Ban Ping's largest compound and most elaborate building is a Buddhist temple made of concrete. The villagers live in wooden or bamboo houses on platforms, raised by posts to about 6 feet off the ground. Under the house, they tie their animals, work their looms, store their firewood, and sometimes rest themselves in the hot season. With few exceptions, each of Ban Ping's 120 houses is situated in its own compound. In 1960 the village had a population of 670.

Ban Ping is about 2 miles from Chiengkham Town. Like other Lue villages, it has a neater and more prosperous air than most Yuan settlements have. Its house-compounds—each with its own granary—are fenced, and their grounds are swept and orderly. Large stands of cultivated bamboo and coconut show that Ban Ping is older than the Yuan villages near Chiengkham Town. More houses are of hardwood, fewer of bamboo. The houses seem higher and are certainly much longer than those of the Yuan. Their walls slope outward from the floor as in the old houses that are considered historical relics in Chiengmai. The people look neater, for instead of the motley and tattered clothes sometimes seen even in prosperous Yuan villages, almost all the men are dressed in a uniform of indigo; the women wear tight jackets of the same color. Their sarongs are of a single, distinctively Lue pattern and are rarely made from the imported cotton prints usually used by the Yuan. Under the sound of the gasoline rice mills can be heard the steady thwak-thwak-thwak of the Lue women weaving. The older women, with their white turbans and looped topknots, could never be taken for anything but Lue. In the roadside Yuan villages which the traveler passes for 30 miles, he sees no looms, no tribal dress, no distinctive hairstyle. But in these Lue villages, despite their proximity to town, are a people who take pride in being economically independent and ethnically distinct.

Ban Ping claims to be more amicable, friendly, and cooperative than other villages. Its members seize upon minor peculiarities of custom and costume as emblems of Lue identity and superiority (Moerman 1967b). In their eyes, the Yuan are lazy, the Lao aggressive, and townsmen untrustworthy. Ethnic pride, community loyalty, a consciousness of kinsmen, and, perhaps, a somewhat more abiding faith in the spirits (*phi*) might seem striking to those with special knowledge only of central Thailand. But in most respects Ban Ping is fairly typical of the north and of Thailand. Its round of life marked by the daily sounds of the carabao on their way to and from pasture and by the annual cycle of the monsoon and the festivals; its insularity complemented by radios and teachers, by merchants and officials; its occasional gossip and scandal countered by the security that men feel for having been born among neighbors with whom they live, worship, and die—Ban Ping, neither huge nor tiny, neither grossly rich nor desperately poor, neither dissatisfied nor unambitious, neither irreligious nor compulsively orthodox, lies comfortably within what one expects of peaceful paddy-growing communities in Theravada Buddhist Southeast Asia.

Ban Ping and the other roadside Lue villages seem to be self-contained communities. Their old fields lie near them. Each village has its temple, its sign marking the headman's house, a shop or two, and a small rice mill. But all these are also bonds to the outside world. Fuel for the mill, the goods in the shops, the authority of the headman, the training of the priests—all come from beyond the village. To pay for them the villager sells his rice, the source of his livelihood and the basis of his life.

RICE: A WAY OF LIFE

We prosperous Americans can scarcely conceive of the importance rice has to the Asians who grow it. Our bread and biscuits, potatoes and pancakes, corn and crackers, doughnuts and dumplings make it difficult for us to understand a continent where all prosperous villagers plan, and poor villagers aspire, to eat the same staple starch every day at every meal. In Ban Ping, rice is the main component of every meal, the major source of cash, and the object of most labor. Its production, consumption, and sale are the most common topics of village conversation. All other activities—economic, political, religious, and social—must yield to the rice cycle and the rains that govern it. Rice is a universally accepted standard and store of value. A ball of rice is the infant's first solid food; a basket of rice accompanies the corpse to the pyre. Village roles are often phrased and perceived in terms of rice farming. Young men are "those who make the fields."[6] Boys of eleven and twelve who are about to graduate from school talk excitedly of how "next year we will be workingmen, we will make the fields." Old women begin each day by bringing rice to the temple; old men care for the carabao that pull the plow. A forty-eight-year-old man signals his desire to be considered an elder by interrupting his lucrative basket weaving to bring his carabao ostentatiously to pasture, even though his two sons are quite willing to do the chore for him.

The verb *to eat* is "to eat rice"; a meal together is a ritual. When a stranger, whether someone from another village or the visiting anthropologist, is invited to join a circle around a tray or a low table, he is often told, "We are all eating together; therefore, we are kinsmen." An outsider, immediately after his divorce from a village girl, is told, "Don't forget us. We are still kinsmen. Whenever you pass this way, you must stop to eat rice and drink water with us." An economic household is phrased as "those who eat rice together." To intimates, one should make interest-free loans of rice when they are in need. At household ceremonies, close "kinsmen" bring a token amount of milled rice.

Village etiquette forbids all but intimates to watch someone eat. Shortly after we arrived in Ban Ping, we were told that it was "unseemly" to eat on our porch since, unlike the villagers' homes, it had no sheltering wall. Village visitors, who would stay for hours poking into every inch of our house, would leave once we unrolled the dining mat. Children would be upbraided for not disappearing, or at least for not averting their gaze while we ate. "They're eating. Get out of here! Buddha, these kids!"

Among the most basic of Ban Ping's social ideas is the distinction between officials, "men who eat monthly money," and farmers, "those who work." In 1960, 91 percent of village households managed farms. All villagers think of themselves as farmers; no officials, not even the

[6] Uncredited quotations come from my field notes of villagers' remarks.

lowest clerk or the poorest teacher, ever do farm work. While villagers may envy officials their leisure, they also pride themselves on being "men who work." "I'm a workingman," said a young member of the Ban Ping school committee, "and can't wait around all day for someone who merely eats monthly money. If the teacher doesn't come . . . when he said he would, workingmen don't have to wait for him."

Not only the production of rice, but rice itself, serves to focus class and regional identification. All Tai eat rice, but the sticky rice (see App. A) of the north is often contemned by Asians who eat ordinary rice. Central Thais, Burmese, or Indonesians commonly consider a diet of glutinous rice to be difficult to digest and to encourage slothful behavior and sluggish thought. Throughout northern Thailand, many young villagers express ambivalence toward their staple food. They claim it prevents them from thinking swiftly and clearly, but add that a workingman could not possibly sustain himself on a diet of ordinary rice. Glutinous rice furnishes the northern peasant with an elegant symbol of his typical feeling that hard work makes him better, and stolidness makes him worse, than city folk.

In Chiengkham, and throughout northern and northeastern Thailand, one can express his social position by the rice he eats. Officials are forced by their position to try to live as central Thais: class becomes culture. The Chiengkham district officer was born and raised in the nothern city of Lampang. But he, and many other high officials who are northern by birth, eat the ordinary rice and coconut-milk curries of central Thailand. People seldom speak of rice as a sign of status, but all recognize it as such. The feast that sometimes follows *tambon* meetings provides a clear example. Village headmen are served glutinous rice and raw *lap*, the highly spiced chopped meat that is the great delicacy of the north. Teachers and other low-ranking officials are often served both kinds of rice and cooked *lap*. At the district officer's table only the ordinary rice is ever served. When an official or policeman eats at the Ban Ping headman's house, ordinary rice is set before him; he may later request the glutinous sort and thereby create a mood of special intimacy in which, among other signs of fellowship, all speak together in a northern dialect. Our own initial rapport was aided by our eating glutinous rice. Villagers had no preconceptions about what kind of rice is eaten in America, but our obvious high status made them assume that we would eat in central Thai style. The acknowledgment, "They eat as we do," provided entrée for us as equals.[7]

[7] In the summer of 1964 I visited a Royal Thai Army Mobile Development Unit in northeastern Thailand. It was rather encouraging to observe that the soldiers ate glutinous rice for lunch.

THE LUE PAST

Southeast Asian high civilization largely derives from India and, to a lesser extent, from China. Geographically, the idea of the frontier is appropriate, for rarely in Southeast Asia and hardly anywhere in Thailand is the image of Asia's teeming masses at all appropriate. Rather, it was long true that the scarce resources for economic or political advancement were population, not riches; labor, not land; subjects, not territory. War was commonplace among the publicly pacific Buddhists of Southeast Asia. The banners of these wars were sacred images and, literally, white elephants; often, the consequence was population raids. With an almost ritual regularity, accounts of Southeast Asian campaigns end with the phrase, "and many captives were taken" (see, for example, Hall 1955:117, 118, 153, 158, 168, *et seq.*). Historians and chroniclers are struck by the fact that nobles and artisans were taken prisoners and often enriched the politics and high culture of their captors; the Khmers played the Greeks to the Thai Romans. Peasant prisoners were, and their descendants are, important to Thailand's demography and economy. There is scarcely a province in modern Thailand without some remnant of a transported population who were once the "slaves" of a noble and successful warrior.

In Southeast Asia, it was the state, not the tribe (cf. Boserup 1965:74), which employed warfare to "secure for itself the advantage of dense and permanent settlement while avoiding the burden of additional hard work in agriculture." The history of Southeast Asian population raids lends some support to Boserup's argument (*ibid.*, p. 96) that the great danger in feudal systems and the cause of their famines are that nobles are tempted to use too many farmers as soldiers, as artisans, as servants, and as workers in places other than the farm, thereby bringing about "rural underpopulation relative to to total population and to agricultural productivity."

The original Lue homeland, which Lue usually refer to as "the old country" (*merng derm*), is the Sip Song Panna; this loosely organized Tai state in southwest Yunnan (long. 100°–101°30′E, lat. 21°30′–22°30′N), although under the vaguely defined authority of the Chinese, was ruled by a Lue "Lord of Life" at Chienghung, which the Chinese call Ch'e-li fu. The Lue of Ban Ping were brought to Chiengkham during the latter half of the nineteenth century, a period that some Tai peoples refer to as "the age of gathering vegetables to put into baskets; of gathering captives to put into settlements."

Chiengkham was then part of Nan, a Tai-Yuan principality whose Lord of Life was subject to the King of Thailand. Along with the other dependencies of Chiengsaen, Chiengkham had become depopulated through the campaigns that culminated in 1804, when the Tai (under Bangkok) took Chiengsaen from the Burmese. Chiengkham's lack of population was a threat to the Thai king, which presumably became more severe as European powers began to annex unadministered parts of Southeast Asia. In the nineteenth century, and even now, it could be officially reported that "land has no real value [in North Thailand] until it is brought under cultivation; whichever state makes the first settlement acquires therefore the best title to the government of the district" (Archer 1888:9). King Rama IV of Thailand, in order to provide land with labor and to protect his frontier while at the same time furthering his campaign against Chiengtung (Damrong 1918/19), ordered the Prince of Nan to get Lue captives from Myang Phong in the Sip Song Panna. In 1853/54 and again in 1856/57 (Anonymous 1954:par. 6), the Lue were brought to northern Thailand; they took with them some rice and some valuables and the names and spirits of their old country villages.

In their version of the tale, the Lue mention neither the name of the Thai king—Mongkut, publicized and defamed in *Anna and the King of Siam*—nor the affairs of state that presumably motivated him. The hero of their story is Mahacaj (see Damrong 1918/19), prince of Phong, who during his war with Cae—a *myang* like Myang Phong under the loose authority of Chienghung—appealed to his *sio*, the Prince of Nan, for aid. By the time the Nan army arrived, Mahacaj had died in a Buddhist temple to which he had been carried after being shot with a poisoned arrow. His followers "scattered into the woods and fields like orphaned children" until the Prince of Nan arrived to lead and protect the dependents of his *sio*. In this way, say the elders of Ban Ping, those like themselves, whose ancestors came from Myang Phong, were not, as were the ancestors of many other Lue in Chiengkham, "captured, herded, and divvied up like carabao and oxen."

According to local tradition, the Phong Lue was first settled at Myang Ngaw (probably lat. 19°40′N, long. 100°17′E) near Therng (see map 2). This was too near the homeland and the Prince of Nan, afraid that they would flee, brought them to Chiengmuan, south of the present Pong District. But because the land of Chiengmuan was insufficient, about a hundred years ago (by genealogical reckoning), the Prince of Nan permitted some of the Chiengmuan Lue to come to Chiengkham, whose fertile fields and excellent irrigation system had barely been maintained by the few Yuan and Shan left after the wars of the eighteenth century. Even in Chiengkham, the Lue did not come under the direct authority of the national government until after the administrative reforms consequent upon the Shan rebellion of 1901–02. Only gradually throughout the early decades of the present century did the nationally oriented officials and merchants of the market town come to exert an influence on village life. Their increasing importance can be traced quite clearly through the movement and production of rice.

In northern Thailand, there is a wide annual variation in rice yields from region to region. In Chiengkham, however, the crop has always been bountiful. Even during the "year of the running star with a tail" (which I take to be 1910, the year of Halley's comet) when the crop failed throughout the north, Chiengkham had a small surplus which strangers came to buy or beg. Villagers ascribe Chiengkham's good fortune to its old irrigation system, the fame of which, they assert, reaches to the King at Bangkok.

By the last third of the nineteenth century, there was a firmly established pattern of trading in surplus rice. Every year, in the dry season, small surpluses were packed onto oxen and taken south through the valley of the Waen and the feeder valleys of the Yom to Orj, Chiengmuan, Sorng, and ultimately to Phrae, about 100 miles away (see maps 1 and 2). As the only customers were consumers, the market was quite small. Between the seller and buyer there were bonds beyond those of supply and demand, motives in addition to immediate profit. As an old rice trader explains it, "Even if there were higher prices to be obtained elsewhere, one followed one's usual road where there were kinsman, fellow Lue, *sio's,* friends, and intimates. . . . If strangers came selling rice, people wouldn't buy from them, but would wait for the man they knew." For some twenty years after the central Thai came to Chiengkham, rice was moved by those who grew and owned it along routes unaffected by the national government's path to Phayao or by the export trade.

The major stimulus for change came when a railroad was completed to Lampang about 1920. Rice then began to move over the government roads to Phayao from whence it could be shipped throughout the north. Ten years later, the Phayao road was good enough to permit the passage of oxcarts and the days of sending pack oxen directly south were over. Chiengkham's rice now moved over the Phayao road to a much larger market than before. Despite the interruption of World War II, it was only a short time before large mills were built, trucks came, and merchants appeared to buy and to transport the villagers' rice. Surplus rice is now sold in Chiengkham at prices over which the farmer has no control; merchant buyers have an oligopsony and farmers must sell because they need to buy other things. No longer do villagers assume the risks of moving and selling rice to its ultimate consumers. Rice is bought by Chinese millers, trucked over

THE PEOPLE AND THE PLACE   15

the Phayao road by professionals, and sold in a market that, to any individual farmer, appears infinite and impersonal.

The number of large mills and the impressive efforts of the truckers to maintain the road there indicate Chiengkham's importance as a producer of rice. The main cause of this importance is the huge increase in productivity which has followed the introduction of tractors.

Before Chiengkham was sacked at the end of the eighteenth century, much of its population was concentrated in the valley of the Ing near Myang Lor. Buddha images and the ruins of temples testify to Lor's former prosperity, but when the Lue came to found Ban Ping, the "fields of Lor," or Thunglor, were given over to swamp, grasses, and heavy forests inhabited by wild elephants and tigers. As fields near Ban Ping became scarcer, young villagers would try from time to time to clear land at Thunglor.

The flooding of the Ing is quite rapid. Since the farmers could not plow or transplant until the monsoon had softened the soil, the rising water drowned their young rice.[8] But the fabled fertility of the vast plain of Thunglor remained alluring, and the occasional discovery of Buddha images of great antiquity and power kept the fascination alive. For a time there was a rumor, not unknown to city folk, that foreign firms intended to take air photos in order to develop Thunglor. Attracted by the tale of Thunglor, an enterprising tractor owner from Lampang went there in 1953. One of his employees taught those who were transplanting at Thunglor how to broadcast dry seeds onto tractor-plowed soil. Seeding was thus possible before the rains began, and the rice, with this head start, kept above the rising waters of the Ing. After a year or two of mixed success, the advantages of the tractor became apparent. Farmers from many villages have since claimed land at Thunglor.

Tractors brought from urban centers have made it possible to cultivate an additional 6,000 acres (2,400 ha),[9] of which Ban Ping owns 550. The villagers of Chiengkham have thus been forced to decide whether or not to use tractors for growing rice. Their decision has modified the earlier relations of village to town and of district to nation.

Rice and the production of rice are central components of Ban Ping's changing relations with other communities. The Chiengkham Lue were brought from the Sip Song Panna to work as farmers. Their

---

[8] Local experts claim that the floodwaters rise too rapidly and fall too suddenly for "floating rice" to be transplanted.

[9] For comparative purposes, and because they conform to official Thai sources, metric units have been favored except in stating land area where the usual Thai practice is to translate rai as .40 acre instead of as .16 hectare.

movements from Ngaw to Chiengmuan to Chiengkham are explicable in terms of farming. Their increasing participation in the Thai nation is, in large part, a matter of farming. Their role in the modern economy is that of peasants who produce rice and consume what the proceeds of its sale permit them to buy.

The villagers of Ban Ping have always grown rice to eat, to share with kinsmen, and to sell. Although rice has always been the heart of the economy and, in the words of an articulate villager, "the bones of the people," no area of village life has changed more than rice and rice farming. The sale of surplus rice, once a source of petty luxuries, is now a major industry. Throughout Thailand, the carabao and the wooden plow are the dominant means of cultivating rice land. In 1960, most of Ban Ping's land was plowed by tractors, although the wheel had been introduced but thirty years earlier. The social consequences of technological innovation and new technological decisions can be studied in Ban Ping while they are still occurring. The tractor and the market are changing the ways in which the villagers behave to one another and to outsiders. Social relations based on rice and expressed in terms of rice are changing. The people of Ban Ping have begun to treat their fellows as they used to treat only strangers. Cash has become basic to present production; price and profit have become major influences on future production. Work is becoming distinct from "fun," and oriented more exclusively toward the rewarded completion of particular tasks. These changes mean that life and farming in Ban Ping are becoming more "commercial," and less "self-sufficient." Such captions, however convenient, take on meaning only through detailed descriptions (Parts Two and Three). Also indicated in these descriptions is the curious constancy that underlies village life and provides villagers with the stable framework within which to make revolutionary technological decisions.

II.
The Problem

In this chapter I describe how my subject matter and goals influence each other and determine the organization of this study. I argue, first, that our ignorance of lowland rice farming in Asia demands the detailed data I present, and, second, that the imprecision of the anthropological concept of "the peasant" recommends the way in which my data are organized. The discussion of technology specifies the ways in which I hope that this book will contribute to the science of ethnography.

FARMING AND PEASANTS

Farming.—The supreme importance that farming has for villagers obligates me to describe it. In addition, it has become an anthropological commonplace that sessile populations, surplus food (Leach 1954; Linton 1939:283–290), watering techniques (Wittfogel 1957), the availability of productive resources (Eggan 1941; Wolf 1957), and other components of agricultural technology have a decisive influence upon the lives of those who grow rice. It is no accident that the best general introduction to the peoples of Southeast Asia is entitled *Hill Farms and Padi Fields* (Burling 1965); these dichotomous and complementary environments and ways of life characterize the region. Yet hardly anyone (Geertz 1963 is an encouraging exception) has examined technology in sufficient detail to establish direct relations between particular farming practices and their specific societal consequences.

If the simple fact of cultivating inundated rice were as important as is often assumed, we should be hard put to make sense of the great diversity shown by the Thai, the Vietnamese, and the Ifugao. We know less than we suppose about the relationships between agriculture and society in general and between rice farming and Asian societies in particular. Our ignorance about Thailand is especially indefensible. Thanks largely to the stimulation of Cornell University, it is probable that during the past fifteen years more social scientists have gone to Thailand than to any other Southeast Asian country. Many of them have emphasized that rice farming, together with Buddhism, is the central Thai institution, or that an understanding of the Thai family requires an analysis of land tenure (Blanchard 1958: 424). Yet no one has seriously attempted to investigate the social implications of Thai agriculture.

In recent years a number of distinguished monographs about swidden farming in Southeast Asia have appeared (Conklin 1957; Freeman 1955; Geddes 1954). Although wet cultivation produces much more grain and supports many more people than swidden farming, and although it is the concomitant of high civilization throughout the region, to my knowledge this study is the first detailed anthropological account of how wet rice is grown in a specific Southeast Asian community. Gourou's classic studies (1936, 1940) of Southeast Asian farming are based on surveys and thus cannot be used to trace the sequences and alternatives that compose a single technological system. Although Thai village life has been the subject of a number of published books, none concentrates on farming. The original Cornell project publication (Sharp *et al.* 1953) was general and exploratory. Another general study (deYoung 1955) lacks clear community focus. Community studies that have concentrated on a particular part of Thai village life have emphasized Buddhism (Kaufman 1960; Kingshill 1960). The best brief descriptions of Thai farming (Barton 1960; Pendleton 1962) are too generalized to take account of regional variations. Of the two studies most closely comparable to mine, one (Rajadhon 1961) is concerned largely with ritual and is based on narratives rather than on direct observation of a specific community. The other (Janlekha 1955) is primarily directed toward developing techniques for objective farm economics and accountancy and thus often does not use categories appropriate either to the local culture or to the task of producing rice. Although the goals of these two last-mentioned studies differ from mine, the reader will see that they have often proved quite useful for comparative purposes.

Rice farming presents villages with numerous alternatives, with numerous occasions for making decisions. Two major decisions—plow versus tractor and glutinous versus nonglutinous rice—imply very different and changing relations with the outside world and especially with its centers of control. Because these two decisions are required by technological innovation, they do demand conscious choice from the villagers and are not merely analytic alternatives which I impute to them (cf. Katona 1951:230 f.).

The Lue share the staple crop of inundated, or wet, rice with all the lowland Tai, with all the plain and valley dwellers of Southeast Asia, and with most people who inhabit the world's most populous continent. Unlike other Asians, however, the Lue, along with most other Tai of northern and northeastern Thailand, Laos, and Yunnan, eat glutinous rice as their staple food. Although this crop thus helps to define and isolate a continuous culture area of about 200,000 square miles, it is given scant and inaccurate mention in the literature on rice (see App. A).

Peasants.—Most of the people in the most populous parts of the world are peasants, a cultural type in which many anthropologists and a growing number of economists and officials are interested. Perhaps the origin of the anthropologists' interest is simply that we have run out of primitives to study. A more respectable source of concern is our awareness that "a community that is a whole all by itself" (Redfield 1956:8) has rarely, if ever, existed since *Homo*, by taking on culture, became man. In writing of Ban Ping as a peasant village, I am not concerned with typology, with the questions of whether the word "peasant" should be applied to fishermen (Firth 1951:87; cf. Redfield 1956:18) or fetishists (Fallers 1961). Along with many other students of Southeast Asia, I am interested in the articulation of multisocietal systems and do not much care which specific societies are called "peasant" (cf. Lehman 1963:223). In 1959, when fieldwork was being planned, I intended to study how members of a Tai hill tribe make decisions that have the consequence of enmeshing them in lowland society. Failing to find any Tai "hill people" (Leach 1960: 69 ff.), I studied Tai "hillbillies" in order to see how an isolated lowland people relates to national society. The research problem is the same in both instances, and it is only for convenience that I call Ban Ping a peasant community. The word describes not what Ban Ping "is," but one of the ways in which this book views Ban Ping.

In the chapter sections on extracommunity relations the concept of peasant is a functional one in that it views activities from their stipulated consequences (Nadel 1957:7) quite regardless of the motives for those activites and of the actors' own understanding of their consequences. As peasants, the people of Ban Ping relate to other communities. In this book, farming is the activity, and relations with other communities are the stipulated consequence.

In the effort to understand peasant societies, anthropologists have made use of impressive concepts like "defensive ignorance," "cultural brokers" (Wolf 1956), or "the dyadic contract" (Foster 1961). Such conceptual tours de force have permitted fresh integrations of previously unrelated aspects of culture and society. Yet, by their very power, such concepts do violence to the unity of activities and institutions in much the same way that the theories of our intellectual ancestors, the early evolutionists, violated the contextual bonds of the traits they culled from diverse traditions. Terms like "defensive ignorance," "cultural broker," and "dyadic contract" direct our attention solely to the substantive components of peasant societies about which we can speak most easily. In doing so, they ignore both the local context of behavior and the data that do not conform to the typology. If ethnographic statements about peasant societies are to be other than haphazard, they must be based on induction from a previously demarcated domain (interactions within the family, for example) and cannot be a mere listing of examples that embody a retrospective insight (some social relations are dyadic contracts, for example). To phrase the issue more generally, if we focus on impressionistically derived concepts, like cultural brokerage or defensiveness, we are doing no more than substantiating the occasional existence of diagnostic indexes found in some of the societies we classify as peasant. In this study, I use the functional concept, *dependent incompleteness,* as an analytic metacultural definition of "peasantness" under which some aspects of all societies can be viewed.

Even if any group can be studied under the aspect of its "peasantness," some groups are profitably called "peasant" and some are not. There are, perhaps, two standards of relative "peasantness" which could both be measured for comparative purposes. First, one might array whole cultures or their institutional components along a continuum from tribal to national. The standard for assigning positions along the continuum would be: How much of the material goods and the actions of these people comes from, is modeled on, or is explicable in terms of communities other than their own? It is with this continuum in mind that I have devoted major attention to *changes* in extracommunity relations. Second, the peasantry is usually considered not merely as incomplete, but also as dependent. The "part-society and part-culture" (Kroeber 1948:284) is partial because it is involved with and leans upon superior centers of control: markets, priests, capitals. It is with this dependence in mind that I have devoted major attention to extracommunity relations that involve the nation and the market, and sometimes to intracommunity affairs that reflect these institutions.

A further basis for concentrating on some areas of peasant life is that peasant producers are the hope and the despair of those concerned with increasing the agricultural production of underdeveloped economies. As anthropologist and citizen I share this concern and have therefore tried to develop data and techniques that relate to the ways in which field ethnographers can be of use to development economists. The farmers of Ban Ping are interesting subjects for this concern because, quite mindless of our conventional conviction that peasants resist innovations in staple-crop technology, they welcomed the tractor for farming rice. In addition, the Agricultural Development Council

(Wharton 1965:7, 19, 60) has assigned highest priority to research on Southeast Asia "which focuses upon the motivational and attitudinal variables as they affect the productive and developmental processes—farmers' goals of production, the nature of farmers' decision making processes, and the influences and patterns of diffusion and adoption of practices and enterprises." In this book on agricultural change and peasant choice in Ban Ping, I attempt just such a focus.

Although all these current interests have influenced the weight given to various kinds of extracommunity relations, they in no way affect the selection of subject matter. Rigid adherence to an objectively delimitable unitary complex of activities (farming, in this instance) should contribute to the rigor (and, unfortunately, to the awkwardness) with which peasant societies can be analyzed.

ETHNOGRAPHY

Those who come to this book because of their interest in Southeast Asia, Thailand, farming, peasantry, or economic change, and who are not interested in ethnography, need not read the remainder of this chapter, for its purpose is to justify the organization of Parts Two and Three in terms of my ethnographic goals.

No small part of the anthropological impulse is a simple, although rarely innocent, curiosity about exotic peoples. Curiosity—whether casual, predatory, or comforting (like that of the evolutionists) —requires little more than entertaining descriptions for its satisfaction. If, however, ethnography is to be something more than pedantic travelogue-*cum*-peepshow, it should have purposes that, with only a little embarrassment, we can call scientific.

Types of ethnographies.—When cultural anthropologists stopped specializing in the exegesis of unrecorded histories, they began to reach too deep and to touch upon too many other disciplines to continue striving for complete description. When the sources of data ceased to be the recollections of a few old informants, it became illegitimate to confuse real with ideal behavior and, without explanation, to ignore history and emphasize structure, to ignore psychological and emphasize social functions. Once the ethnographer could no longer do everything, it became necessary for him to make an explicit statement of what, in fact, he was trying to do. Few of us are so dedicated to Freud, Marx, White, or eschatology that we "relate everything to a single central vision" which determines the universal significance of all data. Rather, we make use of a kind of opportunistic eclecticism which we usually fail to acknowledge. That is, in the terms suggested by Isaiah Berlin (1957:7 f.), we view culture as foxes, not as hedgehogs. But as our eyes dart about, here and there, we fail to explicate the unconscious theorizing and covert concepts by which some facts are included in our accounts and by which all facts are classified. Our miscellaneous information is stuffed into such undefined pigeonholes as "economics," "social life," "government." Rarely is any area of data sufficiently rich to disclose the points of articulation and principles of integration among these or any other categories of behavior. Without stating it, the typical study emphasizes those data that were easiest to come by, or most appealing to the author, or most fashionable at the moment.[1] It would be unfair to demand that an ethnographer define all his categories with equal clarity and provide each with equally good data. The issue, rather, is that the scientist's inexplicit bias, at work while collecting and analyzing data, prevents the reader from gauging the unavoidable distortions between native life and the printed page.

Ethnographers are concerned with the learned, patterned behavior, its rules and its products, as that behavior characterizes the members of a social group. Prolonged fieldwork results in an embarrassing wealth of information. It provides the ethnographer with impressions and hypotheses, with rolls of negatives, boxes of notes, columns of figures, and crates of artifacts which must somehow be arranged into a pattern intelligible to those who have never experienced the behavior upon which it is based, and also intelligible in retrospect to the anthropologist himself. Such data, unlike the replicable experiments of the chemist or the accessible archives of the historian, are unique, private, and thus all but sacred. They encourage the same reverent attitude that motivated "the patient exploration of all aspects of a culture, to salvage and treasure cultural details, which was the method of the old ethnology" (de Laguna 1957:180). But for at least a quarter of a century (Lesser 1939) this "old ethnology" has been criticized as antiscientific. Certainly, many of its products, like many contemporary community studies, are dull compendia of miscellaneous information of interest only to those who have some compelling extrinsic curiosity about the people or practices described. That the Timbara roll logs, the Jivaro shrink heads, and the Tepoztecans beat their wives can hardly be expected to interest anyone except those who may be dropped among them by black parachute in the dead of night.

In order to avoid the pitfall of miscellaneous trivia, the ethnographer may concentrate his curatorial commitment upon a limited segment of the life he purports to describe and analyze. Instead of pre-

---

[1] One can easily distinguish a "modern" from an "old-fashioned" study by the fact that the latter pays some attention to folklore and material culture. Modern studies can probably be divided into various strata: the age of kinship, the age of personality study, the age of a last chapter on acculturation, the age of a chapter on "the community and the nation." For a parallel in another discipline, see Goldhammer 1954.

senting some of all his data, the ethnographer may choose to present all of some of his data. That is, he may sacrifice breadth in order to concentrate on a specific part of community life. Like a general study, this procedure permits a writer to add his data to the anthropological record. In addition, it requires consistency, relevance, and a sense of closure. The author is forced to delimit his universe of discourse carefully, to specify the way in which he views it, and to justify his self-imposed limits in terms of issues significant to the discipline. This path, too, has its pitfalls.

In informal discussion we sometimes dichotomize between traditional ethnographers whose exercises in mindless empiricism have the unrealizable goal of complete description and the self-selected "scientists." The latter, in de Laguna's memorable image (1957), are like pot hunters who destroy the significance of a site by obsessively removing the few artifacts they value. De Laguna's criticism is of studies that "have relied upon brilliant intuition alone to cut through the tedious routine of scholarship, or have sketched major considerations by presenting certain striking features, sometimes even tending to ignore that which did not fit or which seemed irrelevant (1957:180 f.). Her argument is similar to Griaule's (1957:5):

... il s'agit aujourd'hui de mener des études précises et profondes sur données étraites, avec des methodes rigoureuses et non d'abouter à une sorte de petit pantheon de faits sociaux bien choisis [que] les sociologues puiseront pour leurs besoins d'exemplification.... Alors seulement la sociologie pourra procéder à des généralisations et à l'établissement de lois.

Even Leach, despite his occasional impatience with traditional fact grubbing (1954:285, 312), rejects studies in which "insight comes from the anthropologist's private intuition: the evidence is only put in by way of illustration" (1961:12). These anthropologists of divergent views and different nationalities seem to be in essential agreement.

Domains and classifications.—In recent years, the popularity of linguistic analogies for sociocultural systems has been growing at the expense of physiological analogies. To be more than mere imagery, such analogies should concentrate not on the details of linguistic analysis (e.g., complementary distribution, componential analysis), but on first principles. Yet, ethnology has yet to reach the "starting point of ... a [descriptive] science [which] is to define (1) the universe of discourse, and (2) the criteria which are used in making classifications" (Hockett 1942:3). Only from this starting point can we hope to achieve the ethnographer's goal of "culturally significant arrangement of productive statements about the relevant relationships obtaining among locally defined categories and contexts ... within a given social matrix" (Conklin 1964:25). Because of the scope and complexity of our subject matter, and because of the deductive bias of physiological (and especially functional) models, ethnology suffers from inadequate demarcation of domains (i.e., universes of discourse), inconsistent definition of criteria for classification, and confusion among native, Western, and analytic categories.

The clear definition of meaningful domains (e.g., activity systems, institutions, relational patterns, cultures), although prerequisite to objective, comparable, and replicable ethnographic statements, has received relatively little attention (cf. Conklin 1962a:87; 1964). Even the most sophisticated analyses suggest that perhaps we know only our own culture well enough to reject categories of objects and events as irrelevant to a universe of discourse. As a member of the culture whose cognitive categories he is describing, I know that Frake is correct in his offhand judgment that "an Eskimo pie is not a kind of pie" (1962:79). Similarly, as a member of American culture, I know that Wallace and Atkins (1960:60, 67 f.) are wrong in suggesting that we natives distinguish between consanguine and affinal uncles. In the first example, lunch food is a native domain. In the second, the domain—of persons traceable to me on a genealogical grid through consanguine links alone—is native only to the peculiar subculture of anthropologists. If a domain is demarcated inappropriately to the culture described, one cannot make culturally significant statements about its categories, relationships, and contexts.

The domain of this study is rice farming in Ban Ping. The villager who speaks of *het na* and the outsider (whether missionary, agronomist, or official) who describes rice farming must observe much of the behavior and confront many of the data presented in this study. If I am correct in asserting that all villagers and all outsiders agree on which actions constitute rice farming, there is no immediate need to define my subject matter further. Although they agree on what rice farming is, the native and each specialist will, of course, emphasize different aspects of it and delineate different ways in which *het na* is connected to the rest of village life. From this variety of approach arises the necessity of stating criteria of classification. It is here that linguistic models again are appropriate.

A physiologist, one hopes, can always distinguish a liver from a pancreas. When ethnographers used an organismic model, they assumed that such categories as kinship, economics, or politics provided a similarly apodictic analytic scheme. But, with the sort of categories provided by most ethnographies or by books like *The Outline of Cultural Materials*,[2] the fieldworker is like a man who has been

---

[2] *OCM* (Murdock 1950), as it is usually called, states quite clearly that it is not intended as a guide for collecting field data. It has nonetheless been frequently so used.

ordered to bring back chocolate pudding in an egg carton. He can fill the depressions in his box with neatly separated quivering mounds, but his collection shares only local color with the objects of the field. Objective criteria of *tribe* do not demarcate the Lue (Moerman 1965); genealogical notions of *kinship* provide only a crude suggestion of those whom villagers call "kinsman" (Moerman 1966b). Any of us, by reflecting upon his fieldwork, is made aware that no recorded observation, nor even any collected artifact, fits neatly and exclusively into a single substantive category of the sort we usually bring to the field.[3] As Goodenough (1956:28 f.) has pointed out for ethnography, linguists learned before we did that categories developed for comparative purposes distort the workings of specific systems.

Linguists also preceded ethnographers by basing procedures (Lounsbury 1953:404) on a principle to which we often give only lip service: distinctions significant to one culture need not be significant to all. Unlike the other social scientists, we can rarely afford to use the ready-made categories of Western culture for our comparative purposes, but must instead make them to the measure of our metacultural subject matter. We must derive our *intracultural* categories not from "the application of a previously designed typological grid" (Conklin 1964:26), but from the distinctions recognized as significant by the specific peoples described.

The fieldworker cannot possibly record everything he experiences or report on everything he has recorded. One selective device is to arrange individual events (including informants' statements about events) into categories significant either because they are used by natives or because they are useful for comparative and metacultural purposes. The comparative categories of anthropology are sometimes projections of Western folk ideas onto exotic settings. Burling (1962) has pointed out that some of us, when describing other cultures, use the term "economic" for those goods and services that are priced in our own. We anthropologists define politics by reference to a sovereign state that not all societies have. Similarly, social anthropologists may have no foundation for their supposedly universal distinction between consanguines and affines other than the Western folk categories of blood relatives and in-laws, no basis for notions of fictive ("phony," if we drop the jargon) kinsmen and of the "semantic extension" of kinship terms (cf. Lounsbury 1956:193) other than the genealogical bias of Western property law.

To avoid the danger of using Western folk images as analytic categories, it is often best to define our analytic categories, not substan-

[3] Suppose, for example, that one watches as the lay leader of a Buddhist congregation makes offerings at the start of a service. Is his behavior religious (veneration of the Buddha), economic (transfer of valuables), social (deference of an elder to young clergy), or political (the acting out of an elected position of much respect and some authority)?

tively, but as special perspectives for viewing behavior.[4] This study views the events of *het na* from the perspectives of technology and of extracommunity relations. The distinction between these categories is conceptual, for both apply to the same people, to the same actions, and to the same domain of behavior. I have already specified the functional perspective employed in the chapter sections on extracommunity relations. An entirely different perspective, and one closer to the villagers own, is furnished by the chapter sections on technology.

Technology and rationality.—The farmers of Ban Ping grow rice. The chapters that follow begin by describing farming behavior from the viewpoint of technology. By "technology" I do not mean material culture, subsistence production, or any other category based upon the substantive content of the behavior itself. Following Ford, I use technology as an analytic category that views behavior as solutions to problems. While it might prove profitable to view all patterned behavior as problem solving (Ford 1942:555, 557; 1945:90 f.), the intention is more limited. The technological sections of this study are concerned solely with the ways in which the farmers of Ban Ping make use of what we call things, people, and ideas in order to solve the problem of growing rice, as they see it.

Although concerned exclusively with techniques of agriculture, the technology sections are conventionally anthropological in form and goal. In form, a comparative approach is used, the ways in which one component of farming affects others are delineated, and farming decisions are set in the relevant context of the society and culture of Ban Ping. The goals of the technological sections are equally conventional. First, the reader learns how each farming operation "makes sense" in terms of the preceding operations and in terms of the botanical and agronomic characteristics of rice. Second, the reader is told the frequency distribution of each of Ban Ping's many farming alternatives and the results of each alternative, in terms of the amount of rice reaped—the product of the technology. Third, in this study I strive, but less conventionally, to describe the "grammar" (Goodenough 1951:10) of farming in Ban Ping. I view Ban Ping farming behavior as the result of decisions made by villagers in accord with the information and values they have about the problems of growing rice. With the knowledge of farming techniques (Part Two), of land acquisition and labor mobilization (Part Three), and of the amount of rice obtained by each technique (Part Four), the reader will understand how a given category of villagers grows rice. The goal, which has not been fully realized, is a style of

[4] The same events can be viewed under the aspect of society or of culture (Geertz 1957; Nash 1957), under the aspect of social organization or of economics (Burling 1962).

ethnographic description [which] should provide sufficient data to permit the construction of decision-making models in which culturally perceived alternatives are designated, the principles (or factors) which are determinate for choosing between alternatives described, and the relationship between the factors specified [Howard 1963:409, paraphrasing Goodenough 1957].

I am assuming that villagers make use of the environmental relationships they perceive (e.g., irrigated land is better than unirrigated land), together with the relevant rules of their society (e.g., land can be rented), in order to farm in such a way as to gain the most reward (e.g., a large harvest). Moreover, farming in Ban Ping closely conforms to technical definitions of "everyday rationality" (Garfinkel 1962:305–308; Schutz 1953). Ban Ping's agricultural technology makes sense in that the village farmer categorizes and compares, demands a close fit between what he observes and what he talks about, makes judicious use of previously successful means, anticipates the alterations that his actions will produce, plans possible alternative courses of action, is concerned with timing, finds ways to increase the predictable features of his situation, decides his correctness in terms of rules of procedure, is aware of and actually exercises choice, and works to increase the scientific corpus of information he uses for making and explaining his farming decisions and their rewards.

I make this point somewhat elaborately because it is common, yet quite mistaken, to think that peasant "decision-making and technology are traditional and arational" (Wharton 1965:13). Men, whether in Iowa or Ifugao, farm not by instinct, but by consciously using culturally appropriate means to cope with culturally recognized goals. To the naïve outsider, the farming practices found in other societies may appear arational because they make sense largely in terms of a tradition not his own. To the sophisticated outsider, the practices may appear tradition-bound because he views them through the anthropologist's construct of the "cultural dope" (Garfinkel 1964:244),[5] losing sight of the fact, which we all know intimately and directly, that an individual makes use of the rules of his culture fully as much as they make use of him. To speak of a "change from tradition to choice agriculture" (Wharton 1965:10) is to ignore a complementarity quite essential to our understanding of agricultural technology: most farming seems to consist of (and only becomes intelligible when viewed as if it were) the results of decisions made and justified by

[5] With this label I want to suggest, but cannot here explore, a distinction between the "cultural dope" and the "cultural sharpy" approaches to social science. The former, concerned largely with customs, seems to suppose that the members of a society devote their first seven years of life to obsessively "internalizing" a culture that they are then destined to spend the remainder of their lives reproducing. The sharpy tradition sees each person as playing with the rules of his culture in order to increase his share of what he values.

traditional, rational rules for choosing among traditional, rational alternatives. When we believe that farming behavior is determined by a homogeneous entity called culture which men cannot escape, we tend to use "culture" as if the mere word explained behavior. We then feel free to throw up our hands when people will not change their behavior as we would like them to. "The Tai do not use tractors, nor the fellahin fertilizer, because their culture does not let them." To find out why, and thereby to increase the chances of change, we must learn what the Tai or fellahin believe they would lose (money? leisure? predictability?) by adopting an innovation and how they value such things. To introduce an innovation successfully, it is wise to recognize and to analyze the rationality of those who have rejected it.

My mode of analysis supposes that persons act (and categories of persons can be imputed to act) in order to get things they value (e.g., rice, money, religious merit, love) through judicious rational use of the rules and resources of their environment (e.g., rice cannot grow in sand, to receive aid one must give aid). Time—through a person as he matures, through a tool system as it evolves, through a society as it meets other societies—permits changes in the prizes and in the rules, and in the actor's perceptions of both.[6]

This scheme for viewing social activities obviates some scholastic disputes and so permits us to get on with the business of recording, understanding, and predicting the behavior of man. Consider, for example, Leach's "protest . . . against attempts to isolate kinship behaviors as a distinct category explainable by jural rules without reference to context of economic self-interest" (Leach 1961:305 f.). Now, the present study also asserts that human activity involves both rules and self-interest and that any analysis of behavior which ignores either basis for action is false. But I would challenge the way in which Leach distinguishes between the social and the material, and assigns primacy to one. The present study maintains that an individual's perceptions of the rules imposed by his world, material *and* social, limit and direct his decisions with equal effectiveness. It is perfectly true, but only by half, that what the "social anthropologist calls kinship structure is just a way of talking about property relations which can also be talked about in other ways" (*ibid.*, p. 305). Kinship structure is also just a way of talking about personality formation (Kardiner 1945), population dynamics (Birdsell 1957), or sources of religious ideas (Swanson 1960). And, in some societies at least, all these things are also just a way of talking about kinship systems. In any event, there is little reason to assume that property determines be-

---

[6] Although I am not aware of his influencing my approach, it would be churlish not to point out that Charles Erasmus (1961) has carefully developed and elaborated a similar view of cultural behavior.

havior more than personality, religion, or nutrition does. There is still less reason to agree with Leach (1961:304 f., emphasis added) that "kinship *systems* have no 'reality' " while "property *relations*" do. Despite the insulating quotation marks, Leach uses "reality" to mean palpability. Thus, he is clearly correct in asserting that kinship systems are not tangible, and clearly wrong in asserting that property relations are. There are things and there are persons; and they are equally "real." There are folk categories of kinsmen and of property; one is no less "real" than the other. Finally, there are the analytic and relational categories of kinship systems and of property relations; one is just as abstract as the other. Despite Leach's claim (1961:304), he maintains the very dichotomy he criticizes between things "sacred" and things "profane," things "social" and things "material." He merely opts for the primacy of the profane.

We are through, until the last chapter, with the elaborate distinctions and flights of scholastic fancy that concern academic anthropology. The next three parts of this book concern the manure, dirt, sweat, and grain that are the bases of agricultural change and peasant choice in Ban Ping.

PART TWO: *FARMING OPERATIONS*

The following chapters on plow and tractor farming each fall into two main parts: technology and extracommunity relations. The technology sections—for those who have not bothered with the explanations in chapter ii—relate farming practices to each other and to the environment; delineate the underlying physical and social forces that determine the choice a Ban Ping farmer makes among the practices available to him; and, in order to counteract anthropological ignorance of wet-rice farming, offer the fullest descriptions permitted by the author's data and the reader's endurance. The extracommunity relations sections examine each farming practice to see how (or whether) it brings the Ban Ping farmer out of his own village into a wider world.

III.
Plow Agriculture

THE RICE FIELDS OF BAN PING

The people of Ban Ping distinguish among six rice fields (*na*), and name most of them according to their location. For example, *na horngmet* (see table 1) gets it name from the village of Horngmet which lies near it, *na norng than* from its location in the depression (*norng*) once cleared by an elder named Than.

With the exception of Thunglor and the Great Field, I do not refer to these fields by transliterating or by glossing their village names. Instead, I identify each field by its distance from the village and by the way in which water is obtained for growing rice on it, since these are the main environmental influences on farming technique. Thus, I refer to the fields as home flood, home rainfall, semi-irrigated, home irrigated (Great Field), distant flood (Thunglor), and distant irrigated (see fig. 1 for locations).

Although villagers do not literally name individual fields by distances from home and water source, table 1 indicates that their *system* of field names is consistent with these two ecological features. A further confirmation of the ecological basis of the village system of field names is furnished by my observation in 1965 that the former *horngmet* field, which is now watered and farmed in the same way as Thunglor, is now called Thunglor. Much as we take account of social class when using names like Harlem and Beverly Hills, so the people of Ban Ping take account of water source when using locality names for their fields.

To the west of Ban Ping, just beyond the Waen River and but a few minutes' walk from the village temple, are the villagers' 18 acres (7.2 ha) of *home flood field*. These get their water when the Waen overflows. A few steps outside the eastern gate of the village lie 55.2 acres (22.4 ha) of sandy *home rainfall field,* beyond which is a narrow scrub forest where carabao are sometimes grazed. This irregular forest borders on the village's 20.4 acres (8.3 ha) of *semi-irrigated field* watered by the spill-off from the main irrigation system that serves the village's 214.8 acres (87.0 ha) of *home irrigated* land. The home irrigated or Great Field, watered by the Great Dam, is Ban Ping's traditional source of rice, the main agricultural influence on its social organization, and the focus of whatever slight emotional attachment

TABLE 1
Names, Acreages, and Farming Techniques of Ban Ping's Fields, 1960

naj *tunglong* "GREAT FIELD" HOME IRRIGATED 215 acres P;t	*nork*		*phae* RAINFALL 55 acres P,T;t,b	*norngthan* HOME FLOOD 18 acres P,T;t,b	*tunglor* THUNGLOR DISTANT FLOOD 550 acres T;b		*horngmet* DISTANT IRRIGATED 150 acres P;t,b
	phanang SEMI-IRRIGATED 20 acres P;t				*naferng* "straw fields" DEVELOPED LAND	*napa* "forest" fields VIRGIN LAND	

(Header spans: *ban* "home field" covers naj, nork, phae, norngthan; *na* "paddy field" covers all)

Note: Native names are in italics. Quotation marks enclose glosses. Names in small capitals are those commonly used throughout the text. Numbers indicate the acreage owned by villagers of Ban Ping. P = cultivated by animal-drawn plow; T = cultivated by tractor; t = transplanted; b = broadcast. A semicolon separates technique of cultivation from technique of seeding; a comma indicates variation in technique, with the technique most commonly used preceding the comma.

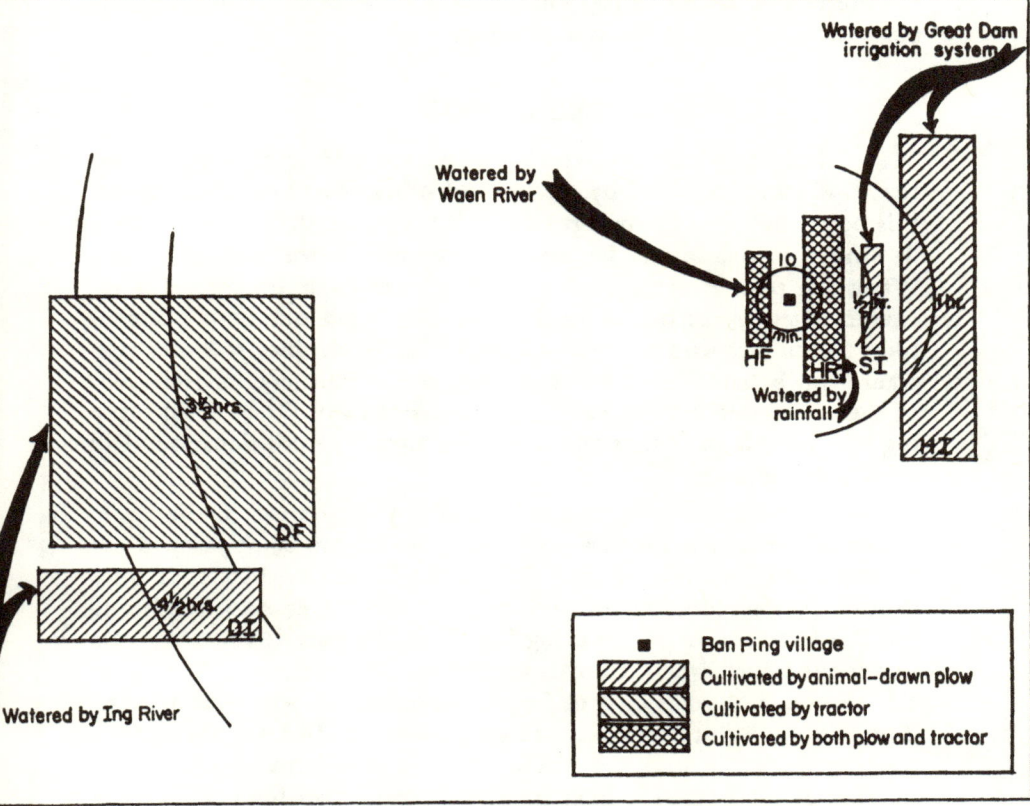

Fig. 1. Schematic diagram of Ban Ping's fields. Distances from Ban Ping are drawn to a scale of typical travel time. The size of each field represents the acreage owned or farmed by Ban Ping villagers.
KEY: HI = home irrigated (Great Field); SI = home semi-irrigated; HR = home rainfall; HF = home flood; DF = distant flood (Thunglor); DI = distant irrigated.

the farmer feels for his land. It takes, at the most, little more than an hour and a half to walk over the narrow dikes and crude log bridges that lie between Ban Ping and its farthest home irrigated land. Along with the other home fields, the Great Field provides the "eating rice," which is the village's insurance against the uncertainties of yield and price to which the "selling rice" from the *distant flood* (550.4 acres or 222.9 ha) and *distant irrigated* (130.4 acres or 52.8 ha) fields is subject. The least distant of these fields (see fig. 1) is two hours by foot or oxcart from the village. When the roads permit, an able cyclist can get to the beginning of the distant fields in about an hour, but as most farmers walk or ride oxcarts, only in extraordinary circumstances would one attempt to go to his Thunglor or to his distant irrigated field and return in a single day. It is the amount of time, rather than the number of statute miles, which makes these fields *distant* for purposes of technological decision making.

TECHNOLOGY

All of Ban Ping's 948 acres (384 ha) are used to grow inundated rice, but some are tilled by tractor and others by plow. Throughout this book, the term "plow agriculture" designates the farming system in which cultivation is by means of animal-drawn wooden plows. When the plow is used, farmers usually transplant; tractor fields are characterized by broadcasting. It is best to begin our description of plow techniques with practices on the Great Field, since practices elsewhere can be considered by us, as they are by villagers, modifications of these. The reader who can endure the details of Great Field farming will be able to understand the more cursory descriptions found in subsequent sections.

Great Field tasks.—FERTILIZING   For the few who use it, the application of fertilizer is the first agricultural operation. Some farmers put ox or carabao manure on their fields; even fewer use chicken or duck droppings, sometimes mixed with ashes of rice straw; none used commercial fertilizer in 1960. During late April, manure is collected from under the house, where animals are tethered for the night. This practice results in a good deal of humus being mixed with the manure. The mixture is put into an oxcart with a long-handled hoe that is then used to spread it onto the still-dry field; a few farmers pile up the manure at the irrigation inlet for the water to distribute later in the year.

IRRIGATING   Throughout the world, the techniques of rice farming depend upon the supply of water. Ban Ping's home irrigated and semi-irrigated fields are watered by the "Great Dam," a wood-reinforced earthen wall 50 meters (165 ft) long and 25 meters (83 ft) wide which shifts the flow of the Lao River westward. Each year every farming household pounds stakes into the dam and then wedges boards vertically across the stakes.[1] To reinforce the smaller dams and levees which irrigate groups of four to ten plots, the farmers weave sections of split bamboo. Heavy strips of bamboo at least 25 mm broad are woven in a simple under-two over-two pattern.

During May, the young men of the village begin to cart wood home from the nearby forests. The wood is cut with hatchets and field knives. A hoe and a small basket are the only other irrigation tools. There are no water-raising devices, and the dipping baskets (Rajadhon 1961: drawing 5, 9), used for irrigation elsewhere in Thailand, are normally

[1] In May 1960 each household sent a young man with twenty (25 mm by 46 cm) stakes and ten (25 mm by 91 cm) boards for each rai of land worked.

used solely for fishing here. In emergencies, however, Ban Ping farmers know how to use these baskets for splashing water onto desiccated seedbeds, if any water is nearby.

PREPARING THE SEEDBED   Almost all of Asia's wet rice is nurtured in a seedbed before it is transplanted to the fields. By the beginning of May, or even the end of April, there are many young men at work on the two types of seedbeds used in Ban Ping: the "forest" and the "field" beds.

Slightly more common is the forest seedbed made on dry land, either on a home rainfall field or on a plot cleared in the forest and used for one to three years. The high winds, which precede the "head-of-the-year" rains, signal the farmer that it is time to burn his forest seedbed. This job is done in the evening, after the wind has died. When there is no woody undergrowth, coconut fronds or thatch are used as fuel, for the burning is considered a source of fertilizer. Manure is sometimes spread on the forest seedbed after its first year of use.

Field seedbeds are made on a plot of land adjoining a main irrigation ditch and used year after year. These field seedbeds are thought to produce somewhat inferior yields. When the land was more plentiful than it is now, even those with choice land near the main ditch chose to clear a forest seedbed on unclaimed Great Field land.

Field seedbeds are tilled by hoeing and weeding (see illus.). The claylike soil is first sliced with a hoe, and the slices are then broken up with the side or back of the blade. Clumps of grass and straw are put on a pile for burning. Unlike the forest seedbed, no coconut fronds or other fuel is added to the fire, and the ashes are not deliberately spread over the plot, for water is considered fertilizer enough.

SEEDING   Seeding proper awaits the head-of-the-year rains which in 1960 fell at the beginning of May, about a week after the completion of all seedbed tillage. These rains are sporadic but heavy showers which normally fall between mid-April and mid-May. A dry spell separates them from the true monsoon, whose total precipitation dwarfs the head-of-the-year rainfall. However, the timing and the predictability of the head-of-the-year rains make them crucial to farming in Ban Ping. Seedbed tillage begins on extremely hard soil sometimes covered with a thin film of dust. Even after tillage, the topsoil consists of firm pellets of earth, often too tough to be broken by a man standing on them. After the head-of-the-year rains, the seedbed soil, while still dry, is more friable and contains enough moisture to permit the distinctive seeding techniques used in Ban Ping.

Work parties place dry grain in dibble holes made in a still-dry seedbed. The dibble stick, a 6-foot fence pole, is tipped with a conical lead weight. The dibble point is pressed into the soil at regular intervals[2] and removed with a twisting motion intended to keep the earth from clinging and so crumbling into the hole.

While the men of the work party are using dibble sticks, the women follow them with basins of rice. In a stooping position, they take a fistful of seed from the basin and direct a stream of grain over their index finger into the hole. Although there is no attempt to measure the seed, about ten to twenty grains are commonly dropped into each hole. Since the women keep their hands quite close to the soil, very little grain misses its mark.

After the seeding, which takes less than a day, the men dust soil over the holes with a branch or palm frond. They then build a fence of closely spaced vertical bamboo stakes to prevent animals from molesting the growing rice.

PLOWING Once a seedbed has been fenced, young men build a temporary field shelter for use until plowing and harrowing are completed. A woman of the household brings food to the fields daily, although the men return home occasionally and sometimes sleep there. Depending on the size of the holding and the number of draft animals, tillage may take from more than a week to about a month. Throughout this period work is confined to the early morning and late afternoon hours because it is claimed that animals, especially carabao, cannot pull implements during the heat of the day.

The earth in low fields is often sufficiently softened by seepage or overflow from the irrigation ditches for plowing to begin immediately. On higher parcels, or those far from a source of water, plowing may be started on dry land, but it is more common for the owner (in agreement with owners of neighboring parcels) to dam the irrigation ditch with earth and so moisten the land.

Carabao and, more recently, oxen pull the simple wooden plows and harrows of Ban Ping's traditional tillage. A cord attached to the animal's left nostril, together with the farmer's shouts of "right! right!" "giddap!" and "whoa!" allow the farmer to guide the plow. With pressure on the handle, the farmer adjusts the depth of plowing and avoids the dikes as he methodically plows each square in closely spaced parallel furrows (see illus.). Ban Ping's plowed fields, like nearly all of Asia's transplanted rice land, are divided by low dikes into small squares (typically $\frac{1}{6}$ acre) which permit precise control over water level.

Immediately after plowing, the water level is raised slightly by building up the downwater dike, and a wooden harrow, reinforced

---

[2] On one field seedbed, which the farmers called "typical," planting holes were 15–20 cm apart and 3.8 cm deep.

PLOW AGRICULTURE 39

with leather or rattan, is pulled by the carabao in order to pulverize the soil and comb out weeds and grass. The harrow's width and the number of its teeth depend on the size of the carabao. The harrowing turns over (*kaw*) the soil into mounds (see illus.). This operation is said to kill the grass and thereby to fertilize the soil, which it also moistens and softens. The water level is then lowered and the mounds turned and leveled (*tyt*), also with a harrow. Some farmers try to delay opening the mounds for a few days or a week in order to allow time for grass and weeds to rot. During this time they may busy themselves with repairing the dikes. Most, however, begin to *tyt* the day after they have finished *kaw*'ing the holding. The final tilling operation is to flatten the mud with a wide harrow converted for this purpose by wedging a long piece of wood into the teeth. Immediate cross-plowing, which often occurs on hard soil, is the alternative to *kaw*'ing. Some feel that this technique hardens the soil [3] and, since all agree that it is easier than harrowing, privately regard those who use it as lazy.

When the fields have been tilled and when the rice, which has been in the seedbed for about seven weeks, is about a *sork* (*ca.* 46 cm) tall, transplanting begins.

TRANSPLANTING If seedlings are transplanted too young, they will be weak and damaged. If transplanted too old, the tillering phase is shortened and the yield consequently reduced (Janlekha 1955:108; Grist 1959:120).[4] It also reduces yields to leave uprooted seedlings unplanted (Thailand 1947:67). In order to minimize these dangers, Asian farmers usually transplant in large work groups which get the task done quickly. In Ban Ping, work groups commonly take two days to transplant each plot.

On the first day the seedlings are uprooted. This is the work of young men who pull the seedlings up out of the ground, knock off the loose soil against their instep or calf, and lay out the seedlings to be bound into bundles with thin strips of bamboo. Once bound, the bundles are brought to an older man who cuts all the seedlings to the same length, commonly about 1 foot (see illus.). A random sample (described in App. B) indicates that men compose 63 percent of the uprooting labor force. Women, who contribute the remaining 37 percent of worker-days, tie the seedlings and prepare food for the work party. Regardless of the sex ratio indicated by the sample,

[3] The one landlord who sometimes charges a fixed amount rather than a share of the crop as rental claims to do so in order to encourage his tenant to raise his yields by *kaw*'ing and thus improving the soil.
[4] There is some evidence (Thailand 1947:68) that slow-maturing varieties are unharmed by delayed uprooting.

villagers consider uprooting men's work. The sexual division of labor permits a household with many men but few women to donate uprooting labor in exchange for planting.

Only field seedbeds are wet at this time. Forest seedbeds are still dry enough to sit on quite comfortably, though the soil has been dampened by the head-of-the-year rains or even by the start of the true monsoon. Thus, in contrast to the way in which inundated rice is usually grown elsewhere,[5] seedlings in the Great Field are often taken from a dry bed to the wet fields. On field seedbeds, the rice is thinned in uprooting so that the bed is left with as many seedlings as the rest of the field.[6]

The next day the male farmers (who contribute 20 percent of planting worker-days) strew bundles of seedlings on the water or on the dikes. The head of the household, sometimes assisted by one of its young women, stays at home to prepare food for the work party.

A party of women, usually young, transplant the seedlings. The planters work quickly, efficiently, and vigorously, but the tone is relaxed and the task seems pleasant. The women begin at the far end of the field and walk backward, stooping over (see illus.). A woman grasps a bunch of seedlings in her left hand and uses the thumb and first two fingers of her right hand to thrust about half a dozen plants into the soft mud. Within about three seconds, she has planted a row of four such clumps and takes a step backward. In about five minutes of fairly continuous work she has completed a four-clump row the length of one field square, or about 18 meters (20 yards) long.

Once a Great Field plot has been transplanted, it needs no more attention until the harvest. Farmers with both a low and a high plot on the home irrigated field usually do not begin to irrigate and till the higher (and therefore drier) plot until they have transplanted seedlings onto the lower. But most farmers dismantle their field houses after transplanting and then can return home to care for their animals and to farm other fields. Occasionally they visit the Great Field to do casual weeding and to adjust the water level by breaking and rebuilding the dikes and by damming and opening the ditches, but the intensive postcultivation practiced elsewhere in Asia

---

[5] Adams (1948:257 f.) cites the *Philippine Islands Bureau of Agriculture Bulletin*, no. 37 (1921), which indicates that dry seedbeds are sometimes used in the Philippines. She also cites the *Malayan Agriculture Journal*, 27 (1939), 40–59, which says: "'Dryland' nurseries for 'wet paddy' are also described in an official report on the Pahang district in Malaya." Pelzer (1945:12) reports that in "the northern Philippines the seedlings are raised in seedbeds that are not flooded and puddled but are left dry." These descriptions conform to the forest seedbeds of Ban Ping.

[6] This practice should permit an agronomist who systematically compares yields from seedbeds with yields from other plots to discover the extent to which rice benefits from transplanting per se. Unfortunately, I made no such comparisons.

PLOW AGRICULTURE

is not known in Ban Ping, where land is plentiful relative to population and the crop provides ample food.

HARVESTING In November, four months after transplanting, home irrigated rice is ready to be reaped by work parties consisting of both men and women. A reaper grasps a bunch of rice in his left hand. Holding the sickle in his right, he pulls it toward him with a quick upward motion which cuts the stalk about 2 feet below the ear. A handful, the product of three or four sweeps with the sickle, is laid on the stubble to dry.

If there is a good strong sun, the rice is left drying on the stubble for about two days, or longer during bad weather. Then it is gathered, usually by men, into conical shocks about 6 feet in circumference and 5 feet tall scattered about the field in places convenient for threshing. Rice is placed in the shocks with the ears facing inward and up in order to protect the grain from possible rainfall.

In Chiengkham everyone threshes by hand, but each ethnic group practices minor variations in technique. The Lue thresh on large mats woven of bamboo, used in pairs. One mat is placed on the ground near the shock; the other, supported by bamboo posts, forms a windbreak around the first. Threshing is done by men working in pairs. One man holds a bunch of rice plants with a flail made of a rope or leather thong fixed to two pieces of wood of unequal length. He pounds the ears against a two-legged inclined table, the lower end of which rests on the mat (see illus.). The grain is thus knocked from the straw and slides down the table onto the mat. His partner beats the straw with short crutchlike sticks to remove any grains left after the pounding.

The rice is winnowed in the field immediately after it has been threshed. While the Yuan follow the rather common practice of throwing the grains into the air, sometimes from metal buckets, the Ban Ping farmer kicks the grains into the air with a slight sideways movement of his left foot, and at the same time waves a thin, closely woven, round bamboo fan over the grains.

The farmers then bring the rice home to the granary in carts that are far more efficient than the pack oxen of former days. But even the young men, who never saw pack trains, listen wistfully when their elders recall the deep, mellow sound that the great ox bells made as the rice was carried back from the field in a long procession. Bringing the rice home, like many other farming operations, is "no longer much fun."

Tasks on other fields.—If everyone farmed in exactly the same way, technological decisions might be merely a device that the analyst ascribes to the native. Villagers, however, vary their farming practices idiosyncratically and in accordance with the characteristics of individual plots. Moreover, there are rather gross differences in technique among the various fields farmed by the plow, to say nothing of the tractor techniques discussed in chapter iv. The environmental differences among plowed fields make the variant techniques intelligible and thereby acquaint us with some of "the principles . . . which are determinate for choosing between alternatives" (Howard 1963: 409).

SEMI-IRRIGATED   On every kind of land, the natural features most often talked about by villagers—source of water and distance from the village—were also observed to have the most influence on farming techniques. In these respects, the semi-irrigated field differs little from the Great Field, and, consequently, the two are farmed quite similarly. Any minor differences in technique are clearly related to slight differences in water and location. For example, it is my impression that the spreading of manure is more common on the semi-irrigated field than on the Great Field. The farmer's reasons are that the former needs manure more because it is somewhat higher and receives less water, and since the semi-irrigated field is closer to the village, it is easier to cart manure there. Similarly the proportion of forest seedbeds is higher on the semi-irrigated field because it is closer to the forest, which is considered more fertile than even the most well-watered field seedbed. In addition, forest seedbeds are preferred generally because they can be used to enlarge one's holdings and, perhaps, because they may permit greater flexibility in the timing of subsequent operations.

The semi-irrigated field is inundated by surplus water from the fully irrigated field. Although this spill-off is as dependable a source of water as primary irrigation, it does not last as long. The Great Field must be completely inundated before the semi-irrigated field is allowed any water; the semi-irrigated field must be drained to maintain the end-of-season water level on the Great Field. Thus, with one exception, each task on the Great Field precedes the same task on the semi-irrigated field. The exception is the harvest; the semi-irrigated field is planted in faster-maturing varieties of rice which, although sown after the seed in the Great Field, ripen earlier. For other fields as well, taking advantage of varietal differences in growing time is a major component of farm management in Ban Ping (see fig. 9, p. 167).

HOME RAINFALL   The home rainfall field is inundated by rain and by seepage from the semi-irrigated field. Its water supply is consequently much smaller, less predictable, and less continuous than that of either irrigated field. Farming techniques reflect this difference. Except in years of heavy and steady precipitation, the home rainfall field produces little rice. If a dry year is anticipated, many owners let

PLOW AGRICULTURE

their farms lie fallow. The soil on home rainfall land is not soft enough to plow until well after the start of the monsoon. Even then, the soil is still so hard that it requires replowing and reharrowing immediately after the initial tillage. Flexibility, provenience, and expansion, factors that discourage the use of field seedbeds for the semi-irrigated field, are even more influential on home rainfall land; consequently, only forest seedbeds are used. During the growing season, the farmer may remove excess water and do some casual weeding. If there is too little water, there is nothing he can do. The difficulty and uncertainty of farming home rainfall fields help to account for the introduction of the tractor there in 1960.

HOME FLOOD The small area of the home flood field does not limit the variety of techniques used to farm it. Like Thunglor, it is subject to a sudden rise in water level. The danger, of course, is aggravated in plots in the lower basin. On such plots the farmer begins to plow the land while it is still quite dry. This extremely hard work, villagers claim and observation confirms, takes about four times as long as Great Field plowing. Upon the completion of plowing, dry seed is broadcast in anticipation of the head-of-the-year rains. The seed is covered either by shallow cross-plowing or by dragging palm fronds over the soil. After seeding, the plot is fenced. The home flood field is near village, so it is not difficult for the farmer to return periodically to resow barren patches. Once the field is inundated, he evens out the distribution of the rice by transplanting the young sprouts from thick to sparse areas.

At the edge of the basin, where flooding occurs later, it is less common to modify plow agriculture by broadcast sowing. Each year, a seedbed is made in a fresh piece of nearby forest where trees are felled, allowed to dry, and burned. After the burning, the scrub is cleared and the soil is cultivated by hoe. At the onset of the head-of-the-year rains, dry seed is drilled into the forest seedbed by means of the lead-weighted dibble. When the field has enough surface water to cover the very shortest blades of grass, it is soft enough to plow. The water rises too rapidly to allow time for *kaw*'ing. Immediately after the first plowing, the farmer cross-plows, levels, and begins to transplant.

DISTANT IRRIGATED Farming techniques here differ slightly from Great Field practices, usually in ways that can be traced to the relative newness of the distant irrigated field. The irrigation system, for example, is less fully developed and serves fewer landholders, who thus must each contribute more wood per rai than is required for the Great Dam that serves the home irrigated field. At the same time, local dams and canals are rather primitive and their maintenance thus requires less labor than do those at the Great Field.

Seedbed and tillage techniques vary on the distant irrigated field, for villagers are not yet certain of the best way to farm its wide variations of soil type, forest cover, and water supply. Variability is further increased because Lue and Yuan work proximate fields; each experiments with the techniques of the other in order to find the one best suited to this still-raw environment. Three major techniques are used for seeding. As an emergency measure, when the monsoon is imminent, dry seed is broadcast among the remaining trees of a newly cleared plot. This method produces some rice, but the farmer thinks himself unfortunate indeed if he has to broadcast dry seed on all of his land. The second major seeding technique is drilling, already described for the Great Field. At the distant irrigated field, however, dry seeds are drilled into the seedbed before plowing only when the local irrigation system is not dependable. The farmer thinks that this drilling gives the seedlings a head start and decreases the chance of their drowning, should he be unable to control drainage adequately.

A third technique now predominates and will probably replace the other two when all the field is cleared and its irrigation system perfected. The new seeding method is the use of soaked and sprouted seeds. The Lue learned the technique from the Yuan, who seem to share it with most farmers in Thailand (Rajadhon 1961:14; Kaufman 1960:43; Kingshill 1960:28). Seeds are soaked for two or three days, although some farmers claim that they may be soaked for more than a week without damage. The evening before seeding they are removed from the water and allowed to sprout overnight. Although most farmers use sprouted seed, they do not yet agree on the best way to use it. Some merely broadcast the seed onto the bed which, whenever sprouted seed is used, has already been tilled. Others make furrows in the seedbed with a plow, harrow, or hoe. On newly cleared plots or when surface water covers the furrow, an unweighted blunt dibble stick is used to make holes in the furrow ridge and the sprouted seeds are placed in these holes. When there is no danger that the sprouted seeds might float on the surface water, they are merely dropped or pressed by hand onto the furrow ridge. Dry unsprouted seed is sometimes introduced into the bed in the same manner.

Minor differences in tillage techniques are also related to the unsubdued nature of the distant irrigated field. On newly cleared plots, a large, square wooden roller pulled by carabao is used for a year or two in order to dislodge tree roots. On light and sandy soil, whether completely cleared or not, plowing precedes inundation and water is admitted for the subsequent harrowing and leveling.

Timing of tasks.—Examining the microenvironments of Ban Ping's various plowed fields has suggested some of the environmental principles that influence choice among technological alternatives. Contrasting Ban Ping's timetable for plowing operations with that of Bangchan in central Thailand highlights some of the ecological and economic factors that underlie farming. In Ban Ping, farming requires a less careful calibration of labor; this difference seems attributable to the village's plentiful land and to its casual marketing arrangements. It is also possible, but beyond my competence to judge, that farming in Ban Ping is comparatively easy because of the plant characteristics of glutinous rice (see App. A). It may well be that the characteristics of ordinary rice do not permit the dry seeding and imprecise schedule of transplanting used in Ban Ping. It may also be that delayed reaping becomes possible only when rice has the high water and soluble starch content that may defer ripening (Burkill 1935:1596). But whatever the significant "specifications" (Ford 1937) of glutinous rice in respect to ripening, it is probable that Ban Ping farmers take advantage of them because land availability and marketing conditions make "harvest losses [more] tolerable (Boserup 1965:51).

In central Thailand there are two "critical periods of rice production" (Janlekha 1955:108): the period between initial cultivation and transplanting, and the period between grain maturity and the completion of harvesting. Whenever wet rice is grown, these are the seasons of most intensive labor, but the Ban Ping farmer does not feel compelled to get the work done on time.

Seedlings can be transplanted only after the field has been prepared for them. Their rate of growth in the seedbed must coincide, therefore, with the farmer's progress in tilling his fields. This progress depends upon water to make the soil soft enough to till and wet enough to receive the seedlings. The farmer who cannot adequately predict the time of inundation may therefore find it an advantage for his seedlings to grow slowly in the bed. Even when soaked and sprouting seeds are used, growth is slower in a dry bed (Grist 1959:116).[7] This advantage is probably increased by drilling dry seeds into the bed rather than sowing wet ones, but Ban Ping farmers, it was observed, leave seedlings in their beds only slightly longer than Bangchan farmers do.[8] In Ban Ping the main laxity in timing is relative, not absolute.

In central Thailand, seedbeds are always made on the field and are prepared by plowing and harrowing. In other words, field tillage and the seedbed preparation, which must precede it, depend on the same

---

[7] Matsuo (1954:86) seems to disagree, for he reports that seedlings on dry (i.e., rainfall) beds grow and root more quickly, but are also more susceptible to blast disease.

[8] Eight Ban Ping farmers, observed in 1960, did their transplanting 42–57 days after they seeded, a period only slightly longer than the 30–50 days reported for the wet seedlings of Bangchan. Had the rains of 1960 been less favorable, Ban Ping's farmers might have been able to delay transplanting still further.

source of water.⁹ As soon as the seeds have been sown, the central Thai farmer must work frantically to prepare his fields for the seedlings. Thus, "this critical period . . . is not only one of physical strain on the part of the farmer but also a period of anxieties" (Janlekha 1955:109). In Ban Ping, however, the presence of forest land permits, and the unevenness of the irrigated field encourages, most seeding to be done by using dibble sticks on dry beds.

In Ban Ping, seeding depends on the head-of-the-year rains while tillage depends on the monsoon which follows later in the year. Plowing and harrowing are hard work, but the Ban Ping farmer rarely needs to fear that he will not finish in time to transplant his seedlings.[10] Bangchan farmers further complicate their tillage-season schedule by planting and transplanting different rices at different dates. On the other hand, Ban Ping farmers usually transplant on the same day varieties that mature two weeks or a month apart.

Similar laxities in timing characterize the harvest season in Ban Ping. Some varieties of rice flower, not after a fixed period of time, but when climatic conditions change (Burkill 1935:1597). Most late-maturing rices flower when the number of hours of daily sunlight reaches a point to which they are sensitive (Grist 1959:10). Since this date is fixed by the solar calendar, and since each variety takes a fixed amount of time to progress from flowering to heading to maturity, it follows that, in any given region, "each [late-maturing] variety will mature on a certain exact date no matter how early or late it is planted" (Janlekha 1955:111). In central Thailand the harvest season, although a time of joy, is thereby made a "second critical period," because farmers fear that "if the harvesting is delayed for even a short period of three or four days, the paddy will be over-ripe, resulting in a higher proportion of breakage and hence in a lower price" (*ibid.,* p. 109; cf. Kaufman 1960:41). In Ban Ping these matters are of little concern.[11]

---

⁹ Rajadhon (1961:13), whose account is based mainly on farming practices in Thailand's northeastern province of Nakorn Ratchasima, speaks of plowing the seedbed while it is still dry.

[10] Ban Ping seedbed technology, however, does allow for other anxieties that may be less common where the seedbed and the fields depend on a single source of water. In 1960 the head-of-the-year rains did not last long and were followed by a period of unusually low humidity and strong sun. Ban Ping farmers, since they use no devices for retaining surface moisture, were afraid that the sprouted seedlings would die.

[11] Timing can become extremely important when the weather is unusually bad. Normally, rice ripens and is harvested in dry fields. The harvest season of November 1960, however, saw unusually heavy rains which proved most harmful to the energetic villagers who had reaped early. Uncut rice can survive flooding for about fifteen days, say villagers (cf. Grist 1959:70), but rice that has been shocked or been spread on the stubble to dry begins to sprout. Every day saw farmers at the frustrating task of raising the ears of the cut rice above the water, sometimes

On the home irrigated field, for example, seven farmers were observed reaping the same local variety of rice between the widely separated dates of November 10 and December 1. On the tractor-plowed distant flood field, rice is left standing long after it is ripe. Some farmers, because they think that it influences eating properties, are concerned with how long they let the reaped rice dry before threshing it. No one, however, is concerned with how long ripe rice stands before it is reaped. The casual timing of harvest operations, which is perhaps aided by the physical characteristics of glutinous rice, is permitted by the land availability and by the marketing arrangements in Ban Ping. The former, together with the consequent scarcity of labor, is probably the compelling factor, and is discussed in subsequent chapters. It is also important that most "selling rice" comes from distant fields where the village has so much that it can be reaped only well after it ripens. The home irrigated field, for the most part, produces "eating rice" in whose milling properties the farmer is relatively uninterested. Moreover, probably because commercial farming has recently come to Ban Ping, villagers have only two markets for their surplus rice: they sell to one another by volume or to Chinese merchants by weight. In both markets, anticipated milling qualities are irrelevant to price.

Farming knowledge.—Knowledge about plow farming is among Ban Ping's most fundamental agricultural resources (cf. Schultz 1964: 3, 133–134, 175–177). This knowledge is distributed according to age and sex, to occasion no anxiety for the future and to assure everyone the respect of his fellows.

Villagers consider it good to farm with ambition and success, but invidious comparisons are very rare. While an occasional young man may boast about how early in the season he started a chore or how quickly he was through with it, peers never berate or even gossip about one another's laziness. The competitive games that figure so prominently in work parties elsewhere in Thailand (Rajadhon 1961: 28; Kaufman 1960:44) do not occur in Ban Ping. Some persons are thought stronger and more energetic than others; these traits are appreciated and desired (especially in a prospective in-law) but more

by means of racks built for that purpose. Those who had already shocked their rice considered themselves lucky, for the straw exterior of the shock protected the rice ears. But as the water level rose to the base of the shocks, the rice ears lying on the soil began to sprout. Since the villagers did not believe that such unseasonable weather could persist, they postponed large-scale efforts to bring the rice home to their granaries. Soon it was too late for carts to reach the flooded fields. Then came a time of great anxiety. With the deprecating giggle that indicates strong emotion, the villagers complained to one another that there would be only maize to eat. Groups of young men got drunk and wandered the village paths complaining of their luck. Only in such unusual circumstances can the harvest season in Ban Ping be regarded as "a critical period in rice production."

is expected of such people. It is interesting that *du,* "very hard working," also describes someone who is "fierce" or "strict." No one is incited to excellence or expected to do more than his age, sex, and physical size permit. "Physical strength" is the main standard for determining what an individual can or cannot do.[12] Only someone who is clearly strong enough to perform a task and who is presumed to know how to do it is ever accused of "laziness." Even adults are not ashamed to admit that they do not have the strength or knowledge to do a task. Only if, like "Grandma" S who cannot stuff mattresses, their inability diverges too much from what is expected of someone their age and sex, are they subjected to mild ribbing. Even fear is little cause for shame. "Grandpa" M, who is squeamish about small furry animals, and "Grandpa" T, who ran away from the tattooer in his youth, can joke about their fears openly and with good humor. For good and for ill, the farmers of Ban Ping permit their fellow his faults, and do not encourage his competitiveness. Differences in skill are not permitted to threaten one's self-respect.

Farming skills are learned casually. Children who are too young to work often watch and imitate an older relative. The little four-year-old girl, who pretends to carry well water in empty condensed milk cans hung on the ends of a tiny shoulder pole, accompanies her mother to the fields and sits on the bank to watch her transplant. As a child begins to imitate them, adults throw out an occasional corrective remark, but there is little deliberate instruction. A child begins with the lighter tasks, imitating elders of the same sex. A little boy tries his hand at weaving the nursery fence while a small girl, following the women, drops a few seeds into the holes.

For any task there are degrees of competence. In Ban Ping, to "play at" a chore describes a child's activities from the time he merely tries

---

[12] Although most eight- and nine-year-old boys herd carabao, one mother pampers her son somewhat and says that he is not "strong enough" for the task because the bulls he watches are larger and fiercer than the cows his friends care for. One sixteen-year-old boy can "work like an adult." Another, who is also considered hardworking, is "too small" and "can plow for a little, but not with the strength and endurance of a grown-up."

Because women's tasks are thought to require less physical strength than men's, girls are presumed to be ready for real work before boys. By the time they are ten or eleven, most girls can "play at reaping" alongside adults. The age at which they are considered fully able to reap varies. A, our "daughter," began "really reaping" for her own household and for close relatives when she was eleven, but was not sent to repay labor debts until she was fourteen. By the time she was sixteen her co-workers were no longer willing to consider her youth an excuse for uneven work. S, who is now fourteen, is counted as an adult because she is sent out to reap to repay her household's labor debts, but K, her friend and age-mate, will not be "strong enough" to do so until next year, even though K has done her share of the household reaping since she was eleven.

to imitate adults to the time he is able to perform productively in short spurts. After this, the child begins to "really work," but it may be quite a few years before he is considered efficient enough for his parents to send him to other households to help repay labor debts. The more distant a "kinsman," the more meticulous one must be in exchanging labor with him.

Work begins as a game and children take some pride in their developing ability. Occasionally, however, a young person may be unwilling for the moment to do a specific task. In describing how to handle such a problem, an informant indicates the serious attitude that Ban Ping farmers have toward work:

A young man is told to work if he's big enough and berated if he won't. Even before he is really able to do the task, he's scolded if he won't practice. One doesn't really scold him, but kids him by saying: "However handsome you are, no girl will have you if you don't work hard." One would say the same kind of thing to a young girl like that one [pointing to a girl reckoned old enough to work for others] who won't work. . . . Children must learn that everyone has to work.

EXTRACOMMUNITY RELATIONS

Just as an automobile can be simultaneously a means of transportation, a source of debt, and a sign of social class, so plow agriculture can be a technological system and an index of changing relations of dependence. Each tool or technique used by the Ban Ping farmer relates him to his fellows and to the outside world. Let us now consider, under the aspect of its consequences for "peasantness," each of the activities already discussed as technology.

Farming tasks.—FERTILIZING Central Thai farmers buy commercial fertilizers (Kaufman 1960:43). Ban Ping farmers use cash, not to intensify present resources, but in order to accumulate new ones. They say that the home irrigated field does not produce as well as it used to and claim that "the land is tired," but new land, increased herds, and tractor rental—not commercial fertilizer—are their answers to declining yields.

Village farmers recognize that the most significant attribute of rice-growing land is the water it receives. Some of them theorize that fertilizer is unnecessary because Ban Ping's fields are close to the mountains and thus get the freshest water with the most plentiful nutrients, but, whatever his theory, no villager has been forced to consider using commercial fertilizer. The home irrigated field provides his "eating rice" without money; there are virgin lands to supplement his production. Fertilizer is seen as a costly substance used by a few Chinese market gardeners and by large-scale citrus growers. To the villager, fertilizer is a symbol of the townsman: largely irrelevant to village farming, but pertinent to the villager's image of himself.

As he carts it to the fields, a village lad calls manure "the fertilizer of the hicks," [13] and so shows that he has begun to make the invidious comparisons used by townsmen. The young people frequent the town more than their elders do; they have seen fertilizer in the shops and talk about it in Ban Ping. This familiarity has begun to invert the traditional hierarchy of farming knowledge, in which old people had been thought to know more than the young.

Central Thai villages are closer to Bangkok; their dialect is the language of the officials. Agricultural officers distribute fertilizer or, at least, systematic information about its use (Sharp et al. 1953:141). In Chiengkham villagers know about fertilizer only when, like the headman, they have special access to the town and its officials and merchants. Sometimes the district officer, as he tells headmen about progress, mentions fertilizer along with toilets and eating eggs (cf. Moerman 1964:36–37).

IRRIGATION The maintenance of dams and canals is the agricultural operation that has always brought Ban Ping into closest contact with other communities. Since it requires large work groups (see illus.), irrigation is sensitive to the increasingly commercial emphasis of village farming. Irrigation is also the only task of plow agriculture in which the government has shown direct interest. For these reasons, in addition to the evolutionary significance often ascribed to it, it is appropriate to examine in some detail how irrigation is organized in Ban Ping.

The tools of irrigation in Ban Ping, unlike those often used in central Thailand, are cheap and are produced locally. Extensive forests are a free source of construction materials for which central Thai farmers must sometimes buy substitutes. Rough terrain obviates the need for water-raising devices used on the Chao Phraya plain. A more striking contrast lies in Ban Ping's independence of "hydraulic despotism" (see Wittfogel 1957) and its bureaucratic successors.

Before Chiengkham came under Siamese administration in 1903, political leaders were not responsible for irrigation. Each village had a "dam chief"; one of them was elected "Great Dam chief" of Chiengkham. These chiefs decided how much wood each farmer was to bring to the dam, directed the work of irrigation, and celebrated its completion with a sacrifice (a pig) to propitiate the "spirit of the dam."

---

[13] No one claims, as farmers are said to elsewhere in Thailand (Thailand 1947:2), that fertilizer encourages growth but produces fewer grains and is therefore harmful. For uneducated farmers manure may, in fact, be superior to chemical fertilizers since it would be difficult to damage the soil by its excessive application. In Rangsit manure "increases yield relative to quantity applied" up to the very heavy application of 400 kg per rai (Thailand 1947:26, 29).

To compensate for his responsibilities, a chief's household was excused from contributing wood and labor. A male dependent helped the chief with his administrative duties, and often attended meetings in his stead. This experience qualified the dependent to succeed the chief. The building and maintenance of smaller dams and levees were usually supervised by the oldest of the farmers whose fields they watered. He and the members of his household did not have to work on their dam.

As irrigation was organized in 1900, so was it organized in 1960. Then the position of dam chief alternated between two elderly villagers with little political influence. While both were fairly prosperous, neither was an especially large landowner. The chief of 1960 succeeded his father-in-law and was assisted by his son-in-law. The chief's household, and that of the village messenger (who also assisted the village council and the temple committee), were exempt from contributing wood and labor to the dam. The 1960 Chiengkham Great Dam chief was a prosperous Lue farmer from a village near town. Neither he nor any village chief in Chiengkham was an official or even a headman.

The pattern—that irrigation is organized and maintained locally without the aid of the national government—is widespread (Wijeyewardene 1965:258 f.) throughout and perhaps characteristic of northern Thailand. The national government, however, has begun to take an interest in irrigation. In May 1960, when the irrigation chiefs met to plan the clearing of the main channel, they were told that government officials would inspect and measure the dam. The officials had also requested a list by village of landholdings and of the farmers who had failed to deliver their wood and labor. The Great Dam chief, who made the announcement, shared the village chiefs' dismay and pointed out how embarrassing it would be for officials to learn how often villagers shirked their obligations. Knowing the village fear of officials, he promised not to disclose the names of individual shirkers. Quite as an afterthought, one of his assistants revealed that the government's interference was not merely an exercise in power, but that its purpose was to implement the district officer's suggestion that the government and the farmers match funds to buy a concrete dam to replace the present wooden structure.

The villagers had been considering a concrete dam for a number of years. Now they were presented with an official estimate of its cost (40,000 baht) and a tentative offer of financial help. Nevertheless, they were highly suspicious of the government's motives. The district officer wanted a new report of landholdings in order to be able to compute the dam's estimated cost per rai. The villagers, who consistently underreport their holdings, thought the government's request was but a device for increasing taxes. For many villagers, the dam would cost too much whatever its price.

A few old men, most of them landowners with a small household labor force, favored a concrete dam. The most fervent advocate was Maj M, the richest villager, who argued in private that a "concrete dam would be good. Our children and grandchildren would have happiness [because they won't have to work hard]. But the other villagers don't approve of this idea; they think it would [make the work] be too easy." Although his annual income exceeds 10,000 baht, Maj M recognizes and often shares the village view that cash is an extremely scarce commodity. When trying to encourage support for the concrete dam, Maj M's public argument was less long range and did not concern capitalizing labor. "The concrete dam would be good," he said. "We'd only have to pay once and then never again have the annoyance of paying 10 cents every single year for every single rai so that the chiefs can buy a pig for propitiating the spirit of the dam." [14] The other elders remained unenthusiastic and repeated the rumor that when money was collected for a concrete dam in another part of the province, a *kamnan* absconded with the cash.

If villagers come to favor a concrete dam, it will probably not be because they are receptive to capital investment but, rather, that population growth has made it more difficult to organize communal labor, that private landholdings have become more important, and that the possibilities of alternative employment are slowly rising. Before there were oxcarts, village farmers and their wives would spend a night or two at the dam, to which they had carried shoulderloads of wood. With the innovation of capacious carts, women no longer accompanied their husbands; the work took the men a single festive day. But gradually, making the dams and channels became more of a chore. There were "too many strangers, too few kinsmen," for the old social controls to operate. People got in one another's way; villagers stole one another's wood. Now, when there are no sanctions, no one works; when there are sanctions, all try to escape them. In 1958 the irrigation chiefs decided to stagger workdays with the result that Ban Ping villagers report to the dam, not with the entire district, but with the three adjoining Lue villages. In 1960, despite the presence of even

---

[14] It is not that Maj M was honest in private and deceitful in public. Rather, the contrasting statements show the sophistication with which he perceives the values of a "progressive" and a "conservative" audience. To the Western anthropologist, he reveals his sincere interest in saving labor and benefiting his progeny. To fellow villagers, he ignores the benefits of capitalization to reveal his equally sincere interest in reducing trivial annoyances and minor current expenditures. Nevertheless, it is difficult for an American fieldworker not to rely on the commonsense suppositions of his own culture and feel that honest opinions are expressed more often in private than in public statements, in drunken than in sober words, in selfish than in altruistic sentiments.

such closely related villages, six Ban Ping households were not "too embarrassed before the others" to shirk their duties. The village chief —instead of threatening to tie them to stakes out in the sun for a full day, as chiefs are said to have threatened to do in the past—connived in their shirking. He later boasted to the village elders that he had protected Ban Ping's interests from the neighbors, "kinsmen," and fellow Lue—all of whom, because of increased population and commercialization, are now often treated as strangers. Only the groups that maintain minor dams and channels are untroubled by shirking. Although they often include farmers from more than one village, no one fails to contribute wood and work, for the groups are small, the reciprocity is immediate, and the benefits for an individual's fields are obvious.

SEEDING Discussions of rice farming frequently begin by distinguishing between wet and dry cultivation, partly on the basis that only in the latter are dry seeds and a dibble stick used (Blanchard 1958: 307; Grist 1959:113; Pelzer 1945:16; Wickizer and Bennett 1941:10). The Ban Ping practice of drilling dry seeds into dry soil in order to farm wet rice violates this distinction and has not previously been reported for other wet rice farming people.[15] The farmers of Ban Ping consider the technique peculiarly Lue and claim that the Yuan, who use it on the home irrigated field, have learned it from them.

Nevertheless, there is some evidence that the practices are more general than villagers (and the literature) recognize and that, despite village pride in their uniqueness, Ban Ping's seedbed techniques may be part of a widespread adaptation to the free forested land, unpredictable water supply, head-of-the-year rains, and glutinous rice of the northern region. Near Nakorn Pathom in central Thailand there is a small settlement of northern Tai (Lao Song) whose ancestors were brought as captives about a century ago. When I told them of Ban Ping's seedbed technique and showed them photographs of dibbling and seeding, they remarked that their parents had used the same techniques in Nakorn Pathom before the fields had been completely cleared of roots and stumps. There is also some evidence that the techniques are used by lowland Tai in northern Laos.[16]

The other point of interest is that marketing considerations are not important to the selection of seed. The Ban Ping farmer decides which rice to plant on the basis of conditions of land and labor. Within

---

[15] Matsuo (1954:105) reports drilling by Japanese who farm dry rice through crop rotation.

[16] Halpern (1958:16) describes the Laotian "wet rice field" by quoting a lengthy text collected by William A. Smalley. Unfortunately the text is Khamu, so that one cannot be sure whether its references to burning and late plowing describe Laotian practices or modifications of Laotian practices made by the swidden-farming Khamu.

these constraints, he plants the particular local variety of rice he prefers to eat. No one plants nonglutinous rice; the few who cull grain for seed use culinary criteria such as aroma, texture, and adhesiveness of the steamed rice. Even those who are most commercially oriented do not consider such characteristics as grain weight, milling properties, and minor differences in yield. On the Great Field, price and profit are not guides or incentives for production.

TILLING As he plods behind his plow, the Thai farmer, even in progressive Bangchan (Janlekha 1955:97), seems a symbol of timeless Asia. But, in Ban Ping at least, the image of the unchanging peasant is illusory. Although no innovation on the home irrigated field is as dramatic as the acceptance of the tractor on other fields, the farmers of Ban Ping have sometimes altered their plow techniques and learned new ideas from the outside world.

In Ban Ping there are three styles of wooden plows, all metal-shared and drawn by animals. The oldest of these is the "pig's head" plow illustrated in Phya Anuman's sensitive appreciation of the Thai farmer (Rajadhon 1961:illus. 14) and quite like the triangular Chinese plow (Hopfen 1960:fig. 34*b*). About fifty years ago the "deer antler" plow made its appearance. Choice between the two is solely a matter of personal preference. Some use the deer antler plow because they find it easier to avoid bumping their knee against its handle which is an S curve continuous with the slide board. A more basic change than the esthetically pleasing deer antler is offered by the third form, the ox plow, which came to Ban Ping about fifteen or twenty years ago. It has a long beam specifically adapted to fit a team of oxen rather than a single carabao. Because a team of oxen is said to plow less well than a single full-grown carabao, some farmers prefer renting carabao to using their own oxen, especially if they own low-lying land where the water and mud are too deep for oxen to work effectively. Nevertheless, as more and more young farmers invest in cart oxen, the new plow's popularity grows. Tillage by oxen and the ox plow that permits it came from Laotians who had settled near Phayao. The innovation was introduced only after the road to Phayao had been improved sufficiently to permit the passage of carts, so increasing the number of ox owners in Ban Ping.

Chiengkham's growth in population and the expanding market for its rice have had consequences beyond improvements in the road. Individual as opposed to household farming has become more prominent. This shift has altered the techniques of tillage as well as its tools. Middle-aged villagers say that it is not as common as it used to be to *kaw* and allow time for the grass to rot in the mounds. Formerly, farmers of contiguous plots would combine their labor and carabao to plow and then harrow, beginning with the plot farthest from an irrigation ditch or from the village and moving inward, each helping to till his neighbor's field. Now, they say, neighbors often do not even consult each other about their tillage schedules. Immediate cross-plowing is common because many farmers fear that careful harrowing would require them to continue using their carabao after intervening plots have already been planted. In such an event, the slow, superior farmer would have to bring his animals home circuitously or through the irrigation ditch to prevent them from eating or trampling his neighbor's young rice. Some farmers who *kaw* and delay *tyt*'ing take their carabao home after dark so that no one will see them trample their neighbor's rice.

TRANSPLANTING With their characteristic eagerness to distinguish themselves from the Yuan, Ban Ping farmers volunteer the opinion that walking backward when transplanting is peculiarly Lue. "The Yuan now do it on the home irrigated field only because they are embarrassed to be different from us." In Ban Ping the sex division of labor at transplanting time is explained by saying that only men are strong enough to uproot, while women have more nimble fingers and thus excel at the delicate work of planting. Nonetheless, when practical circumstances require it, women do uproot and men do plant. Townsmen say, however, that the division of labor is a matter of propriety: it would be improper for women to raise their legs in order to knock the soil from the roots of the seedlings.

HARVESTING The sickle, still Ban Ping's only reaping tool, was, like all iron goods, once bought from Haw (Panthay or Yunnanese Moslem) traders. The Haw sickle was a broad, smooth blade, one end of which was bent around a fairly wide wooden handle. As Chiengkham's ties to Thailand increased, the Haw trade diminished. The modern toothed sickle is made in the village or bought from Tai traders who get it in Lampang or Chiengmai. Unlike the Haw sickle, it has a narrow and acutely curved self-sharpening blade set into a narrow wooden handle. The change from old to new sickle took place gradually about thirty years ago.

Ban Ping's present threshing technique is an innovation made after the introduction of the cart. Before then, a single harvest mat, rather than the pair of today, was used. The rice was threshed by barefoot men who stamped it while supporting themselves on crutch-like sticks now used solely for beating the rice.[17] Although one man, now dead, is reputed to have been able to stamp in a day as much as three-quarters of what can be pounded now, villagers estimate that a typical worker stamping the grain could thresh only a fourth as

[17] In 1960 a few villagers reverted to the older technique when unseasonable rains had made their fields too wet for mats and their rice too wet for effective pounding.

much per day as is able to be done by means of the new technique.

The use of oxcarts made it possible to bring threshing tables to the field,[18] but this does not explain why farmers should want to bring them there. The development of an infinite market and the opening of tractor-plowed fields mean that individuals farm far more land than they used to. "If we tried to thresh in the old way," says one informant, "we'd cripple ourselves." The use of threshing tables came about because of increased rice production; it also provides some small sign of the way in which resources in things are becoming more important than resources in people. The same informant goes on to explain that, in the old days, although an individual stamper could thresh little rice, daily production was often quite high because there were many "kinsmen" who worked together. "Now that people think only of themselves, daily capacity is limited not by the number of one's kinsmen, but by the number of threshing tables."

Farming tools.—Home irrigated land is expensive but the cost of farming is low because tools are cheap and no one buys fertilizer or seed. On the other hand, in central Thailand, with its scarce land and long-established markets, farmers spend money in order to intensify their production.

In his extremely thorough study of a rice-growing village in central Thailand, Janlekha lists the farming tools that are "indispensable or essential for good crop production" (1955:95) in Bangchan (see table 2). To farm effectively, a central Thai peasant needs 1,892 baht worth of tools, of which the most expensive are the boats and irrigation equipment required by the water regime of the central plain. A Ban Ping farmer needs only 212 baht.

Some Bangchan farmers also buy devices Janlekha terms "unnecessary but contributing to convenience"; most important are costly gasoline-operated irrigation engines and the increasingly popular winnowing machine (about 500 baht). The only comparable tool of convenience in Ban Ping is an oxcart that may cost about 1,000 baht but is not actually needed for the home irrigated field. Farmers buy it for use on their distant fields, and also for nonagricultural reasons.

---

[18] Before the use of carts became general, a few Ban Ping farmers had threshing tables which were much larger than the present tables and were rarely used. The Yuan, on the other hand, often used such tables for cooperative nighttime threshing. A Yuan host who planned to thresh at night would tie his rice into sheaves before shocking it. All the workers who came to help him could grab a sheaf and hit it repeatedly against the table. The sheaves stayed in their hands; the rice slid to the base of the table. No grain was lost on the threshing floor as it would be were stamp-threshing used at night. The Lue did not use this technique. They never threshed at night, nor were their cooperative groups as large as those of the Yuan. The Lue developed a small table better adapted to the size of their work parties, their threshing mats, and their carts than the large tables used on Yuan threshing floors.

PLOW AGRICULTURE

During the rainy season, when the fields need no attention, the road to Phayao becomes a morass over which only oxcarts can transport goods. Cart owners are able to earn significant amounts of cash by carting out milled rice and returning with goods from Lampang for merchants in Chiengkham Town.

TABLE 2

FARMING TOOLS IN BANGCHAN AND IN BAN PING

Bangchan		Ban Ping		
Tool	Price (In baht)	Tool	Price (In baht)	Source of implement [a]
yoke	12	yoke	0	v
hoe	14	hoe	5	p
basket	15	basket (pair)	10	pv
sickle	24	sickle	5	pv
harrow	30	harrow	50	v
plow	80	plow	35	v
broom	6 [b]	field knife	8	p
pitchfork	2	sheath	3	v
shovel	3	hatchet	12	p
rake	5	water container	0	v
weeding knife	19	digging basket	0	v
boat	944 [b]	dibble point	1	pt
noria for irrigation	309	plowshare	15	pt
		rope	0	v
windmill	429	bamboo ties	0	v
spade	?	animal bell	0	v
roller	?	harvest mat	30	v
spatula	?	threshing crutches	0	v
Total	1,892	flail	0	v
		threshing table	35	v
		winnowing fan	3	v
		Total	212	

[a] v = village; p = peddlers; t = town.
[b] Average price of more than one variety.

In addition to documenting the low cost of Ban Ping's essential farm tools, table 2 indicates the village's comparative independence of urban centers, for almost all the tools of plow agriculture (*v*) are made in the community by the farmer or one of his "kinsmen." Most metal goods (*p*) are bought from itinerant peddlers. Although these goods originate in northern centers like Chiengmai or Lampang, the villager is unaware of his dependence on the town because the peddlers who bring them are country people much like himself. Indeed, some Ban Ping lads have sold Chiengmai sickles in their own and other villages. The only item that must be bought in town is the optional and unimportant metal basin used in seeding. In central Thailand, on the other hand, most major farming tools seem to come from urban centers.

Each Ban Ping household owns all the tools needed for Great Field farming.[19] In Bangchan 36 percent of the farmers (Janlekha 1955:95) lack major irrigation equipment. Central Thai farmers can borrow windmills only when they are least needed (*ibid.*) and obtain gasoline engines only by renting them at a high daily cost (Kaufman 1960:42), often from fellow villagers who own them, not for farming, but for profit (Sharp *et al.* 1953:134). The low cost of Ban Ping's essential equipment precludes such concentrations of wealth and power. When a tool is not quite suitable, or is in use, or out of repair, one commonly borrows another from a neighbor or a close "kinsman" who receives no payment.

Unlike essential tools, carts are expensive. Almost half (44 percent) of Ban Ping's farmers own one along with a team of oxen to pull it. To borrow a cart for transporting seedlings, one has only to ask a neighbor or close kinsman. For such a brief loan to an intimate there is no direct reciprocation. But if one's intimates do not own carts, one must use more distant ties. Though some villagers deny it, this requires clear reciprocation. A village carpenter, a few days after he "merely came to help" the headman repair his cart roof, borrowed the headman's cart to transport his seedlings. "I've come to ask my kinsman for his cart," said the carpenter, though his genealogical ties to the headman are rather distant.

The unseasonable rains of 1960 made a cart more than a mere convenience for harvesting the home irrigated fields; it was foolish to leave the rice in the fields any longer than necessary. As his cart rumbled out to the fields with those of his neighbors, a young villager turned to explain that "we kinsmen are all helping one another." But analysis showed that his and other communal carting groups consisted solely of cart owners, often not especially close kinsmen, who were repaying one another immediately and directly by working together. This arrangement permitted the rapid harvesting required by the flood emergency. When they carried rice for villagers who did not own carts but were just as close genealogically, they charged 10 percent of the load.

Farming knowledge.—In Ban Ping it is assumed that everyone knows how to farm. All have acquired their knowledge within the village. The elementary school, which children now attend for four

---

[19] Because everyone owns all essential tools, no "sociogram" of borrowings was attempted. For the use of such a device in the study of an American farming community, see Leonard and Loomis (1941:47).

years, has recently begun to teach some aspects of gardening and woodworking (including bamboo weaving). The dedicated head teacher wants to give his students more instruction in the care of pigs and poultry than the national syllabus permits. Perhaps some villagers will consider that such instruction compensates for the fact that the school has delayed the age at which children learn some basic productive skills (cf. Hanks 1958). No villager thinks it possible for the young to know more about traditional farming than their elders. No one in Ban Ping has ever attended an agricultural school; no officials ever instruct the villagers. All adults have equal knowledge, so only skill and effort, together with material resources, are believed to influence success.

The reward of labor is prosperity. Unlike central Thai (Pfanner and Ingersoll 1962:354), the villagers of Ban Ping do not attribute success in plow farming to religious merit. Good land and hard work are the only explanations they know. In their farming, the villagers of Ban Ping are empiricists, eager to try promising innovations. Just as they were quick to accept the tractor, they were disappointed at my inability to provide them with seeds for new crops.

Farming operations include no agricultural rituals. The first plowing ceremony, the offering to the rice goddess, the harvest offering, the sacrifice to the spirit of the rice, which are all so important elsewhere in Thailand, do not enter Ban Ping's rice cycle. The oldest farmers and those most versed in the spirits say that, even in their parents' tales of the Sip Song Panna, such rituals were not a regular part of Lue farming. One must propitiate the spirits of the forest before felling trees, and villagers do so when clearing new land or cutting lumber. One may sacrifice a chicken to the spirit of the rice before reaping it, and the chicken is offered no less frequently than it used to be.[20]

Although Ban Ping's knowledge of farming techniques is durable and self-sufficient, villagers must, of course, obtain current information in order to make successful technological decisions. The home rainfall field provides an intriguing example of how such information is obtained and used. The field lies fallow if there is insufficient precipitation for it to be farmed, but how do villagers predict precipitation? Home rainfall farming operations begin before the monsoon has started. Tilling and transplanting, the most difficult steps of plow agriculture, must be completed too early in the season for anyone to be sure of the amount, duration, and frequency of rainfall. So plans are made on the basis of a farmers' almanac that predicts

---

[20] Only one old ritual has fallen into disuse: the divining of auspicious days for putting the rice into the granary. While all are said to have performed this ritual in the past, no one younger than forty-five did it in 1960–61.

the relative amount of total precipitation and the number of heavy showers to be expected of the next monsoon. Two of the wise men of the village possess perpetual astrologic calendars which permit this information to be computed for any year.

Very few villagers, however, make use of these books. Instead they consult the brilliantly colored pictorial calendars annually printed and distributed by chemical firms, oil companies, and similar urban sources. This annual weather forecast, although it comes from the city, is expressed in traditional visual terms which even the illiterate can understand. All villagers are concerned with the calendar's prediction of total rainfall, which most of them seem able both to interpret and to describe in terms of the number of Nagas (mythological serpents) depicted on the calendar.[21] In February 1961, five men who own land at the home rainfall field happened to be together in order to settle a divorce case. Conversation soon turned to the calendar that one of them had seen at the home of a headman in a neighboring village. It showed seven Nagas (indicating very little total precipitation) and, further, predicted only thirty heavy showers (rather than the fifty predicted for the last monsoon). The calendar also indicated that there would be some flooding, because most of the season's rain would fall at one time, and that half of the rice crop would be lost. It also predicted the ratio of rice planted to rice harvested. The landowners concluded that they would plant little home rainfall field. It should be emphasized that this was not a group of rude and simple men, for three of the five are shrewd, widely traveled traders. It should also be emphasized that despite the earnestness of their discussion and the sincerity of their plans, they probably did plant their home rainfall plots because 1961 developed into a very wet year. Whatever they finally did, decisions to plant or to let land lie fallow are based on nonscientific information which, although "old-fashioned," is tested against observation of reality and has as its preferred source the urban world outside the village.

SUMMARY

Villagers live neither by instinct nor rote; plow farming in all its variations is orderly, intelligible, and rational. I have traced two

[21] Only some of the villagers understand the cosmological connection between Nagas and rainfall. According to one explanation, the "rains come when the giant Nagas fight together in the water of a certain mountain [presumably Meru]. The noise from their battle is thunder; the spray of their battle is rain and hail. Dry weather comes when there are too many Nagas, five or six of them, and each tells the others not to fight, not to play, not to waste the water which the *thewadas* bring to us as rain." To the owners of the home rainfall field, of whatever degree of cosmological knowledge, the Nagas and other calendric devices are important influences on production. Phetsarath (1959:122 ff.) describes similar devices in Laos.

culturally recognized features of the environment, water and land—water's amount, duration, dependability, timing, and flooding; land's hardness, sandiness, ownership, amount, and distance from Ban Ping and from other plots—for these features underlie and justify the interlocking technological decisions that constitute farming in Ban Ping.

The relative elaborateness of task descriptions has been dictated by the degree of variation in village practice and rationale, not by the number of acres on which a particular technique is employed. To assume that a technique's significance for decision making is independent of its statistical incidence is quite basic to the approach of this study. The practical (as opposed to theoretical) justification for this assumption is my conviction that native principles of perception, cognition, and decision provide a better means of anticipating and manipulating future actions than does a mere inventory of behavior.

Farming decisions based upon the culturally recognized environment have consequences for Ban Ping's external relations. The pioneers from the Sip Song Panna would have little difficulty mastering present techniques, for Great Field agriculture has been conservative. Plow farming is still relatively uncontrolled by urban centers. Peculiarities of Lue farming custom have been retained with pride. Success as a farmer is based on tools, knowledge, and standards native to the village. Compared with farming in central Thailand, farming in Ban Ping requires little cash. Townsmen have no influence on what the villager plants or on when he harvests. Nevertheless, tillage, transplanting, and harvesting now include new tools and operations. Every step of Great Field agriculture shows the individuation of landholdings (based on increasing population, a market for rice, and the customs by which new households obtain their land) which has made it more difficult for villagers to farm together. Formerly, there were far fewer persons and each of them needed little more rice and he could eat. Now, the market will take all that can be produced. Increasing population and expanded demand would have caused even greater changes in plow agriculture had not fresh lands been opened by the tractor.

IV.
Tractor Agriculture

The tractor is a dramatic innovation, yet its introduction in Ban Ping and even the changes it caused were presaged by plow agriculture. Socially, the individuation of landholdings, accelerated by the tractor, was already basic when, in order to obtain their own plots, young men first went to Thunglor. Like the cart, the ox plow, and the serrated sickle, the tractor came from a northern city beyond the reach of everyday life. Technologically, the alacrity with which the village accepted the tractor is consistent with the pragmatism of Ban Ping's traditional farming. The water regime, already so important to variations among plow techniques, required the tractor. Moreover, the total technological system of plow agriculture, not just its separate elements, prepared Ban Ping to accept the tractor and thereby helped to preserve many extracommunity consequences of traditional plow farming.

TECHNOLOGY

This description of tractor technology in 1960 is briefer than the description of plow technology because many operations required by the plow are obviated by the tractor; many technological decisions are not the villagers' to make; many practices are still idiosyncratic.

Farming Tasks.—There are eleven tractors, all owned by townsmen, which plow the approximately 6,000 acres (2,430 ha) of Thunglor, including the 550 acres farmed by Ban Ping villagers. Tractors are kept working night and day from February, as soon as the crop is harvested and the ground is dry, until August, when the soil is wet with rain and flood. Work on Ban Ping's part of the Thunglor fields usually begins in March; the February plowing starts at faraway Therng District (see map 2) and the late plowing occurs on inferior land of which Ban Ping fortunately has little. In early or mid-March, at the convenience of the tractor owners, the people of Ban Ping begin to work on the distant flood fields (see fig. 9).

The first task is "pointing at the fields." Landowners, accompanied by members of the tractor crew, put markers at the corners of their plots and help the tractor crew to measure them with a standard link chain. The farmer pays the tractor owner according to the amount of land plowed. Knowledge of plot size is thus far more accurate on the distant flood than on the home irrigated field.

Land must be cleared before the tractor will plow it. On land previously cultivated, the farmer uses the pointing day to burn off grass and straw. Virgin land requires more time and effort, for trees must be felled and their roots cut away before the tractor owners are willing to plow. Farmers with heavily wooded land, like that near the river Ing, use carabao to uproot the trees. It may take them quite a few seasons to convert such a holding into cultivable land. Even those with sparsely wooded land often cannot clear their entire holding in a single season. For everyone, however, the major obstacle is not the time and the work of clearing, but the inability to accumulate enough money to pay for plowing the entire plot. The tractor owners charge 25 baht for plowing a rai of cultivated land and 50 baht for each rai of newly cleared land. A few farmers with newly cleared land pay a little extra for a second plowing.

Use of the tractor is no longer confined to the distant flood field. At the home flood field, which is subject to the same rapid rise in water level as Thunglor, two owners hired tractors in 1960. The difficulty and uncertainty of conditions in the rainfall field caused eight of its thirty-one operators to hire tractors in 1960. Other landowners were quite interested in this innovation and said that they would decide whether to hire a tractor next year on the basis of the yields obtained by this year's tractor users. However, yields were not very impressive, largely because sowing (followed by fence building) took place immediately upon plowing, leaving no time for grass to die and rot; the success and durability of the innovation cannot yet be determined. Sowing hastily on the rainfall field was necessary because tractor owners were willing to bring their machines to the small home rainfall field only after they were finished with the more profitable plowing of distant flood lands. In 1961, after we left Thailand, no one practiced tractor agriculture on the rainfall field. The failure to use tractors, however, was probably not caused by disappointment in the 1960 yields. In 1961 there were widespread floods in northern Thailand; in Chiengkham, rainfall was unusually heavy and began quite early in the year, undoubtedly a major influence on the decision not to use tractors. I do not know, however, whether the decision was made by the tractor owners because the ground was too wet for the machines, or whether villagers decided not to incur the cost of hiring tractors in a year when the rains promised to make farming productive without them.

Few farmers visit their distant flood fields between the day of pointing and the time of sowing (see fig. 9). Only those who have some nonfarming reason—such as a desire to fish in the Ing—do get there. While there, they clear away grass left by the tractor, pile it into mounds, and burn it.

Ban Ping farmers have precise ideas of how and when to sow. At the end of April, a villager said, "It's too early to sow. One must wait until it has rained more. After the ground is thoroughly wet, one broadcasts the seed." The real timetable, however, is somewhat less precise. If the rain is late, if there is a convenient lull in other activities, if many fellow villagers anticipate rain, if one's friends or neighbors on adjoining fields want to sow, then the time has come. Scarcely two rainless days after his remarks, this villager and everyone else had become impatient and only old men, children, and women were left in Ban Ping.

To reach his plot, a Thunglor farmer rides in an oxcart for from three to four hours. In addition to his seed rice, he packs the cart with pails and water containers, a chopping board, a day's supply of steamed rice, peppers, salt and spices, pickled tea and tobacco, dried meat or preserved vegetables or salted fish, milled rice and the equipment for steaming it, some bedding and spare clothing, mats, candles or a lamp, a fishnet and basket, and the invaluable strips of bamboo. If he is one of the few who owns a gun, he will bring it to hunt for birds, rats, or squirrels for *lap*. Rarely does he bring enough straw for his oxen.

The sowing itself takes less than a day, but burning the grass, fishing, hunting, and visiting friends make many stay for two or three days. The nights are spent in the tractor shed, under an oxcart, or in one of the few field houses.

After unpacking the cart and releasing the oxen to graze, the farmer may begin to burn the straw or wood left by the plowing. The large clumps of earth turned up by the tractor are broken down with hoes by the more energetic farmers. A few impatient farmers may begin to sow on the evening of their arrival, but most wait until the next morning when they awaken before dawn to take advantage of the cool weather and of the slight moistness of the soil.

Because the distant flood field is the last to be harvested, everyone sows late-ripening rice. All know the technique of culling seed by fanning it to remove light and empty hulls, but no one practices it. Farmers usually pour the rice from a sack on the cart into a basket or pail held near the ground some 2 or 3 feet away; inadvertent culling may result.

Sowing techniques have yet to become standardized; each farmer sows his own plot in his own way. Removing a handful of seeds from a pail or pliable basket, he throws the seeds forcefully onto the ground, or casts them horizontally, or appears to be merely walking about throwing rice into the air. Many farmers make use of twigs or clods of earth to keep track of the area sown. One young man broadcast his seeds deliberately, paced carefully, and used a set of wood and paper flags to record his progress. There is no evidence, however, that careful technique affects the yield. By 6 A.M. most have begun to sow. Even with the pauses to rest and to burn odd clumps of straw, it takes no more than two or three hours to sow 4 acres (1.6 ha).

In their descriptions of how to farm, villagers recognize the advantages of covering the newly sown seed. They say, "One turns over the soil by having an ox pull a mat made of five to seven palm fronds. If one leaves the seeds on the ground without covering them, birds, insects, and rats will eat them and one will not have a good harvest." Yet, once again, real and ideal farming diverge, for in fact hardly anyone bothers to cover his seed. Most villagers seem to view the Thunglor harvest as a windfall because the techniques of tractor agriculture are new, its success is beyond the villagers' control, and its product is luxury "selling rice." "Yes," said one farmer, "the birds eat the uncovered rice seed. But they don't eat all of it. We get more than they do."

Soon after sowing, farmers return to Thunglor in order to reseed barren patches. In 1960 quite a few resowed their entire plots because the head-of-the-year rains were so late and so brief. Aside from resowing there is little to be done during the growing season. Along with providing the main incentive for tractor agriculture, rapid flooding prevents farmers from caring for their crop. Occasional trips to Thunglor soon become little more than fishing expeditions.

The tools and techniques of harvesting the distant flood field are no different from those employed on the home fields; but since the ripe rice stands for so long, some farmers claim that it is dry enough to be threshed merely by rubbing it in their hand.

Timing of tasks.—Unlike the task of plow agriculture, trips to Thunglor and work there are scheduled, not on the basis of plant growth stages, but on the basis of the demands of machines and the convenience of their owners. The Ban Ping farmer goes to measure and "point at" the fields when the tractor owner says he should. Sowing can be done only after the tractor has plowed. The ripe rice is harvested after other fieldwork is done.

Plowing time, which fixes the schedule for all other operations, is set by considerations of mechanical efficiency. Tractor owners prefer a schedule in which contiguous plots of similar slope and soil cover (e.g., cultivated, sparsely wooded, heavily wooded) are plowed at the same time. Soil and slope conditions determine the number of weights and disks the tractor pulls. To keep his machine in profitable operation, an owner wants to change weights and disks as seldom as possible. Aware of this aspect of tractor technology, the more sophisticated farmers sometimes describe a plot by specifying how many disks are used to plow it.

The villager prefers a schedule that would get his plot plowed earliest, in this way both getting things over with and taking advantage of the fact that the earlier the plowing, the more time there is for grass and roots to dry in the sun before the April head-of-the-year rains announce the start of the sowing season. When their optimum schedules differ, the tractor owner, not the farmer, gets his way. On tractor-plowed home rainfall land, villagers noticed that the rice at one plot seemed more bountiful than at any of the others. The parcel belonged to a wealthy young man who, perhaps because of his rather extensive holdings at Thunglor, was able to get the tractor owner to plow his rainfall plot quite early in the season.

Once they have cleared their land and measured it for the plowing, the farmers return to their village. From then on, the main item of daily conversation is the whereabouts of the tractors on the distant flood field. Only after his plot is plowed can the villager sow.

In sowing their fields, the Ban Ping farmers make the same kind of decisions, albeit with much less anxiety, as those made by swidden farmers who must time burning to follow a drought but to precede the rains. Tractor agriculture is a defense against the rapid flooding of the Ing. To maximize his advantage, the farmer must sow as long before the monsoon as possible, for otherwise he is little better off than those who once used carabao and transplanted at Thunglor. But the farmer must also time the sowing to come just before the head-of-the-year rains, for if the seeds stay dry too long on the land, the yield will be less, largely because of pests. Almost everyone burns the plowed stubble immediately before he begins to sow.[1] To assure the best possible burn of the stubble, the farmer wants to sow after the longest possible drought. Those who sow too early return to resow. One man

---

[1] Villagers burn because it is the easiest way to get rid of the stubble. It is probably fortunate that they do so, because there is some experimental evidence that burning is the best available way to clear the soil. In 1933-34 the rice experiment station at Rangsit obtained the following yields from various techniques of treating grass and stubble:

Technique	Yield (kg per rai)
plow under	221.6
early plowing	252.7
green manure plowed under	271.5
burn	289.3

Green manure competed with the crop; plowed-under stubble rotted too slowly. The experimenters concluded that "burning stubble is usually best" (Thailand 1947: 27).

who finished sowing only hours before the first heavy rain was considered extremely fortunate and many commented that he "must have a lot of [religious] merit." Since all farmers have the same considerations of optimum timing, almost all sow within a fortnight. The almost simultaneous sowing presumably has the added benefit of discouraging birds and rodents from concentrating their attentions on any one plot or section of plots.

No one harvests green rice. Beyond this stipulation, the timing of Thunglor harvest operations is determined by social, not agricultural, factors. Only after the men have harvested and stored their household's home-field rice are they available to get the rice at Thunglor. Moreover, carts are needed to bring the rice home from the distant field. Even if an individual farmer wanted to harvest early, he would have to wait until his neighbors had cut and removed the rice standing between his plot and the cart track. Therefore, everyone harvests at Thunglor at the same time; no one starts until all have finished harvesting at home. Rice at the distant flood field, waiting until long after it is ripe, dries and hardens and falls prey to pests. For people used to the wearying work of plow agriculture, however, the yield still seems excellent. The rice from tractor farming is a bonus whatever its amount, since Ban Ping's basic needs are amply supplied by other fields.

EXTRACOMMUNITY RELATIONS

The consequences of tractor farming for extracommunity relations are numerous and complex. The tractor has created a new dependence of village on town, yet the townsman also needs villagers to whom he is often connected by old institutions in new garb. In addition, Ban Ping is just beginning to pay the human costs of technological development.

Work and fun.—Anyone who lives in Thailand soon becomes familiar with the phrase, "lots of people, lots of fun." A large number of individuals in casual interaction (Phillips 1965:59) is central to the ideal of enjoyment. Crowds gathered for transplanting, for a funeral, or for riding a rice truck are all "lots of fun." The absence of this pleasure is a striking feature of tractor agriculture. More precisely, tractor agriculture exhibits a dichotomy between work and fun which is new to Ban Ping, however familiar it is to Americans.

The farmer's first task is to measure and mark his land for the tractor operators. Because Ban Ping farmers were among the first to claim land at Thunglor, many villagers own land there and their plots are contiguous. In addition, most Ban Ping farmers hire the same tractor owner who thus finds it convenient to bring them all to Thunglor on the same day. He calls for them in his four-wheel-drive truck;

the thrill of riding in the vehicle more than compensates for the discomfort of the trip. With the passengers shouting, laughing, telling stories, the hour-long trip to the distant flood field is clearly "lots of people, lots of fun." The fun continues, somewhat abated, after arriving at the rude tractor shed where the farmers plan fishing trips, pretend to speak knowledgeably about the machinery, admire the coffeepot and other urban-style appointments. As the day proceeds, each farmer in turn leaves with one or two others who have contiguous plots and goes with a tractor man to mark and to measure. The small groups treading over the rough straw are very different from the large jovial parties waiting in the shed or riding on the truck. The very first operation of tractor agriculture, then, signals the separation of work from fun which distinguishes it from most traditional male productive activities in Ban Ping.

Some six weeks after pointing, the farmer returns to the distant flood field for sowing, which is solitary rather than group work and so shows the same dichotomy. When they are not actually clearing their plots and broadcasting seed, the farmers visit one another, go in groups to tend the oxen, form small hunting parties and large fishing expeditions. But each farming operation is done by one man working alone. As I watched two brothers, otherwise inseparable, each sowing his plot, I was reminded of the social isolation of contemporary industrial society symbolized in Bellamy's *Looking Backward* by a painting of rain-threatened Bostonians, each desperately holding onto his own umbrella.

The third and last trip to the fields is for the harvest. On all fields, the harvest is a time of joy, but the large harvest bees of plow agriculture do not occur at the distant flood field. Each farmer reaps and threshes alone or with one or two hired assistants. Only when the day's work is over do people enjoy themselves. Fires are lit and lads go courting. "When the harvesting is done, there are large fishing expeditions. Lots of people, lots of fun."

Commercial crops.—Five years after the tractor first appeared, Ban Ping farmers began to grow more than the small plot of ordinary rice necessary for sweetmeats and starch for yarn. The purpose of growing ordinary rice was purely commercial, for the villagers eat only glutinous rice. Shortly after the introduction of the tractor, then, price and profit became major standards for crop selection. The desire for profit dominates Thunglor and is fulfilled there. On the Great Field, all rice, even the surplus beyond subsistence, is glutinous; in this way, as in others, the tractor has helped to preserve the traditional character of plow agriculture.

In deciding whether or not to grow ordinary rice at Thunglor, the villager thinks only in commerical terms. In 1960 hardly any ordinary rice was sown because its relative price had been so low in 1959.

Nevertheless, the Ban Ping farmer is a comparative newcomer to the large-scale rice market. In at least two ways he is less deeply involved in producing for it than are sophisticated townsmen in Chiengkham. First, he is less knowledgeable. The assistant district officer, a large landowner, laughs at the foolishness of village people who react to last year's price. A low price for ordinary rice, and they sow none; a high price, and they sow nothing else. The assistant district officer is proud of his policy of always sowing both kinds of rice. Second, even those village farmers who are most market-minded still think first of subsistence. No one plants ordinary rice unless he is sure that his other fields will provide more than enough glutinous rice for his family to eat, to entertain with, and to contribute some to the temple. No one would take advantage of the high price of ordinary rice by planting it so that he may sell it and buy back glutinous rice to eat. In 1960, for instance, one farmer was forced by debt to do this. Although he later boasted of it, other villagers did not think it a good idea. Even when they predict a high price for ordinary rice, Ban Ping farmers still plant enough glutinous rice for their own needs. Since they have no reliable information about future rice prices, the practice of keeping "eating rice" on hand follows the rules of good business as well as of traditional subsistence.

Toward the planting of crops other than rice, their caution is equally reasonable. The difficulties of the home rainfall field made one old farmer consider planting peanuts on his comparatively large plot. Peanuts, grown in small gardens and forest clearings, were getting a good price from Chinese merchants in town. Furthermore, a young tractor driver had observed that the rainfall field's sandy soil was suitable for peanuts. The old man's vague plans will probably never be realized. Other villagers, including the few who had planted substantial amounts of peanuts, pointed to the risks involved. "The price may be high, but the price may be low. Furthermore, one can't eat peanuts [as a staple]." However acute the peasant's entrepreneurial ambitions, peasant rationality precludes planting commercial crops that threaten subsistence (cf. Muscat 1966:90).

Access to tractors.—The tools of traditional agriculture are cheap and easy to obtain, whereas the tractor and the oxcart needed on the distant flood field are expensive and cannot be made in Ban Ping. To obtain either of these tools the village farmer must spend money and deal with outsiders. For tractors, he subjugates himself to townsmen; for carts, as we shall see, he can mask commercial relationships with the terminology of kinship. Access to either tool can be described only through sociological analysis.

The natural environment of Thunglor requires the tractor; the social environment of Ban Ping prevents villagers from owning one. No individual is wealthy enough to buy a tractor; no technique or institution exists which permits the villagers to pool their resources to buy the tool collectively. In January 1960, Maj M suggested that Thunglor landowners buy their own tractor, but no one was interested. Villagers pointed out that a common tractor would cause constant dispute about its maintenance and plowing schedule. The only common property in the village is the temple; even secular supplies have to be deposited there or else become the exclusive possession of a single household (Moerman 1966a:161).

Insofar as class pertains to ownership of the means of production, villager and tractor man are distinct classes. In other ways, as well, the gap between them is wider than any gap between people based on plow agriculture. The rice grower and the tractor man live apart: the farmer in villages, the tractor owner in the city or the market town. They differ vastly in political and economic influence, which in Thailand is determined by those to whom one has easy access. Aside from the few farmers who have personal connections with an official, villagers can influence governmental action only by avoiding its agents. In economic matters, no villager, aside from the wealthy Maj M, has enough rice to bargain with the millers who set its price. The much more powerful position of the tractor men is suggested by the genealogy sketched in figure 2. C (#1 in fig. 2), who owns the tractor that most Ban Ping farmers hire, contracts for his own customers. Nevertheless, his prominence is based on membership in a coherent group united by ties of kinship and self-interest. The men in figure 2 share extensive official and commercial contacts. When a rival tractor owner lowered his price by 5 baht per rai, the group met and boasted that they formed a "corporation" that could monopolize Thunglor plowing. At first they considered lowering their prices below cost in order to drive rivals out of business. They also considered having the *kamnan* (#4 in fig. 2), who holds the Shell Oil agency for Chiengkham, make it difficult for their rivals to receive fuel and lubricants. Although neither policy was enacted, the group may well have had the power to enforce both. In 1960 they chose to lower their price to that of their competitor.

Although they differ vastly in power, position, sophistication, and degree of solidarity, the farmer and the tractor owner still need each other. They are members of a single society and must often confront each other. In these meetings, both amicable and hostile, can be seen the main aspects of relations between two classes.

The first large-scale meeting takes place when the fields are pointed at and measured. It is rather pleasant for the villagers of Ban Ping that so many of them use the same tractor. They gain the excitement of a truck ride and of a social occasion shared with their fellows. The villagers' social benefit is, of course, a significant economic benefit for C. The social unity of Ban Ping assures him that almost all its 103 customers, with their relatively large and conveniently contiguous holdings, will use his tractor and will arrange for their plowing at the same time and at his convenience. In return for their business, C does more than merely take their money and plow their fields. To a fortunate few, he is a patron willing to intercede with officials or to permit an occasional payment to go past its due date. He jokes and gossips with all the farmers, and instructs and advises them. Most tractor owners permit and encourage such broad-based social relationships. The farmers of Ban Ping find C and his brothers especially acceptable

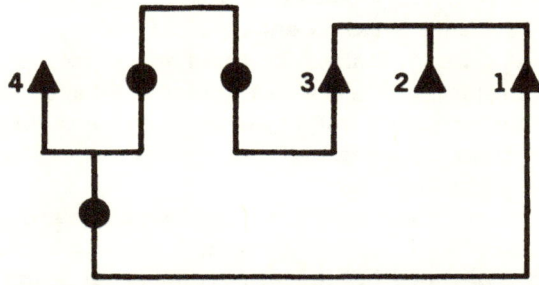

Fig. 2. Schematic genealogy of tractor owners usually hired by Ban Ping farmers.

KEY: 1 = C, who owns tractor most Ban Ping farmers hire; 2 = assistant district officer, also a tractor owner; 3 = manager of largest rice mill in town, district representative to Provincial Assembly, not a tractor owner; 4 = *kamnan* of market borough, wealthiest man in district holding major interest in largest mill, sole agent for petroleum products, also a tractor owner.

because they, like the villagers, are Lue. When the farmers were driven to the fields, C talked and joked in the broadest Lue although he never uses the dialect in town, presumably lest it embarrass him there by its provinciality. In manipulating his ethnicity in order to gain entrée into villages, he is like his brother, the assistant district officer, who said at our housewarming, "You see, I talk Lue to them and they like it. They like me. I am a Lue too, so I am their friend."

On pointing day there is a strong feeling of camaraderie. Although C behaves with a minimum of condescension, almost every interaction between him and the villagers indicates clearly that he is thought to be superior. C offers the villagers purchased—and thus more prestigious (Moerman 1964:35)—food and drink; the villagers show reluctance to initiate interaction with him and use the pronouns of respect. C's occasional asides in central Thai and his frequent references to Bangkok and even international events demonstrate his superiority. It is through the tractor men that villagers learn much of what they know of the outside world.

Although C speaks Lue, neither he nor any of his employees at the tractor shed could ever be mistaken for a peasant. However work-

and grease-stained their clothing becomes, it bears no resemblance to the indigo-dyed, home-woven dress of the villagers (see illus.). The one village lad who smoked C's brand of store-bought cigarettes was soon embarrassed by C's jocular references to his evident prosperity.

The villagers, observing life in the shed, comment that the "tractor group can afford to eat well; they have meat every day." C feeds his crew well in order to retain them; villagers bring only their most portable and least favored rations. The impression that the two groups are greatly divergent in wealth is thus exaggerated. To the villager, C seems wealthy, knowledgeable, friendly, and supportive. His control of a tractor is merely one aspect of his respectfully acknowledged social superiority. Unlike the brash young men who drive and maintain the tractors,[2] C acts as a patron should act and therefore is not resented. He and the other tractor owners are able to assert their new dominance by means of old institutions: age-mate relationships and the bond between patron and client.

Formally acknowledged age-mates (*sio*) are supposed to treat each other as kinsmen. While no villager would dare claim that a *sio* relationship with C obviated fulfillment of commercial obligations, C can use his *sio*'s to obtain new commercial services. Maj J, a former Ban Ping headman, has little land but has always prospered as a merchant. Formerly in the cloth and tobacco trade, he now earns cash as an itinerant tradesman. He is of a respected village family, well liked, widely traveled, and commercially astute. Next year (1961), he will solicit customers for C's tractor, keep records of landholdings and payments, and care for the tractor shed. In return for these services, C will give Maj J land and will plow it without charge as long as Maj J works for him. But Maj J refuses to consider himself an employee and rejects such commercial terms as "hire," "salary," "commission," or "payment" when applied to his arrangement with C. Nor does he refer to his own willingness to leave home (his daughter is grown and his wife deranged), his own business abilities, or his extensive friendships. C made the offer, he insists, because Maj J's father and C's father were *sio*'s; the prosperous son feels it his duty to aid the poor one. A commercial relationship is explained and reinforced by a traditional relationship; Maj J becomes more acceptable and thus, presumably, more effective as a salesman.

[2] The youth of these agricultural students, in their early twenties, is inconsistent with the respect that their knowledge and position demand from the villagers. They come from Chiengmai and other large northern towns. Impatient with the "backwardness" of the villagers, the students favor purely task-oriented behavior foreign to Ban Ping Lue and to most tractor owners. The majority of the tractor owners, in their wisdom and in their provincialism, participate in the more total relationships compatible to the villager, who then deals with them as superior members of his own society.

C's arrangement with Maj J is rather like the old bond between patron and client, the basis of the traditional Thai polity, through which subjects were granted land by their lord in return for military service and corvée labor. This ancient transaction is also part of contemporary tractor agriculture. Land at the distant flood field has value only when it is cultivated. Before a tractor can plow it, land must be cleared of trees and roots. Only the laborious efforts of men and carabao can clear the heavy forest that grows near the banks of the Ing. C has title to about 200 rai of this heavily wooded land; two vigorous and rather sophisticated villagers have agreed to clear it for him. In return, C has given them half the land and promised to plow it for them without charge during the first season of cultivation. Thus, C's capital is exchanged for the villagers' labor and both benefit. Since the undeveloped Thunglor land cost C nothing, his only present sacrifice is the artificial consideration of what his tractor, were it employed full time, might have earned in fees were it not occupied in plowing his clients' land. For their labor, C gives his clients 100 rai of land; without the labor, the land is valueless. C can afford to be generous because he has other land, other interests, other sources of income.

The rare villager who attempts to copy the ways of his superiors loses sight of the fact that his own economic base is weak. Such an instance is furnished by Ban Ping's headman, whose schemes and ambitions often subject him to severe criticism from his cautious co-villagers. The headman, like C, claimed a great deal of land near the banks of the Ing. Almost all of his 150 rai was too heavily wooded for him to clear in time for planting. During the height of the rainy season he went with some of his "close relatives" to uproot the trees with carabao. In return, the headman proposed to give his helpers some of the cleared land. But the mud, leeches, and mosquitoes interfered; only between two and five rai were cleared after a week of work. He complained to his wife, upon returning from the fields, that one main reason for lack of progress was that everyone was interested only in clearing his own plot. With neither the inducement of free plowing nor the influence and authority of a true patron, the headman cannot control his helpers. And with only his land to support him, he cannot patiently await gradual clearing.

The pressure of time makes the villagers most vulnerable to the control of tractor operators, who determine the plowing schedule. The farmers, many and unorganized, all want their fields plowed in time for the weeds to die before the rain. In this regard Ban Ping, although without either the knowledge or the organizational capacity for using it, has the potential for collective bargaining. Farmers from other villages, where landholdings are not large and contiguous, constantly approach tractor men to "beg" that their fields be plowed soon. Only rarely need a Ban Ping farmer plead in this way.[3] When he does, it is clear that the individual farmer needs the tractor man far more than the tractor man needs him. Tractor owners, as their abortive price war indicates, use economic incentives to influence villagers. Villagers, who have no economic incentive to offer tractor owners, instead make use of such social incentives as personal service and excessive respect.[4] Although such devices may succeed in altering the plowing schedule, close relations with townsmen have little effect on tractor fees.[5]

Tractor fees are payable at about the time of plowing, and during April the village is busy with the continual comings and goings of C and his agents. At least half the fee must be paid in cash or in its rice equivalent. Many farmers arrange to pay the balance of the fee after harvest, but this credit is expensive; rice is worth more before planting than it is just after harvest. Farmers, merchants, and creditors in Chiengkham commonly price rice futures, called "green rice," at half the current market value of rice. The form and date of payment are subject to constant negotiations which emphasize the practical value of maintaining good relations with townsmen. The farmer's predicament can best be understood through the following fictious example in which the tractor owner insists upon the most favorable terms. In 1960 rice sold for about 10 baht per hap during May, when many farmers paid their fees. A farmer with 10 rai of forest field could therefore pay his full fee of 500 baht with 50 hap of rice. If, on the other hand, he feared that he would not have enough rice to last until the harvest, he might arrange to owe half the fee and sell only 25 hap to pay the other half. The price of a hap of green rice was 5 baht, so the farmer agrees to give the tractor man 50 hap of rice after harvest in payment for the 25 baht owed for plowing. If the tractor man presses his advantage, he can collect 75 hap rather than the 50 hap he receives

---

[3] As an extreme example, one villager continually "begged" the tractor owners to plow his field from the beginning of April until the middle of September; he had to spend weeks at Thunglor.

[4] One villager, desperate to have his riverbank field plowed early, served for two weeks as cook for the tractor crew. He received no pay hoping, instead, to obligate his employers. "I help them, they will help me," he explained. Incidents like this one indicate that conventional Western distinctions between economic and social transactions often are inappropriate to peasant choice in Ban Ping.

[5] Of twenty-four farms sampled (see App. B for description of sample), 75 percent paid 20 baht per rai. Those who paid a higher rate probably had their plowing done before the new price was announced. At the smaller home rainfall field, on the other hand, relations with townsmen seem to have influenced prices as well as timing. Of the four plots about which there is information, two were plowed for 30 baht per rai, one for 20 baht, and one for 15 baht. The headman, whose relations with various townsmen are intricate and close, paid only 15 baht. The farmer who paid 20 baht fed the tractor crew while they were in Ban Ping and also promised to clear land for C.

from farmers who are able to pay their fee in full. Unlike villagers, tractor owners are sufficiently wealthy to withhold most of their rice from the market until its price is right. To them, for the most part, 10 hap is worth twice as much as 5 hap no matter when received. By postponing payment for seven months, the tractor owners earn an additional 50 percent.

Access to carts.—Oxcarts, although cheaper and less revolutionary than tractors, are no less essential to farming at Thunglor. It is therefore necessary to examine the consequences of the techniques by which they are obtained.

All the carts used in Chiengkham are made in Lampang,[6] but few Ban Ping farmers obtain them there. Many village households (44 percent) own a cart; most are used carts, bought from neighbors or from nearby villages. New carts are bought in Ban Ping itself or in Phayao, closer than Lampang, but where the prices are somewhat higher. Most years, after harvest, when the roads are dry and the farmers solvent, teams of cart traders come from Phayao or Lampang to stay at a village home. These cart dealers are men much like the villagers of Ban Ping in background, behavior, and aspirations. They are referred to as the "kinsmen" of the villager who puts them up. When villagers are pressed about this kinship, they say, "The cart people are not K's true kinsmen. They are people he knows. They help one another. If K needs a new cart body, they will make him one. He met them when trading in Phayao. They put him up there; he puts them up here." Actually, this friendship called kinship is based primarily on commercial arrangements. Thus, K receives a commission of about 60 baht for each new cart his guests sell. Nevertheless, because the commercial transactions by which carts are bought can be masked as kinship the villagers are insulated from the feeling of subordination which is part of the hiring of tractors. Short-term reciprocity has always been one of the ways in which a villager honors and activates some of his many kin ties. Kinsmen help one another; those who help one another can be called "kinsmen." By retaining this vocabulary, the Lue of Ban Ping can participate in economic and social relationships that extend far beyond their village and yet avoid feelings of impersonality and subjugation; dealings with outsiders often create such emotions in other peasants in Thailand (Moerman 1966*b*).

At Thunglor the demand for carts is so great that those who do not

---

[6] Variations in cart form provide interesting but uninvestigated examples of environmental adaptations and of regional patterns of trade and influence. The carts of the riverine central plain have high walls tapering to a very narrow floor and are clearly not intended for general transportation. In the north, where land transport predominates, the cart floor is much wider and so can move families and their possessions. Lampang carts lack the elaborately carved backboards seen in Chiengmai.

own them cannot obtain another's through the "kinship" or generalized reciprocity which often suffices at home fields. When carts are most needed, access to them may require a substantial exchange. When a carpenter spent a few days helping another villager repair the body of his cart, he explained it as "helping my kinsman" although the kin relationship was not close. In private, the carpenter was asked whether he would be paid for his services. He replied, " 'Father' T has a cart, but he's not a carpenter. I'm a carpenter, but I have no cart for the Thunglor harvest. We're kinsmen, so we help each other. I'll borrow his cart." At Thunglor, even cart owners must hire additional carts. Those with home fields can easily cart their harvest to their granaries in a day or two, for the fields are sufficiently close to permit a number of trips in a day. A round trip to either of the distant fields, on the other hand, takes a full day. Consequently, those who farm there hire cart owners from Ban Ping and other villages to bring the winnowed rice from the distant fields to their granary. Although the carters' fee is substantial (7 baht per load), they are paid with money that comes from the crop they carry, so that there is no possibility of indebtedness. Tractor fees, on the other hand, threaten a villager's solvency because they must be paid when he is little able to afford them.

Farming knowledge.—Ban Ping farmers learned to broadcast-sow from townsmen hired by the tractor owners. Everything that village farmers have learned since or hope to learn comes from outside the village. Unlike plow farming, tractor agriculture is not learned gradually through example and instruction, passed on from the older generation to the younger. Instead, it is taught by townsmen to the villagers they favor. It is the young villagers who find C and his brothers most congenial; they speak easily of "three-disk land" or of rivalries among tractor groups. Unlike knowledge of traditional agriculture, information is passed from the young to the old; the women know nothing at all. Knowledge of tractor agriculture depends not on position within the household and the village but on contact with outsiders.

Tractor owners are often well educated. They are wealthy and well traveled, and are on intimate terms with the prominent merchants and officials. They know far more than the villagers do about the international and national markets for rice. They are better able to predict changes in prices, laws, and transport and storage facilities. Like everyone of influence in Thailand, tractor owners have a coterie of supporters and admirers. Some Ban Ping villagers are on the periphery of these groups. Although in 1960 the entire village buzzed with the rumors they picked up, it seemed likely that such coteries would learn to keep valuable inside tips to themselves.

There would be precedent for this policy, for Ban Ping is not a community of homogeneous knowledge. It has always had extravillage economic relations; the rice traders of the nineteenth and early twentieth centuries kept their slim trade secrets to themselves. In a Buddhist rice-farming village that makes its own clothing and utensils, most things relating to the regular round of life are known equally to all individuals of like sex and age. However, some areas of knowledge—medicine, religion, architecture—are the province of recognized specialists who must be rewarded for their services. Knowledge of external events is unevenly distributed; government news must be transmitted by the headman, and ecclesiastical information is announced by the priest or the temple committee. Other information is considered private; no one is obliged to tell his neighbor unless such information relates to a pressing emergency that affects the entire community (Moerman 1967a). One is permitted to keep to himself information about such things as life in Singapore or local variations in the price of peanuts. When negotiable information from the market town—news of special prices, insecticides, fertilizer, changes in the law —becomes important to village economic life, there will be few sanctions to prevent those with access to it from benefiting themselves at the expense of their neighbors. It might then be possible to describe Ban Ping in terms of a stratification of knowledge as well as of wealth and power. Differences in knowledge of tractor agriculture already distinguish villager from townsman and may soon distinguish villager from villager.

The beginnings of such distinctions may be discerned in town and in village knowledge of insecticides. The two most serious threats to tractor agriculture are water and insects.[7] Against drought and flood, all are equally powerless. Against caterpillars, the most destructive of insects, responses vary. The people of Chiengkham, in their knowledge of insecticides, demonstrate that the dependent relations of village to town are becoming an ever more prominent feature of their lives. The most highly trained men in Chiengkham Town—the few who have been to college, the Bangkok-born policeman who spent a year in England—are convinced that commercial insecticides are the only effective weapon against caterpillars, but the majority of townsmen do not yet worship modern science. Religion, their first line of

---

[7] Irrigation and propinquity minimize these dangers on the home fields. Crabs, often so destructive in irrigated fields elsewhere in Thailand (Rajadhon 1961:26 f.), do not seem to trouble the villagers, perhaps because so many crabs are used in the traditional Lue crab paste (*nam pu*). Villagers never indicated that they broadcast the chopped bark of Manila tamarind (*Pithecolobium dulce*) in order to drive away crabs (cf. Thailand 1947:12).

defense against pests, represents a canny mixture of tradition and cautious spending. As the wealthy *kamnan* put it:

> Last month when I asked you about insecticides, there were caterpillars at my Thunglor field. I hired priests to read a special portion of the scriptures and the caterpillars left. My son at the College of Agriculture doesn't believe it, but I know that it worked. Skeptics should be willing to see for themselves. Yes [laughing], you're right. It was much cheaper than insecticide would have been: it cost only 20–30 baht. Moreover, insecticide might not have worked against caterpillars since they attack the underside of the plant while the spray works from the top.

In town, everyone knows about insecticide; some use it; the rest rely on the priests; all hope for abrupt changes in water level that will either drown or wash away the pests.

In Ban Ping, no one uses either insecticides or the Buddhist rites which have become popular in Yuan villages. Although insecticide is available in shops that all frequent and is occasionally a subject of government announcements, few villagers are aware of it.[8] The few who do mention it—the headman, an ex-policeman, former schoolteachers—have all had some intensive contact with the outside world and interpret its ways to the village. Of these men, only one rejected insecticides on straightforward economic grounds: "It's very expensive. A small can with a small spray gun costs 40 baht and would not be nearly enough to cover a plot." The others have no such detailed information; they view insecticide as something that pertains exclusively to townsmen. Since it is a symbol of the town, the headman, whom his fellow villagers sometimes criticize for "wanting to live like an official," would like to use it some day. For the same reason, the villagers who are aware of insecticide dismiss it from their minds. While P, a former teacher, was describing insecticide as "something townsmen use," his father-in-law returned home. The older man had never heard of insecticide although P had been living and farming with his father-in-law for more than ten years.

In tractor as in traditional agriculture, success is a matter of how much rice one harvests. The standard of success is clear and the desire for it universal. In plow agriculture, the villager knows how to influence his success by careful seedbed techniques, proper crop selection,

---

[8] Awareness is an imprecise concept. What is meant here is that in response to the question, "What can one do if insects eat the rice?" the usual answer was, "Nothing except make offerings [of a few sweetmeats] to the guardian spirit." When pressed with further questions (e.g., "Isn't there anything else one can do? What if the offerings don't work?"), even young men who have traveled to and lived in towns and cities were not sufficiently aware of insecticide to mention it. In one instance, the questions were put to a farmer immediately after he had complained about the failure of World Health Organization agents to spray against mosquitoes. He saw no connection between insecticide and rice pests.

permitting weeds to rot, replowing, determined harrowing, proper water control, and good dike maintenance. In tractor agriculture, success seems beyond the farmer's control. The villager feels that well-cleared level land that has already produced good crops is the best guarantee of success. But beyond choosing or yearning for what he considers the best land, the farmer finds his success dependent on the plowing schedule and at the mercy of water and insects. His techniques for influencing the tractor schedule are hardly more satisfactory than his abilities to influence the water and the caterpillars. When a concern as basic as farming success is beyond empirical control, one is not surprised to see people turn to religious devices and explanations. It is only on the modern tractor fields, never on plowed fields, that villagers make animistic offerings and townsmen ask Buddhist priests to read from the scriptures. Only for broadcast sowing were some villagers interested in determining the traditional "day on which rice was born." At Thunglor, villagers explain differential success not in the empirical terms used for plow agriculture but by means of religious merit *(bun)*.

SUMMARY

Tractor agriculture.—The plow and the tractor form a single farming system. So, for example, labor demands at the Great Field delay the Thunglor harvest; labor demands at the distant fields alter the varieties of rice planted at home (see chap. vi). Yet there are, obviously, definite differences between plow and tractor agriculture. To the villagers themselves the most striking differences are in the work rhythm and in the rewards for labor. In traditional rice farming, the nursery is first seeded under a grueling sun; tillage requires weeks behind a carabao that pulls crude wooden implements through deep mud; transplanting makes the women complain of backache. All the tasks of traditional agriculture are arduous, although fun to do in a group. At tillage, transplanting, and harvesting, the pace of work can become extremely demanding.

The work rhythm of tractor agriculture is very different. Except for the clearing of some kinds of land and for the work at harvest time, it demands relatively little effort. First, the farmer "points" his fields to the tractor driver. Some time afterward, he returns to his holdings to scatter the seed. Months later, he harvests.

The tractor, however, is more than a laborsaving device. It also creates a new relationship of farmer to land, of village to town, and of neighbor to neighbor. The tractor has changed the farmers as well as the farming of Ban Ping. The cooperation and large-scale work parties of the Great Field can hardly be found at Thunglor. Cash, not animal and human labor, is the major outlay for tractor agriculture. In the agricultural techniques and beliefs connected with Thunglor there is nothing distinctively Lue. Plans for future production are geared to predictions of price and profits; success or failure seems beyond the villagers' control. The village is totally dependent on the town for cash and for credit; for the timely plowing that means success; for the insecticides that improve the crop or for the Buddhist rites that seem to; for predicting the prices that influence what kind of rice shall be sown; and for all significant knowledge of how to farm. More precisely, villagers are dependent on townsmen. By virtue of their age or intelligence, their ambitions, status, or experience, some villagers are closer to townsmen than others. This differential accessibility, together with the easily manipulable reciprocity which has always been the main cement of village social structure, means that tractor agriculture provides a basis for the development of economic stratification within Ban Ping.

Tractor agriculture exemplifies fortuitous and temporary good fortune. Rapid flooding, ignorance, dependence on the townsman's timetable, and an attitude of opportunism make farming practices rather casual since they prevent villagers from plowing more than once,[9] from covering their seeds, from weeding, from optimal harvesting. These fortuitous decreases of labor expenditure, added to the efficiency of the machine itself, increase the agricultural productivity upon which sustained prosperity must be based. It is less fortuitous that the expansionism, practicality, and individualism of Ban Ping's traditional agriculture prepared her to take advantage of the tractor which, in turn, has exaggerated these qualities and increased the well-being which they, and the ample lands upon which they were based, had produced.

Farming operations and economic development.—Part Two suggests that the people of Ban Ping are bad farmers, or so an extension officer,

[9] It is possible that casual practices may inadvertently increase yields as well as directly increase labor productivity. The Thai government's 1933–34 experiments with broadcasting produced the following yields from different means of cultivation:

Technique	Yield (thang per rai)
Animal plowing	18.2
Tractor plow, allow soil to weather, light second plowing	19.3
Tractor plow, broadcast onto clods	20.8

Weathering and double-plowing produce a fine tilth which encourages thick growth but makes the ears bear less rice (Thailand 1947:28). Barton (1960:160) suggests that cross-plowing followed by heavy rain may either bury the seeds too deeply (by breaking down the soil) or produce a crust through which sprouts cannot pass. When there is little rain, large clods are also best.

a Japanese, or even a central Thai might be likely to think. Ban Ping farmers rarely use fertilizer, do not select their seeds, and hardly ever weed. Seeding, plowing, transplanting, reaping, and threshing are all done at a time and in a manner that suits villagers' convenience. Although it has been suggested that Ban Ping's casual handling of "the two critical periods" may in part be permitted by environmental factors,[10] it is nonetheless probable that adoption of central Thai techniques (well-cultivated seedbed, tillering period lengthened by earliest possible transplanting, reaping at peak quality) would raise the yield and the quality of Ban Ping's rice. Since I have shown that rice is valued and have assumed that villagers are rational, why do not all farmers adopt the superior operations practiced by some and why have not the more elaborate operations of central Thailand developed in Ban Ping? One answer is that, even before the introduction of the tractor, the availability of land permitted farmers, and tenure and household arrangements (see chap. v) encouraged them, to expand production at the expense of unit quality. To phrase it another way, since land was plentiful (a product of the natural environment coupled with cultural resources) and labor scarce (a product of social resources as well as of demography), the utility of labor was higher than that of land and, hence, labor productivity counted for more than yield per unit area. In this crucial sense, Ban Ping was free of a major halter that so crippled economic development elsewhere in Asia.

In a recent book (1963) Clifford Geertz develops the stylistic notion of "involution" into an "analytic concept—that of the overdriving of an established form in such a way that it becomes rigid through an inward overelaboration of detail." He demonstrates that the concept applies to the agriculture of colonial Java in which farming operations were characterized by "increasing tenacity of basic pattern; internal elaboration and ornateness; technical hairsplitting, and unending virtuosity." The whole Javanese rural economy was distinguished by a process in which "tenure systems grew more intricate; tenancy relationships more complicated; cooperative labor arrangements more complex" (1963:82). Geertz points out that wet-rice cultivation has "an extraordinary ability to maintain levels of marginal labor productivity by always managing to work one more man in without a serious fall in per capita income." He argues that this "labor stuffed" pattern of production is an "ultimately self-defeating process" (*ibid.*, p. 80). Geertz portrays the Javanese *sawah* as a God-given make-work

---

[10] The physiology of glutinous rice, along with irregular terrain, plentiful land, and the head-of-the-year rains may provide the environmental basis for the Ban Ping farming methods: disregard of fertilizer, private irrigation, forest seedbeds, dry seeding, and delayed harvesting.

program which always permitted labor intensification through "pregermination, transplanting, more thorough land preparation, fastidious planting and weeding, razor-blade harvesting, double-cropping, and a more exact regulation of terrace flooding" (*ibid.*, p. 77). This "involuted" mode of adaptation in Java he likens to "treading water faster and faster," and contrasts with the "increased agricultural productivity *per worker*, not just yield *per terrace*" (*ibid.*, p. 132) exemplified by Japan.

Geertz indicates (*ibid.*, pp. 132, 135) that the agricultural differences between Java and Japan which became crucial to national economic development are differences in the productivity of farm labor. As Schultz remarks (1964:119) in a wider context, it is "convenient to use 'farm output per man-hour devoted to farming' as a proxy for the modernization process." Thus the importance of differences in labor productivity between Java and Japan cannot be overemphasized. It is misleading, however, to imply that their major basis is Java's elaboration of labor-intensive tasks. Labor productivity is a fractional expression in which the amount of rice harvested is the numerator and the amount of labor used to farm it is the denominator. Its value, like the value of any fraction, is influenced by both numerator and denominator.

The following list of agricultural operations (from Matsuo 1954: 78–100), though perhaps somewhat idealized, is sufficiently accurate to illustrate the great elaboration of farming tasks in Japan. The tasks indicate that Japanese farming is far more labor intensive than Thai farming and probably more labor intensive than farming in Java. The Japanese farmer selects good varieties of seed, culls by winnowing or flotation, stirs and changes the water in which he pregerminates, and disinfects the seeds before putting them in the bed. On the bed itself, he plows roughly, crushes the resultant clods with a hoe, allows the clods to weather before inundating, puddles several times in all directions, and applies compost. While the young seedlings are growing, he adjusts the water level daily to control temperature, thins the plants, weeds them by hand and through the application of burned rice hulls. On the field, he repeatedly plows, cross-plows, and puddles. To transplant, he inundates the bed in order to soften the soil, pulls the plants one by one, washes their roots, and eliminates damaged plants. He drains the field and stretches string across it in order to make sure that the distances between plants are perfectly regular. He raises the water level for the first days in order to facilitate rooting and then gradually lowers it in order to encourage tillering. He tries to keep the soil barely moist toward the end of tillering, dry before the earing, and wet again once earing is established. During the entire growing season, he weeds and hand cultivates to such an extent that this operation, rare in Ban Ping, takes 20–25 percent of the total expenditure of labor. He harvests by hand and either threshes immediately or prepares racks on which the reaped rice can dry. Despite these elaborate procedures, Japanese agricultural productivity is quite high. This productivity, then, must result not from the absence of involution (the labor of the denominator), but from very large harvests (the rice of the numerator).

Geertz suggests (1963:136 n. 30) that Japan's temperate climate may have made her premodern agriculture produce less rice than Java's. Although this point is not essential to Geertz's argument, it should be pointed out that rice reaches its highest yields in temperate, not in tropical, countries (Grist 1959:362; Rivet 1953:vi). Although differences in technique and in soil selection rule out direct comparison of climatic determinants, it is not unlikely that Java, and the monsoon tropics in general, suffer from reduced hours of sunlight during the growing season (Pelzer 1958:131). But this climatic difference is clearly insufficient to explain Japan's high yields. These yields, I think, are to be ascribed to modern farming techniques in general and, specifically, to the use of chemical fertilizer. The Japanese farmer applies fertilizer before sowing, before and after plowing, and during the growing season (Matsuo 1954:81–100). As Geertz (1963:134 n. 29) acknowledges, and as others have pointed out (Ohkawa and Rosovsky 1964:53; Johnston 1951:505), this application of fertilizer seems to be the basis for the high yields that permitted agriculture to contribute to the economic development of Japan. In Ban Ping, the parallel, and more dramatic, capital input is the tractor.

A further difference between Java and Japan is the latter's political independence and "extremely heavy land taxation . . . reserved . . . for, as it turned out, future investment in an indigenous manufacturing system" (Geertz 1963:135 f.). Since undeveloped and noninvoluted Thailand also preserved her political independence, compulsory saving for reinvestment in industry would seem to be crucial. In any event, when the significant factors are fertilizer, tractors, and capitalization, the anthropologist is left with the uncomfortable conviction that economic and technological factors are more important to development than are such concerns as agricultural involution and colonial values.

To phrase this concept more generally, albeit simplistically, the main component of economic development is economic development. This does not mean that the anthropologist has nothing to contribute, but from Geertz's study and from my own experience it would seem that his chief contributions are, first, to translate the abstract (and covertly ethnocentric) formulations of the economist and policy maker into locally appropriate categories and activities and, second, to help predict the effects of development programs and their consequences upon other parts of culture and society. I will not discuss the latter problem because it has already received a good deal of attention in the literature on "applied anthropology" (see, for example, Sharp 1952; Holmberg 1954). Moreover, I rather fear that the anthropologist's notions of cultural systems and of institutional interconnections are so imprecise and opportunistic that he has no special competence, aside from immersement in native life, to make the predictions that his job description and self-definition often demand. Let us instead consider the first responsibility, to translate the indexes and concepts of macroeconomics into locally appropriate categories.

The variety and abundance of the land available to Ban Ping's farmers explain why they prefer farming techniques which, irrespective of the farmers' motives, increase the productivity of labor. Yet, the economist's use of one standard index—population density—obscures the prosperity that the index purports to measure, prosperity that is so essential to technological decisions which provide for Ban Ping's economic development. Population density, the ratio of men to land, is a popular statistic for comparing the wealth and potential of nations. Of greater apparent precision and importance (Georgescu-Roegen 1964) is nutritional density (or economic density), the ratio of population to cultivated land. Especially within the confines of a single nation, one would expect the latter statistic to reflect accurately the scarcity of land. In Thailand about 90 percent of the cultivated area is owned by those who farm it (Thailand 1957:1), or, seen another way, 80 percent of Thai farmers own their own land (Thailand 1961:2). Northern Thailand seems especially prosperous because it lacks the unfavorable working conditions of many mines in the south, the barrenness of the northeast, and the indebtedness characteristic of the central plains. All authorities (Dobby 1956:277; Blanchard 1958:316; Zimmerman 1931:208; Andrews 1935:300; Pendleton 1962:167, 171) agree that the central Thai farmer is more hungry for land and more deeply in debt than his northern compatriot. Yet as table 3 records, nutritional density is highest where problems are least pressing, and lowest where they are most acute.

It would clearly be a mistake to equate the nutritional densities of lands devoted to crops that differ in yield per unit area. In Thailand (Ruttan *et al.* 1966:10) the slightly better general yields of the north and the high incidence of double-cropping on the Chiengmai plain tend to compensate for its greater nutritional density. Moreover, some of the apparent high nutritional density of the north is produced by unreported swidden holdings (Judd 1964:4).[11] In addition it is clear

---

[11] Although swidden farming is undoubtedly important in Nan, neither Judd's evidence nor my experience seems to support his contention (1964:5) that "it is

that Ban Ping's farmers do not handle land as a homogeneous category. Gross and subtle differences in agricultural technique are based on distinctions of soil age, location, and water source. These technological differences form a complex system in which each influences the others. Planned economic development demands a detailed understanding of the local categories of productive inputs. In efforts to develop the agricultural economy of northeastern Thailand, for example, analogous

TABLE 3

NUTRITIONAL DENSITIES IN THAILAND, 1960

Region	Population (In thousands)	Rice land (In thousands of rai)	Nutritional density (In persons per cultivated rai)
North	2,952	2,588	114
South [a]	3,687	4,510	82
Center [b]	8,328	15,104	55
Northeast	9,640	20,465	47
National	26,260	43,172	61

[a] Regional figures for south omit industrial Phuket.
[b] Regional figures for center omit Bangkok.
SOURCE: Computed from Thailand 1965:table 27.

distinctions must be made between upland and lowland and among other resource features (e.g., soil type, plant cover, and visibility from the village) relevant to the local technology (Platenius 1963:31–34).

When reasoning from nutritional density to hunger and rivalry for land we must also consider tenure arrangements. The ratio of animals to their range tells the biologist a great deal about the life of a herd. Peasants, unlike reindeer, do not merely roam the earth, but work and own it. Patterns of ownership heavily influence incentives for production, but are not recorded in measurements of nutritional density. In Thailand, where no one starves, who owns the land is often of more significance than how many people live on it. In Ban Ping, and probably throughout the north, the ownership of land is far more evenly distributed than in central Thailand.

A further consideration concerns the forces that limit the area under cultivation. If, as is true in Chiengkham, there is virgin land exploitable by native techniques (Muscat 1966:92), an unfavorable nutritional density represents shortage of a productive input other than land, not land shortage, yet upon which cultivation is based. Regardless of nutritional densities, land is not scarce where people want little more

obvious that more land is involved in swidden agriculture than in paddy rice culture in Northern Thailand, probably more than twice as much."

than they have; it is scarce where people can never have as much as they want. It is hardly an exaggeration to regard the former as characteristic of Ban Ping (and of the north) and the latter as characteristic of central Thailand. Part Three indicates that an apparent scarcity of land is, in reality, a scarcity of the kinds of credit and labor that local agriculture and social organization make appropriate to use for clearing land. Just as national shortages of some kinds of labor are better viewed as shortages of capital (Georgescu-Roegen 1964:158), so apparent shortages of land in northern Thailand should be viewed as resulting from the scarcity of some forms of labor and credit.[12]

In this context, it is important to realize that labor and credit are no more homogeneous in the way they affect peasants' technological decisions than land is. A shortage of young men who are expected to clear land, for example, has technological implications very different from a shortage of old men who manage land or of women who grow and market vegetables. Cash and credit, like other resource components, must be viewed through the specifications of a local technological system if we are to anticipate and understand their effects on that system. Even ignoring "social" considerations (e.g., "Will my creditor take advantage of me?" "Can I take advantage of him?"), it is likely that of the various kinds of credit available to the peasant borrower—rice and cash, planting season and dry season, consumption and production—each is quite different in regard to demand, repayment, and productivity. The engineering of economic development requires detailed knowledge of rural technology (of the sort that anthropologists traditionally furnish), not because rural producers are irrational, but precisely because they "exhibit a strong tendency to make the most of economic opportunities and possibilities within the limits imposed by the state of their technical knowledge and [by their understanding of] the availability of co-operant resources" (Bauer and Yamey 1957:92). Schultz (1964:164) is quite correct in asserting that peasants react to the "profitability" of new factors and factor combinations, but they do so as *they* view profitability through the constraints of their own technological systems. We must analyze those systems, *as they appear to the native,* if we are to understand and manipulate those constraints.

Boserup (1965:68 f.) is probably correct when she suggests that "diminishing returns to labor" is a common cause of resistance to technological change; but her hypothesis requires, rather than obviates, "the explanations ... offered by anthropologists, sociologists or social psychologists" because these disciplines are able to discover

[12] It is not unlikely that land shortage in the neighborhood of Chiengmai resembles that in central Thailand in its causes, severity (Wijeyewardene 1965:256), and inequity (*ibid.* p. 258).

whether and why those who make effective productive decisions—those who accept or reject the innovation—believe that returns to labor would be diminished. For all economic variables, as for tenure (Schultz 1964:112), "what matters is the relationship of each of these components to the state of economic information on which production decisions are based and the state of economic incentives and rewards for making efficient decisions." The relevant information, incentives, and rewards can be learned only through analyzing local systems of production decisions in their own terms.

By emphasizing the importance of locally appropriate technological and economic specifications, I do not want to imply that "social" factors are irrelevant. The agricultural progress of Japan was based on matters of marketing, political stability, occupational freedom, and secure property (Lockwood 1955:186–188) as well as upon fertilizer, machinery, and technicians. The importance of such considerations is their relevance to the ways in which the variables of concern to economists (e.g., price, profit, capitalization) impinge upon peasant producers and enter into their calculations of how to farm. The tractor, for example, did not supernaturally appear one morning to Ban Ping farmers in their fields. It came from some definite place, brought by some particular person who had to explain how and why a farmer should use it and what his own interests were in their doing so. The acceptability of the innovation depended upon the ways in which specific farmers viewed and judged the specific features of the specific context in which it was presented to them. The Thunglor pioneers already understood that rapid flooding was a threat, that early planting could circumvent that threat, that pregermination of rice was possible. To judge from the course of subsequent innovations, from villagers' attitudes toward their government (Moerman, 1967*a*), and from the legitimate primacy of self-interest (Moerman, 1966*a*), it was probably not irrelevant to its acceptability that the tractor came from businessmen and not from officials. In Thailand, those who control tractors are permitted to profit from them and have the resources to maintain them. In Japan, landlords presumably demanded that tenants, who farmed about half of the arable land, use fertilizer (Ohkawa and Rosovsky 1964:51). At the very least, we must know whether the local social system is such that the persons who pay for innovations, whether in cash (Epstein 1962:69) or in labor (*ibid.*, p. 64), will also benefit from them. Considerations conventionally given such labels as "ideals" or "social structure," for which anthropologists are presumed to have some special competence, are intimately involved in the local productive decisions that economists want to influence.

PART THREE: *RESOURCES IN LAND AND LABOR*

In order to farm, the villager must acquire land and mobilize labor. In the following two chapters I examine alternatives in acquiring land and mobilizing labor, and discuss the implications of the villager's choices for the changing relations between Ban Ping and other communities.

V.
Land Acquisition

TECHNOLOGY

To understand how a villager acquires land, one must consider the amount of land that his tools and his knowledge make available, his resources for acquiring land, and the purposes to which he puts his land. All three considerations have both physical and social components; all have changed during the history of the village.

Availability of land.—The founders of Ban Ping left Chiengmuan for the plentiful land of Chiengkham. The remains of an old temple indicate that there probably had been a village near Ban Ping before the present settlement. The oldest villagers report that their parents told them that some land had already been cleared on the Great Field when the first Lue arrived. There was, they say, already an irrigation system which merely needed improving and enlarging, but most of the Great Field was unclaimed land. The jungle pressed close about the village, and tigers and monkeys abounded.

Land was acquired then by the effort of clearing it. In time, the home irrigated field, "on which there used to be land enough for us to leave uncultivated roadways wide enough for carts," became completely filled and the less choice land began to be developed. The semi-irrigated field was cleared first, the rainfall field and high ground on the Great Field next; small parcels at the two latter fields are still being developed. A generation ago, hopeful young families began to clear fields farther and farther from the village. The earliest attempt, and the closest, was made at the home flood field which consists of a single small depression in which plots are now owned by Lue from Ban Ping and a neighboring village. About 1925, adventurous young men had tried to develop it, but "the spirits were fierce and numerous" enough to make one pioneer contract a severe arm infection. Then, about 1949, a villager returned to the home flood field, and cleared some without mishap. Since then, more have acquired land there. "In former times," explains a villager, "the spirits outnumbered the people, so we feared them. Now, people outnumber the spirits, so they fear us."

By about 1935 the quest for land had become fairly pressing. A few young men tried to develop farms as far away as Huej Khaw Kam (see map 2). In 1953 those who were trying to develop land at Thunglor were taught to use the tractor. In 1955 young farmers from Ban Ping first began to acquire land on the distant irrigated field which had been discovered by Yuan villagers.

Virgin land was neither consistent in quantity nor uniform in quality, but it was always there to give to the village an aura of prosperity and to the villagers a relief from anxiety. "If there was no new land to clear anywhere," an old man says, "things would be hard, but there usually is land. If it's not irrigated, then one clears more of it and trusts to luck. If it produces well, then good. If it produces badly, well, that's that." While it has not been uniformly easy for the young villager to obtain fresh land, he has always been fortunate in the land available to him. This good fortune is not a simple matter of demography, geography, and material culture. Residence patterns, rules of inheritance, trading ability, and pride in making things at home—as well as the folk concepts of "things with a price" (commodities) and of "private" (*lork*) rice—were all essential to the availability of land. These intangible factors supported and constrained farmers no less than the purely physical environment did, thereby permitting Ban Ping's steadily rising population to become an incentive for effective economic development rather than a cause for despair (cf. Boserup 1965).

Techniques of acquisition.—Land at the various fields—home irrigated, semi-irrigated, rainfall, home flood, distant flood, and distant irrigated—has not all been obtained in the same way. Although the farmer sometimes receives a plot as a gift or as a wage for clearing land, his most important techniques for the primary acquisition of farmland from forest are clearing and claiming. Secondary acquisition of someone else's already developed farmland comes through inheritance or purchase. No villager chooses among these techniques with complete freedom. Which technique he uses depends upon his social and economic resources and upon the natural features and economic purpose of the type of land acquired.

Clearing land is a struggle between natural conditions and the energy that can be mobilized by village technology. Moist and swampy land is more difficult to develop than dry land; heavy forest is harder to clear than light forest; grassland is easiest of all. On any type of land, the more people who work together, the easier the task. Siblings or other close kin often cooperate in clearing a tract and then divide the resultant rice land among themselves. It has also always been possible to hire strangers as well as poor or distant relatives. Such workers may be given money, rice, a share of the crop, or some of the cleared land.

A pioneer usually claims more land than he can clear in a single year. Little by little he increases the area under cultivation. During the early years, a part of the plot may be clear enough for normal cultivation; a part may have rice sown haphazardly among the trees; a part may not be used at all. Even on sections of the well-developed home irrigated field, this year's forest seedbed may become next year's plowland.

Ban Ping is no tropical paradise of effortless living. Clearing land often requires desperately hard work, and its yield is sometimes disappointing. Heavy trees are uprooted by carabao; the water buffalo are also used to pull large square wooden rollers that dislodge roots and pulverize the soil during the first few years of its use.

The comparative ease of clearing distant flood land (except from jungle at the very banks of the Ing) means that the filing of legal claim papers is the central act for the acquisition of land at Thunglor. Until 1960, by which time all land was claimed, Thunglor was a free good that squatters could obtain by fulfilling the requirements and properly completing the forms established by the government for a "claim of initial ownership" *(baj capcorng)*. The requirements are that the claimant be between the ages of twenty and forty-five (if younger than twenty, he must be married) and not already a large landholder. After three years, the claimant requests permanent title. He must then show that there are no better claims than his, that the land is suitable for farming, and that he has continuously used it for his own farming and not for speculation. An appropriate official is then supposed to interview witnesses and measure the plot in order to fix its size and boundaries. Land the claimant has not developed within three years reverts to the common domain and may then be claimed by someone else.

Secondary acquisition comes through inheritance or purchase. The abstract rule of inheritance is quite straightforward. A widow receives her husband's property which, together with her own, is divided at her death equally among the social[1] issue of both parents regardless of the heir's sex or age. This rule, however, is insufficient for understanding the inheritance of real property. I start with it because the villagers do, and in order to emphasize the absence of primogeniture and unilineality, and the preference given to viable social bonds over purely formal ties of genealogy.

---

[1] By "social" issue is meant those whom both parents raised as children in their home, even if biologically they are the offspring of only one parent (remarriage) or of neither (adoption).

One formal qualification of the rule of equal inheritance concerns the house compound. It is inherited by the oldest child among those still living at home after both parents had died. His share of the remainder of the estate is diminished proportionally. Since a couple normally lives to see their older children established in their own households, not infrequently it is the youngest child who inherits the parental home. I suspect that this circumstance, rather than a formal rule of "ultimogeniture" (cf. Blanchard 1958:424; Kaufman 1960:22; Kingshill 1960:54), conditions the inheritance of the parental house and its compound throughout Thailand.

It is unnecessary to consider complexities of inheritance by minors or the distribution of plots of uneven quality. The supply of land is sufficient, so that such issues are not contested.

The rule of partitioning inheritance is qualified by a common practice whereby one child buys from his siblings their share of the estate. Throughout Thailand, all children are supposed to inherit with approximate equality. But in Ban Ping, unlike central Thailand, this custom has not produced a fragmentation of holdings which forces some families off the land (Kaufman 1960:64) and makes the survivors farm inefficiently (Sharp *et al.* 1953:150). In Ban Ping, ownership can constantly be rationalized because land "has a price." It has always been bought and sold at prices that reflect the supply of money and the demand for developed land rather than at prices determined by the social relations between parties to the transactions. The social institutions of trade and of self-sufficiency have helped one of a set of siblings to accumulate enough money to buy the inheritance from the others and thereby to keep intact the original holding. The ecology and economy of Ban Ping have provided the sellers with fresh lands to clear or with Yuan holdings to buy.

Throughout the history of Ban Ping, farms could be acquired by purchase; cash could be substituted for the labor of clearing the jungle. Many plots at the Great Field were bought by their present owners, or by their parents, for *bi ngern*, the silver buttons that preceded minted currency. As farms became scarcer and the demand for land increased, the frequency of purchasing and the price for land rose. In the past, as now, transactions with strangers were entered into and recorded with more formality than transactions with "kinsmen." But it must be emphasized that cultivated land has always been a commodity for which kinsman and stranger alike have had to pay the market price.

Certain techniques of acquiring land are associated more with some fields than with others. Table 4 records the techniques by which contemporary owners of each field acquired their farms. Of the generations that cleared the Great Field, few people are still alive. Most con-

LAND ACQUISITION 95

temporary holdings were acquired through inheritance, although purchase of this expensive land is also quite common.

On the semi-irrigated field, the next to be cleared, there is now hardly any undeveloped land. Many of its older owners, however, were able to clear their land themselves, while younger men often received their plots through inheritance.

Most home rainfall plots were cleared by their present owners;

TABLE 4

TECHNIQUE OF ACQUISITION BY TYPE OF FIELD

Field	Percentage of plots acquired by each technique [a]						Number of plots
	I	S	G	C	B	?	
Great Field	50	9	5	3	35	—	74
Semi-irrigated	30	10	—	25	15	20	20
Home rainfall	18	3	5	50	18	8	40
Home flood	—	—	29	43	14	14	7
Thunglor	—	1	14	54	31	—	107
Distant irrigated	—	—	—	14	83	4	29
All fields	18	4	8	33	35	3	277

[a] KEY: I = inherited; S = bought from siblings; G = gift; C = cleared or claimed; B = bought; ? = technique unknown.
SOURCE: Survey of all plots owned.

little of this land has been used for rice farming long enough to have been inherited. Perhaps more people would have bought rainfall plots had not Thunglor become available at about the time that most rainfall land had been cleared.

Uncleared home flood plots are of scant value, so few have been bought and sold. The usable land has been cleared too recently to have changed hands much, except for two incompletely cleared plots that a middle-aged man gave to his sons when they married.

Thunglor land has also been too recently acquired for anyone to have either inherited some or bought out his siblings' inheritance. Of the fifteen plots acquired by gift, most were given by brother to brother or by father to son. No one bought Thunglor land during the first few years of tractor agriculture and few bought while land there could still be acquired merely by filing claim papers. The progressive increase in the frequency of purchase as a means of acquiring Thunglor land is shown in table 5. Primary acquisition of Thunglor is no longer possible since all of it is now owned, although some land will probably revert to the common domain by reason of the owner's failure to develop it. Of the plots that have been acquired by purchase, very few (under 15 percent) were bought unless they had already been cleared by their preceding owner and cultivated for at least one year. As long as there were "forest farms" (*na pa*) for the claiming, there was little reason for buying one from someone else.

TABLE 5

Purchases of Thunglor Plots, 1956–1960

Year	Number of plots	
	Developed land	"Forest" land
1960	13	3
1959	11	0
1958	4	2
1957	1	0
1956	0	0
Total	29	5

Source: Survey of all plots owned.

Like other recently developed fields, no distant irrigated land has yet been inherited. Few from Ban Ping discovered the distant irrigated field early enough to acquire any as squatters. Most of the twenty-four plots purchased were bought from members of other, usually Yuan, villages who first developed the still-imperfect irrigation system. Unlike the neighboring flood field, plots of distant irrigated land are quite marketable even before their trees have all been felled. This is true because farming with an animal-drawn plow is possible on incompletely cleared land, especially if it is irrigated.

Resources for acquisition.—The discussion of techniques of acquisition and their incidence demonstrates that material artifacts and animal energy are not the only resources a farmer has at his disposal. The labor of other persons, kinship position, credit, and official connections are perhaps of even greater importance. Technology, as I have been using the concept, is not limited to the manual manipulation of material objects.[2] Nevertheless, the very centrality of rice farming to village life makes it impossible for me to explore all the institutions that touch upon farming in this study. Some institutions, however, recommend themselves for discussion by their overwhelming significance for both technology and extravillage relations and by the clarity with which they distinguish between plow and tractor agri-

---

[2] Most anthropologists who discuss technology unconsciously project our own folk image by limiting themselves to the ways in which physical tools are used. Aside from Mauss (1948:73), few explicate or justify this usage.

culture. In discussing them, I do not wish to imply either that the institutions cause the farming practices or that the farming practices cause the institutions. Rather, the farming activity—land acquisition in this instance—makes use of the social environment as much as it makes use of the physical environment.

Ban Ping established itself by clearing the Great Field. Clearing required concentrated labor; people lived in fear of the spirits and wild animals in the nearby jungle. We can understand then, why the early villagers lived in longhouses accommodating four or five or sometimes even seven families. Lowland Tai elsewhere rarely live in longhouses [3] which tend, in Southeast Asia, to be restricted to pioneering regions. Younger longhouse members were expected to clear and farm their own lands as well as those lands that fed the longhouse and its elders. In this way, new families accumulated the individually owned (*lork*) land and rice with which they would someday found an independent household. It was also common for young men to buy cultivated land from either the Yuan or from siblings after both parents had died. Some of the money for these purchases came from surplus rice sold by trading caravans composed of close relatives, often members of the same longhouse. Venturesome trade in other goods—carabao, tobacco, ponies, gold, elephants—was a more important source of investment capital. In these ventures, too, the young were aided by their senior kinsmen.

A longhouse of numerous kinsmen permitted young men to save money as well as to make it. Many longhouses were large enough to include every village specialist (except for headman and priest) whose services were thus available to coresident young men free of charge. Moreover, young men were not expected to spend money on expensive rituals. It was considered improper for them to sponsor funerals and ordinations; their weddings were cheap; and all the expenses associated with building a new house were restricted to the old.

No one now lives in a household larger than three families. Longhouse organization seems to have begun to disintegrate about 1930, when, with the completion of the railroad, rice "began to have a price" and the demand for private handholdings presumably increased.[4]

[3] The multifamily longhouse found among some Lue (Srisiwasdi, n.d., I:4,13; II:chap. 1), but not among others (Chiang 1950; Wissmann 1943:22 and drawing 6), is more typical of the Black Thai (Loeb and Broek 1947:415; Izikowitz 1962:80).

[4] There is some evidence that Ban Ping's few Yuan households left the village at about this time. It may well be that Chiengkham's growing participation in a market economy increased the rivalry for land. It may also have been that the Yuan began to acquire the taste for cash-bought goods and services which still distinguishes them from the Lue. The Lue's proud conservatism has the consequence, if not the purpose, of saving money and of discouraging ethnic intermarriages which would diminish their patrimony.

In the days when married siblings remained together in a single longhouse, the house and its land were administered by the oldest resident. The longhouse, then, was a corporate group in which the continually changing member households cooperated when they farmed their "eating rice" (*xaw kin*) on longhouse lands and worked separately when they farmed their "selling rice" (*xaw xaj*) on individual (*lork*) lands. Although no one now lives in a longhouse, the dichotomy of parent-household-subsistence property versus child-individual-venture property is still basic to the acquisition of land in Ban Ping. For the most part, the social and economic distinctions between "household" (*hern*) and individual (*lork*) rice coincide with the technological distinction between plow and tractor farmland. In 1960 many nascent families were fed by their parents' home irrigated field while they established their independence by means of their own distant flood field. Tractor farming has become the functional equivalent of the "private" rice land that supported nascent households in the days of the longhouse. One aspect of this equivalence can be seen from the fact that persons under thirty-five own only 10 percent of Ban Ping's 73 Great Field plots but own more than 60 percent of the village's 104 plots at Thunglor. A further aspect is that most Thunglor plots acquired through kinsmen (see table 6) were gifts of uncleared land made by fathers to their children and by elder to younger brothers.

TABLE 6

BASIS OF PLOT OWNERSHIP BY TYPE OF FIELD

Basis of ownership	Great Field plots		Thunglor plots		Total number
	Number	Percentage	Number	Percentage	
Kin tie [a]	49	67	15	14	64
No kin tie	24	33	89	86	113
Total	73		104		177

[a] Includes inheritance and gifts or purchases within the nuclear family.

Despite this equivalence, there are, of course, crucial differences between the resources used for acquiring land at the two fields. Throughout the history of Ban Ping, a villager who cleared land for plow farming was limited almost exclusively by his resources in labor: by the strength of his body, of his kinsmen, and of his animals. In clearing land for tractor agriculture, the villager is limited almost exclusively by his resources in money and credit. Most of the forest at Thunglor is composed of thin trees which stand rather far apart, and so are rather easy to uproot, fell, and burn. Yet many villagers are unable to farm all the land they own. Maj K, who claimed 20 rai of distant flood field in 1958, is typical of these. During the first season he could afford to hire the tractor to plow only 5 rai. In 1960 he cleared and had the tractor plow an additional 2. Each rai cleared means a rai plowed at the cost of 50 baht, and Maj K wants to spend no more than 250 baht each year to increase his tractor farmland. He, like most villagers, agrees that "people like us can grow wealthy only little by little, as a small bird builds its nest."

Before Thunglor, the typical villager—supported by his parents, clearing new land, trading, buying from his siblings—continually acquired land through ties of kinship mediated by money. As table 6 suggests, the acquisition of land at Thunglor depends on ties to powerful outsiders.

Reasons for acquiring land.—Land has value because it produces rice and can be owned. The value of owning land lies in the owner's immunity from involuntary loss of the land or its product. The Ban Ping farmer has secure title and is sure of receiving payment if he sells or rents his land to others. Since the sale of land has already been considered, albeit briefly, this section discusses the protection of title and renting.

The size and intimacy of Ban Ping make tenure on home fields quite secure. One need not fear misappropriation by one's "kinsmen," and even small children know the boundaries of each plot. Acquisition is well publicized and the limits of each holding are annually demonstrated to the large work parties needed for plow agriculture. Nevertheless, the government requires that all land be registered with it, a regulation that, on the Great Field, the villager regards as motivated solely by the desire to raise revenues. Since the acreage in a title need not be accurate to protect tenure, the Ban Ping farmer underreports in order to save land tax. The discrepancy between government records and actual holdings cannot be determined precisely because no farmer need ever measure his plot in official units, but I believe that the discrepancy is very wide. In response to my survey, it was not unusual to receive a reply like this: "I have 45 rai, but the officials know about only 18." [5]

At Thunglor, on the other hand, official records are quite accurate. Although the same laws of registration apply to both fields, the operations of tractor agriculture make the village landowner dependent upon correct records in order to acquire and protect his farm. His plot

---

[5] The solidarity and isolation of Ban Ping probably make its landowners underreport more than is usual. Nevertheless, there is little reason to believe that official land records are sufficiently accurate anywhere in Thailand to merit the credence they have been given in most published studies of village life there.

is sometimes bordered by forest or by the plots of strangers. Even were his neighbors all close kinsmen, they could not, with all the goodwill in the world, always be sure where one parcel ended and another began. On the distant flood field there are no dikes, and the tractor progressively obscures topographic features. To grow his crop, the farmer does not rely on fellow villagers who constantly witness the extent of his plot by working on or near it. Rather, he depends on the tractor men who must be paid according to precisely measured areas and who can annex land by using their machinery to develop it. After his tentative claim (*capcorng*) has expired, the villager owns not a square inch more than the area plowed by a townsman and measured and recorded by the government.

To discover why villagers choose to rent land, one must distinguish between the motives of landlords and those of tenants, even though the same individual sometimes plays both roles during a single farming year. The Ban Ping landowner farms his land unless he lacks an essential factor of production, but as techniques vary from field to field, the same factors are not scarce everywhere. Home rainfall land may go unused if there is insufficient water. Thunglor lies fallow when there is not enough money to pay for its clearing and cultivation. Rental to others results when the owner is short of labor, the third factor essential to production. The village landowner considers himself a farmer and rents land only when his household lacks sufficient labor to cultivate it. With the increase of neolocality, parents are not infrequently deprived of all young workers, thereby increasing the frequency with which they rent their land, without changing their reasons for renting it.

Fields that need little labor are rarely rented. Among Ban Ping's 103 cultivable plots at Thunglor, only one, owned by a widow with no grown children, was rented. Distant irrigated fields are also rarely rented. They have been acquired quite recently, so that their owners, who had to labor to clear them, still have enough labor to farm them. Of the twenty-nine distant irrigated plots, the only one rented out was owned by a man who preferred working his home irrigated farm because his wife was too advanced in pregnancy to accompany him to the distant field. Since the labor-intensive Great Field and semi-irrigated field account for almost all the land rented by Ban Ping owners, the following discussion is limited to these two fields.

Whatever his motives, the landlord is rewarded with a payment of rent, the amount of which has "always"[6] been set by a rule known and quoted by all villagers. The owner provides the seed, since his

---

[6] "Always" is set within quotation marks both because, as is common in anthropology, it refers to a period of time no longer than informants care to remember, and because, as will be discussed shortly, the rule has in fact been modified.

rice is best adapted to his field. If the tenant furnishes the carabao, he pays a rental of one-third the crop. If the landlord furnishes the carabao, the rent is one-half the crop.

Most landlords rent in order to gain rice from land that they have insufficient labor to farm. The motives of tenants are somewhat more complicated, but one can distinguish between those who rent because they do not have enough land to support themselves and those who rent in order to help their landlord, a distinction commonly made by villagers themselves. Unfortunately, other published studies do not mention this distinction or the factors upon which it seems to be based, so I do not know its generality. Nevertheless, its economic importance may be comparable to that of the distinction between those who borrow for consumption and those who borrow in order to invest (Muscat 1966:133).

To understand the technological factors underlying the distinction

TABLE 7

Tenancy on Home Fields: Size of Plot and Type of Tenant

Plot size (In rai)	Tenant outside village		Tenant in village	
	Lue	Yuan	Nonkinsman	Kinsman
Less than 5	1	2	1	7
5–10	4	8	2	3
More than 10	2	3	1	0
Mean size of plot	7.8	7.8	7.4	3.8

in motive, we need to consider the size of the plot rented and the kinship bonds between landlord and tenant. Tenants on fourteen of the thirty-five parcels of home irrigated land rented in 1960 were fellow villagers. Table 7 indicates that the ten plots rented by "kinsmen" of the landlord were, on the average, much smaller than the plots rented by nonkinsmen. The figures simply reflect the difference between those who must rent enough land to support their families and those who rent merely as a minor convenience to themselves or to their landlord kinsmen. In terms of this distinction, and the plot-size index that reflects it, there is little difference between nonvillagers and those within the village who are not close kinsmen; there is no difference between Yuan and fellow Lue. Transactions with those who are not close relatives are almost purely commercial, and are discussed under extracommunity relations.

Table 8 records all rentals within the village made in 1960. In the first four transactions, land contiguous to the tenant's inheritance was rented from a sibling. This device permits the efficiently unified operation of a fragmented inheritance. The tenant in the first transaction of the table, for example, inherited 1 rai to which he added 4 rai bought from siblings. It was presumably only a lack of cash which prevented his buying the remaining rai which he now rents from his sister (fig. 3).

The rental of an estate among siblings permits even greater flexibility than would its purchase. Consider, for example, the second and third transactions, which both involve the same household as tenant. "Mother" N's household, now quite large (twelve members), is able

TABLE 8

RENTALS WITHIN BAN PING, 1960

Transaction	Plot size (In rai)	Kin types [a]
1	1	yB
2	9	eS
3	2	yS
4	2½	yS
5	1	ex-H
6	3½	SHS
7	1½	eB
8	3½	s
9	6	d
10	8	Sd
11	4½	none
12	7	none
13	7	none
14	11	none

[a] Kin types record landlord's closest kinsman in tenant household. See Key to Genealogical Information, p. 210, for explanation of abbreviations.

to farm the land of two siblings as well as its own inherited land. From her elder sister's small (five-member) household, Mother N rents the 9 rai (transaction 2) that comprise the bulk of the original inheritance bought by the elder sister's household from siblings some fifteen years before. From the other sibling's household (eldest brother, deceased), now sufficiently small (with only four members) to rent out its maternal inheritance as well (transaction 1), Mother N rents (transaction 3) the remaining share of the original inheritance. These relationships are summarized in figure 3. By means of renting, the use-rights of a fragmented estate can be united by the household whose dependents, labor force, and other landholdings most require it. This flexible arrangement works to the advantage of both landlord and tenant.

The households involved in transaction 4 are both extremely wealthy. The two young men of the landlord household farm their

LAND ACQUISITION   103

distant flood fields and the household rents out its more than 20 rai of Great Field. The tenant household, with about 50 rai of its own, is the wealthiest in the village and rents out more than half of its large holding. The home irrigated land it does farm, however, is contiguous to a parcel inherited by the landlord of transaction 4, because the women of the two households are sisters. The tenant accommodates

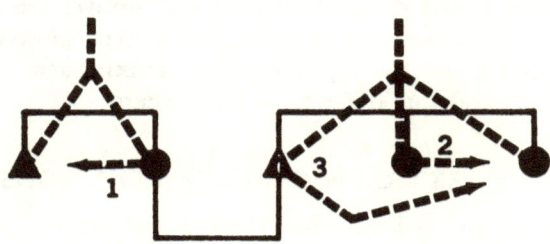

▲ dead

Fig. 3. Schematic genealogy: inherited land recombined through renting. Numbers correspond to transactions recorded in table 8. Vertical dashed lines represent inheritance; horizontal dashed arrows point from landlord to tenant.

the landlord by renting about 2 rai of Great Field; the tenant already has enough Great Field property to rent out 30 rai.

The renting of inherited land is not the only type of transaction in which the tenant's major motive seems to be that of helping his landlord kinsman. In the next three transactions (5, 6, and 7) as well, the owners' need to have the tenants rent from them was greater than the tenants' need to rent the land,[7] and the tenants are wealthier than their landlords.

Transactions 8, 9, and 10 are also motivated by the desire to help kinsmen. They represent prematurely independent young households that support themselves by renting some of their parents' land.

Considerations other than immediate income probably often enter into decisions of whether or not to rent land. In the more modern of the south Indian villages described by Epstein, for example, a landowner who emigrates to town often gives tenant relatives rent-free use of his land, apparently in order to facilitate his returning to the village should he have to do so (1962:211 f.). Published accounts of

[7] In transaction 5, the small parcel is the landlord's only Great Field land. She got it for marrying the old man whose household is now her tenant. The parcel was part of 11 rai, 10 of which are still owned and farmed by the tenant household. No other household, not even the owner's, would otherwise trouble to farm so small a plot.
  The landowner of transaction 6 is an old widow who lives alone. In 1960 the sister of her sister's husband was the tenant. The preceding year it was a genealogically more distant relative who, in his phrase, "took pity and farmed her land for her."
  In transaction 7, an elder brother agreed to rent a Great Field plot from his younger brother who wanted to farm at the distant irrigated field instead.

tenancy in Thailand consider renting a purely commercial transaction. From the Ban Ping evidence, it would seem that they are wrong to do so. Among fourteen instances of rentals within Ban Ping, only the four transactions with nonkinsmen (11-14) are intelligible in purely commercial terms. Like the renting of land to nonvillagers, these four transactions involve larger parcels than do the ten kinship transactions. When close kinsmen rent land, the motives are not purely commercial. The relative importance of commercial motives is reflected in the size of plot rented. By this index, nonkinsmen differ little from nonvillagers and Lue differ little from Yuan.

EXTRACOMMUNITY RELATIONS

Availability of land.—Ban Ping's social organization and rules of inheritance are predicated upon the constant availability of new farmland; Ban Ping's wealth acts to preserve the village, maintain its unity, and influence its ideology of production. In these ways, the abundance of land both depends upon village social life and affects it.

Since there is land for all, no one is forced to leave the village. Ban Ping thus presents a sharp contrast to land-hungry central Thailand, where many families are disintegrated by poverty (Janlekha 1955:31-33) and their members forced to find urban employment (Kaufman 1960:64).

Ban Ping's prosperity encourages almost all villagers to think of themselves as farmers; few young people desire any other career. In a questionnaire, the graduating class of the village school was asked to list the advantages and the shortcomings of roles familiar to them: farmer, teacher, headman, policeman, priest. They were then asked what they wanted to be. Almost everyone replied that he wanted to be a farmer. There is no feeling that economic possibilities are hopelessly circumscribed by growing rice. There is little feeling that a better life is possible in town. Unlike neighboring villages (which Ban Ping preceded to Thunglor), Ban Ping practices few secondary occupations such as sugar growing, fishing, and cutch production which compete with rice farming.

The availability of land helps maintain the unity and uniformity of village society. Land, for example, is hardly ever a subject of dispute. Of thirty trouble cases recorded from February 1960 to March 1961, only one was concerned with land.[8] In Bangkhuad, on the other hand, disputes over land were sufficiently common to be a major topic of village conversation (Kaufman 1960:167).

Another component of unity and uniformity is the relative absence

---

[8] Even in that case, land was far less a contested scarce good than a symbol of equable relations between the families of a man's deceased wife and of his new wife.

of economic stratification. Compared with central Thai villages, Ban Ping suffers no conflict between landlord and tenant, no feeling of economic subjugation, little conspicuous difference among levels of living. In central Thailand the ownership of land is distributed quite unevenly. Less than half of the farmers of Bangchan own enough land to support themselves; almost everyone (89 percent) does in Ban Ping.

The peasants of Ban Ping do not maintain "an intimate and reverent attitude toward the land" (cf. Redfield 1956:63 f.). To them, land is a commodity that has always been bought and sold quite freely with very few restrictions on its alienation. Some have a vague feeling, to which no one gives more than lip service, that a man who sells his inheritance has somehow disparaged his parents. Of slightly more significance is the feeling that someone with land to sell should go first to his siblings and other close kinsmen. The issue here, however, is the practical one that close relatives are likely to have inherited plots contiguous to the one for sale. No one is ever criticized for selling land to nonkinsmen or to people from other villages if they offer a better price or more immediate payment than one's kinsmen can. No one objects to land leaving village ownership.

In this regard, incidentally, land is rather different from cash, toward which, it would not be absurd to say, the villagers have a somewhat "reverent attitude." A given amount of cash often seems to have a higher value than anything it might buy. At village meetings, or in descriptions of Lue self-sufficiency, it often seems that parsimony and keeping cash within the community have a high, almost moral, importance. Land, however, changes hands quite frequently and the village attitude toward it is frankly speculative.[9]

Its easy access to land makes Ban Ping more durable, united, and entrepreneurial than it might otherwise be. Throughout the history of Ban Ping, there has never been a class of landless farmers. The natural environment, as used by village technology, and the social organizations have permitted all to clear, to buy, and to own rice land. For the basis of his livelihood, no villager is directly dependent on the town or the nation.

Techniques of acquisition.—The ways in which land is acquired are influenced by and also modify the social environment. The incidence of clearing affects relations among siblings and between old and new households; the incidence of purchasing reflects Ban Ping's changing relations to the outside world.

In Ban Ping, the "solidarity of the sibling group" is no mere ab-

[9] When he needed money for a new cart, one farmer, for example, decided to sell land rather than rice which then had a low price. Another, upon hearing of new lands available in a distant district, went there in the hope of buying some to resell for a quick profit. Another young man sold his 3.2 acres of distant field in order to buy a plot of equal size at half the price from "a man who lives far away and thus did not know the value of land" locally.

straction. Brothers are often close friends who work together, cooperate in economic activities, constantly exchange visits, and rally to each other's aid in disputes. This fellowship is in striking contrast with the situation in the Ceylonese village Pul Eliya, where "the relationship between full brothers is marked with strain" (Leach 1961:107). Leach demonstrates that the hostility between Sinhalese brothers results from their rivalry over the control of parental property for which the abstract rule (all children inherit equally from both parents) of inheritance is exactly the same as in Ban Ping. In Pul Eliya land is quite scarce; the farmers of Ban Ping consider land plentiful. Moreover, throughout Ban Ping's history, brothers have obtained property through helping one another clear land, through trading together, through amicable sales and purchases. Cooperation, not rivalry, with one's siblings is the best guarantee of land.

In central Thailand, where land is scarce and the longhouse nonexistent, parents try to give the married child who resides with them "a kind of annual bonus locally called *lampai*" (Janlekha 1955:38). The *lampai* may be a gift of cash or of usufruct from a specified portion of the family fields. When the young couple leaves to start an independent household, the parents are expected to provide them with capital. The young, then, must await for arbitrary bounty of their elders; their prosperity is fixed by that of their parents. In Ban Ping, the establishment of a new household need not deplete the land and capital of an old one.

Resources for acquisition.—The social resources of which a farmer avails himself in order to acquire land have further social consequences. The primacy of labor as a source for acquiring land, coupled with a social system that makes cooperators of one's kinsmen and kinsmen of those with whom one regularly cooperates, is certainly not irrelevant to the easy fellowship that seems to characterize village life. In a less general way, the manner in which parents provide land for their children influences the relations between the generations. The fact that it is increasingly difficult for parents to make such provision forces young men to become more dependent upon subordinate relations with townsmen and so threatens Ban Ping's prosperity and self-sufficiency.

To judge by those whose advice is sought and who, in more formal ways, dominate public affairs, only men thirty-five years and older are reckoned mature enough to take active part in village government. Ownership by the young of economically significant resources will undoubtedly affect seniority in village society. At present, the main discernible social consequence has been on residence and household formation.

Before the discovery of the distant flood field, only orphans owned land before their marriage. Now, quite a few unmarried young men own and operate distant flood plots of their own. Until recently, most villagers followed the traditional Lue rule of residence: "Leave for three years, return for three years." Upon his marriage, a man lived and worked for three years with his wife's parents. The couple then went for three years to the husband's parents. Although the rule was modified in practice to take account of the parents' labor needs and of the young couple's wealth, new households were normally expected to have a long period of nascence. Since the introduction of the tractor, many young men, landowners when still single, build houses for their families almost as soon as they become fathers. Through this change in residence arrangements, the innovation of tractor agriculture has also helped maintain the equanimity of village life.

In all communities there is probably some conflict of interest between the young and the old. In communities that, like Ban Ping, have recently been presented with large numbers of thrilling new stimuli, it would certainly not be surprising to find friction and estrangement between the generations. Ban Ping's increasing commercialization and diminishing self-sufficiency form the only world that young villagers have known. Only men younger than thirty-five have worked as soldiers, policemen, or teachers for the national state; only women younger than thirty have gone to school; only girls younger than twenty regard a milling machine as a normal convenience of daily life. In their dress, dialect, deportment, and dreams, the young are devoted to things their elders never knew. Yet there is no war between the generations. Youngsters, at moments of annoyance, do sometimes exclaim, "Old people don't know anything." Old men do sometimes complain, "Young people nowadays don't show proper respect."

There is little evidence, however, that such acerbity is any sharper than it ever was. For advice and support, the young still seek their elders. To settle their disputes, they eagerly apply ancient standards and procedures. For fantasy and romance, they are fonder of tales of "the old days, the Lue days," than of stories of modern urban life. At the up-to-date weddings and housewarmings of the modish young, aged guests are vied for. When a lively young man, his face concealed by darkness, disturbs a hearing by shouting, "The old men want to go home; they're only getting stiff backs," it is easy to imagine that fundamental disrespect exists between the generations. It is more significant, however, that the hearing was called at the request of village adolescents who felt that only their elders could stop them from quarreling.

Ban Ping's resources for acquiring land are forces for solidarity between the generations. The young men of the village are aided by their parents when they develop their distant flood fields and, soon after marriage, establish their own households. Yet a youth's fashionable luxuries—his wristwatch, white shirts, tight trousers, fountain pen—are provided by money from his own field at Thunglor and not from the grudging generosity of elders who consider them foolish extravagances. Between young and old there are now greater differences of experience than ever before in Ban Ping's history. Tractor-based prosperity, however, now permits young families to live alone. Helped by parents but not dependent on them, guided by parents but not under their direct control, the young can revere the ways of their elders and need react with neither froward obedience nor destructive rebellion. But this idyll may not last, for even those who have obtained land from kinsmen must maintain title to it against increasingly ambitious townsmen. The productivity resulting from the use of the tractor, which has made Ban Ping so prosperous, seemed, in 1960, to threaten that prosperity and the independence it supports.

Without the townsmen who taught them the techniques of tractor agriculture, few villagers would want distant flood fields. Without the townsmen who control the means of developing one's claim, no villager could acquire land there. Of the Ban Ping farmers who discovered Thunglor, none has as much land as he originally claimed. Some they gave away to kinsmen who could afford to develop it, but more was lost to townsmen who control the means of development.[10]

The tractor owner is so powerful that, in extreme cases, he can make a villager lose his land merely by altering the plowing schedule. Although a delay in plowing is usually caused merely by a field's inaccessibility, if the holding is large and contiguous to the tractor owner's own land, a blatant conflict of interests can develop. "I gave C a deposit of 500 baht [for plowing a huge tract]. He didn't even use the money to plow the 10 rai it would pay for. He lied time after time in telling me that the fields were just about to be plowed. In this way he hoped to delay until it was too late for me to arrange the plowing with another tractor owner. Then he could just take over my plot [as reverted land]." The charge, even if untrue, illustrates that the relationship between tractor owner and villager is not precisely analogous to the traditional bond between patron and client whose interests were rarely opposed. In 1960 most tractor owners felt that it would be profitable to ignore village smallholders and plow only their own land. Not unless their tractors were otherwise idle would they plow

---

[10] The experience of one pioneer is not untypical: "I claimed 70 rai of which 15 remain. Most of the land was lost to wealthy tractor owners because I didn't have the money to plow it. The tractor owners merely plowed the land and took it as their own. After they had cultivated it for a few seasons, they sold it at high prices."

Few villagers seem to consider such losses unjust. From a Western point of view, it might also be argued that plowing is more expensive and far more productive than the mere discovery and claiming of a parcel of virgin land.

for hire. To accomplish this plan, of which the villagers seemed unaware, the tractor owners needed huge landholdings. The *kamnan*, for example, planned to bulldoze and cultivate 400 acres of ranch and orchard. Although regulations are supposed to limit the amount of land that one can claim, "for large landowners," says the assistant district officer and *kamnan*'s brother-in-law (see fig. 2), "the law permits exceptions."

Tractor owners can expand their holdings only at the expense of villagers. They can foreclose on those who, unused to money-credit as a means of production, are sometimes unable to pay their debts. They can develop and then claim another man's land. Their education enables them to claim land in the correct manner, while their official connections assure them that the laws about effective land development and limited size of holdings will be interpreted in their favor. In 1960, the distant flood field, so essential to Ban Ping's prosperity, seemed threatened by the efficiency of tractors and the power of their owners. Unlike feudal lords, modern patrons can prosper by damaging their clients.

Purposes of acquisition.—How title is protected and how rental is arranged have already been indicated. Both practices involve Ban Ping in relations with other communities. Rental ties Ban Ping to other villages; title registration ties her to the national state.

For fields near the village, the official title form proves that one is a landholder. It may serve as evidence of solvency or, if one is so unfortunate, as collateral for loans. To outsiders who want to buy land, the registration paper shows that one owns such and such a plot, the actual size of which can be measured later. Each paper stands for a piece of land; in some instances the piece has been divided and redivided so often that only the villagers, all of whom know its history, could recognize it. The official paper may bear the name of some owner now dead who, like any living villager, was undoubtedly shrewd enough to underreport his original holding and then secretly add still more land to it. Legal ownership is thus established by an official title which stands for some past or present parcel that it never described accurately. Home fields registration papers are tokens in a continual contest between the peasant and his government.

At Thunglor, on the other hand, accurate official title is essential to secure tenure. This new dependence upon the government has changed the internal structure of the community, since most relations with officials are mediated by the village headman. Officials do not authenticate claims at Thunglor until the time of proving firm title and, even then, their inspection is often quite casual. For collecting land records, the national government uses the headman, who is consequently often besieged by villagers asking him to suggest answers to the government's questions, to write for them in his neat hand, and to sign as witness to their statements.

Ban Ping's headman served his villagers well by sometimes failing to record a claimant's other holdings, by emphasizing the number of his dependents, or by exaggerating the amount of land he has worked to develop. The shrewd conniving for which villagers so often criticized their headman was a great advantage when they acquired land at Thunglor.[11] At the time that land claims were to be filed, Ban Ping's headman disappeared for some ten days, "because he was embarrassed" by his misuse of public monies. Villagers complained more about the timing of his absence than about its cause. His disappearance prevented them from taking advantage of the shrewdness that had given him cause to flee. As land registration, taxation, and government services become more important to farming in Ban Ping, villagers probably will become ever more dependent on their headman or upon others with strategic access to townsmen.

Renting out its land is one of Ban Ping's most important economic ties to other villages. Other things being equal, a Ban Ping landlord might be expected to find his tenants first in his own village, then in contiguous villages, and finally in more distant ones. Such an ordering reflects both the frequency with which the landlord meets people and the likelihood of his land being conveniently accessible to prospective tenants. But Ban Ping and its Lue neighbors have long been prosperous owners of Great Field land. Ban Ping's early discovery of Thunglor added to this prosperity and provided a new outlet for the labor of an already busy community. Lue villagers are now unable to cultivate all their land. Only fifty-five of the seventy-four Ban Ping households that own Great Field and semi-irrigated land farmed all their holdings in 1960. Since Ban Ping and its immediate neighbors are so prosperous, Great Field land is more often rented outside the village (21 plots) than within it (14 plots); most nonvillage tenants (13 of 20) are Yuan.

Almost all these Yuan tenants come from two villages at the far edge of the home irrigated field. Ban Ping has long exerted a measure of unacknowledged economic dominance over these villages. It was to them that Ban Ping's few Yuan families moved when "they became shy of the Lue."[12] The ethnic distinction between Lue and Yuan thus has some slight relation to renting, but is irrelevant to the price of rental.

[11] Even by townsmen, the headman was considered an expert on land claims at the distant field. Although most valued knowledge moves from town to village, rural people do sometimes know things that townsmen want to learn. Early in 1960 the headman was visited by two teachers who wanted to claim land at Thunglor. He suggested unclaimed areas to them, drew a map, and offered to accompany them to the field. Such services or, rather, the patronage they elicit increases a headman's influence in town and so may benefit his villagers.

[12] Yuan from these two villages also furnish labor, discussed in chapter vi.

LAND ACQUISITION 111

The most important point about rent is that all tenants pay it. Kinsmen who pool their inheritance, the elder brother who helps his junior, the son who is supported by his parents—all must, like the Yuan stranger, compensate the owner if they farm his home irrigated land. The Great Field has always been so much a "thing with a price" that even the closest "kinsmen" (except for household members) must pay for using it. All villagers, even the oldest who are so sensitive to any change and so quick to disparage it, agree that rental has always been part of Ban Ping's economy. "In the old days," they say, "if one rented from a close relative, the landowner might give a little

TABLE 9

Share of Crop Paid as Home Field Rental,
1960 Frequency Distribution

Type of transaction	One-third	Two-fifths	One-half	Unknown and other
1. Land only, to kinsman in village	5 [a]	3	0	2 [b]
2. Land only, to nonkin in village	0	2	0	0
3. Land only, to Lue outside village	0	0	3	3
4. Land only, to Yuan outside village	0	0	12	1
5. Land only, to unknown outside village	0	1	0	0
6. Land and carabao, to kinsman in village	0	0	2	0
7. Land and carabao, to nonkin within village	0	0	1	0

[a] Includes one rental to a younger brother in a neighboring village made by a man recently married into Ban Ping from that village.
[b] Includes one parcel of which a trader gave his daughter rent-free usufruct.

extra if he really loved and pitied his kinsman. But the rental for kin and nonkin was the same." However tempting it might be to assume otherwise, the universality of rent is not an aspect of increasing commercialization in general or of the recent growth in demand for land in particular. Nevertheless, the cash market for rice has affected the rental prices recorded in table 9.

Lines 3 and 4 in table 9 show that, despite the rule mentioned earlier, nonvillagers now pay half share even if they supply their own carabao. Villagers claim that this rate for outsiders began "about two or three years ago when land became scarcer." This high rent probably does not indicate a sudden increase in population; rather, it is a culmination—based on the introduction of tractor agriculture—of the accelerating demand for land that began about 1920, when the railroad from Bangkok first came to Lampang. Although fellow villagers are still protected by the traditional rule, which requires half-crop shares only when the landlord provides the carabao (lines 6 and 7),[13] even within Ban Ping rentals are changing to favor the landlord. About half the kinsmen tenants who supply their own carabao and all such nonkin (lines 1 and 2) now pay a rate quite close to the half share demanded of outsiders. The landlords of Ban Ping still feel that it would be wrong to charge a fellow villager the new rate of half the crop. For this reason, Maj M, the wealthiest villager, has decided to rent only to outsiders in the future. It is probable that either the rent within the village will rise or more large landlords will come to think as Maj M does.

In Ban Ping, land has always been "something with a price"; villagers think it improper to give land away, except to their closest intimates. From table 9 it can be seen that the degrees of intimacy significant for renting land are "kinsman," fellow villager, and outsider. Between Lue and Yuan outsiders (lines 3 and 4) there is no difference; the major distinction is between fellow villagers and outsiders (compare lines 1 and 2 with lines 3 and 4). Within Ban Ping, the distinction between kin and nonkin is also important. Most kinsmen pay the old rental of one-third of the crop (see line 1); all non-kinsmen pay two-fifths of the crop as rental (see line 2). When tenants rent carabao, the distinction between kin and nonkin is even more pronounced, but it cannot be represented in a table because both pay the same rental (see lines 6 and 7). Although the two kinsmen [14] who rent carabao are from prematurely independent households, both "rent" by Western definition and as villagers use the term *pha*. As such, they illustrate the way in which the people of Ban Ping use a single rule to cover many gradations of behavior. Both these transactions, even though they involve substantial rents, could well be considered instances of cooperative farming, since young people of the landlords' households made substantial contributions of free labor to their tenant kinsmen.[15] In the transactions with a nonkinsman (line 7) the landlord contributes no labor and the tone is quite different, yet the same term (*pha*) is used and the same rental is charged.

---

[13] Some clever young landowners suggest that a tenant from another village might be charged three-fifths of the crop if he used his landlord's carabao.

[14] One is the "child" of his landlord, the other his landlord's "nephew-in-law." They appear as transactions 8 and 10 in table 8.

[15] In referring to these rental arrangements (*pha*), one landlord described the transaction as "helping my nephew-in-law." In the other instance, the tenant spoke of himself as "helping my father farm."

LAND ACQUISITION 113

In describing purchases of carts, I referred to commerce disguised as kinship. Renting land and carabao to relatives might be called kinship disguised as commerce. Presumably, it is precisely transactions of this sort which are described by the statement, already quoted, that "the landowner might give a little extra if he really loved and pitied his kinsman. But the rental for kin and nonkin was the same." Such transactions have permitted Ban Ping to produce a marketed product and yet remain an isolated village, to master the techniques of commerce without corrupting the ties among "kinsmen." Such transactions, in sum, compose the "part-ness" of the peasant community.

Were land to become scarcer, dependence on purchased products more complete, and the social resources for acquisition less effective, the incidence and social consequences of tenancy within the village would probably change. The form tenancy might then take can be suggested by a comparison with central Thailand where all these conditions exist. Nearly half of Bangchan's farms are cultivated by tenants, while, in Ban Ping, tenants cultivate only one farm in twenty. Few Ban Ping households are entirely supported by rent; none think of themselves as landlords. Renting land is seen not as a way of life but as an expedient means of cooperation between a household with too few able-bodied members to work all the land it owns and a household with too many members for its land. Landlord and tenant are not distinct social classes but, rather, are best seen as transient stages through which anyone might pass during his career.

In the central plains, emphasis upon commercial production creates an infinite demand for land which results in the concentration of ownership in a few hands. The demand also loosens the bonds of mutual service and respect among kinsmen and fellow villagers and replaces them with more purely commercial ties. The central Thai tenant is dependent upon the bounty of wealthy landowners who can thus exact from him contributions of farm labor and personal service (Janlekha 1955:67; Kaufman 1960:30, 104) unknown in Ban Ping where land is too plentiful and its uses still too traditional for its owners to exert social and economic domination. In central Thailand, the anonymity of urban landlords and the pressing demand for land permit rents to rise beyond the point at which the tenant can farm at a profit (Janlekha 1955:67). In Chiengkham, for the most part, "absentee landlords" are peasants from prosperous villages like Ban Ping. They are members of the same economic and social stratum as their tenants; they are subject to the same social controls and share the same aspirations.

In Ban Ping all rents are in kind. In central Thailand, where money can buy almost anything and few things can be obtained without it, rents are collected in cash. This system penalizes the tenant since he always finds it difficult to save money and usually finds it impossible to withhold his crop from the market and wait for the best price.

SUMMARY

The chapter began with a brief history of how the farmers of Ban Ping developed their fields. For these farmers, the bogey of "population pressure" is really just a father with more mouths to feed, a son who aspires to become a householder. In Ban Ping such persons are fortunate in their natural and social environment, for they find plenty of forested land, a value placed on thrift and hard work, a pattern of cooperation within the family and household, the possibilities of long-distance trade and of a market for land, and the incentive of growing "private" (*lork*) rice that can be sold for cash.

To establish order among a villager's many opportunities, I distinguished between primary and secondary land acquisition and analyzed the ways in which certain factors underlie a farmer's decision of which technique to use for acquiring different kinds of land. These factors are the value of a plot for specific productive purposes, the farmer's access to specific economic and social resources, and the availability of alternative plots. Discussion of such resources as longhouse organization, with its labor pool and enforced savings, and kin-based reciprocity enabled us to see the similarities and the differences between developing "private" rice in former times and developing tractor fields today. We then saw how the single purpose of secure ownership and uniform cadastral regulations explain different forms of land registration, depending on field location and farming operations. By examining the landlord's purposes, we were able to predict the incidence of rental on different types of field. The size of the plot rented provided an index of the tenant's purposes, a factor ignored in other studies despite its importance to village society and to farmers' decisions of how to acquire land.

We then considered the ways in which the abundance and acquisition of land affect commercialization and dependence. No one is forced to leave Ban Ping; most villagers think of themselves as and want to be farmers; there are few disputes over land and little reverence for it. These characteristics of life in Ban Ping, as compared with peasant life in central Thailand and elsewhere, depend upon the abundance of land.[16] The techniques commonly used to acquire land

---

[16] The Ban Ping villager's attitude toward his land is probably part of the general economic optimism which seems characteristic of northern peasants. Land is probably especially venerated where the larger economy seems undependable (cf. Epstein 1962:212). In even the poorest of northern Tai villages, on the other

were then shown to influence sibling solidarity and household solvency. Their implications for risk taking and capital formation are discussed later.

The resources used to acquire land encourage amicable relations between generations whose extremely different experiences and aspirations might otherwise make for hostility. The resources for acquiring and maintaining land at Thunglor in 1960 involved potentially dangerous dependence on powerful townsmen whose interests conflicted with those of the villagers. The way in which home fields were registered was interpreted as an expression of the villagers' attitude toward the government. The way in which Thunglor plots were registered was changing the internal structure of Ban Ping by increasing the importance of its headman. Land rental, although shown to have always existed, is changing in its price and frequency. These changes indicate the play between commerce and kinship as principles for determining social relationships and suggest the future courses of rental price, source of tenants, and economic stratification.

hand, "land is easily and fairly frequently bought and sold" (Wijeyewardene 1965:255).

VI.
Labor Mobilization

Every farming household occasionally uses more labor than its members can provide. Ban Ping's natural and social environments permit large and varied landholdings. These, in turn, limit and direct the techniques by which labor is mobilized. In the present chapter I describe the various categories of laborers, delineate the choices made among techniques for mobilizing them, and then discuss the implications of those choices for Ban Ping's relations with other communities and with the world of commerce. At the end of the chapter I comment on some economic development issues suggested by Ban Ping's use of its resources in land and labor.

CATEGORIES OF LABORERS

The abundance of land makes most villagers landowners; like landowners everywhere, they prefer farming their own plots to working for others. The variety of field types owned by potential laborers means that neither the supply of nor the demand for labor is constant throughout the agricultural year. During the tillage season (the time of transplanting and cultivation) those who practice plow farming require a great deal of labor which those who practice only tractor farming are free to give them. At harvest time, on the other hand, farm operators at both the Great Field and Thunglor are all busy on their own land. Abundance and variety thus complicate the ways in which labor is mobilized. These ways can be simplified, however, by supposing that people work only when rewarded for it, and by distinguishing three main types of reward: fellowship, exchange, and goods.

Rewards to laborers.—I use the word *fellowship* for rewards that are neither reciprocated farm labor nor payments in valuables. Fellowship exists in purest form among the members of a household who, except on land that produces "private" (*lork*) rice, work together at all tasks in accord with their sex and age. In return, each shares in the crop according to his needs. Fellowship is not limited to those who live together, for it is also the reward received by close kinsmen and other intimates who "merely come to help," to *coj*, at various tasks. Those who come to *coj* do not explicitly expect a specific return. They come

Villagers going to "point to" the Thunglor fields they want to be plowed by tractor. C is in the foreground; his younger brother is at the wheel.

Clearing a main irrigation channel.

Initial cultivation of a Great Field seedbed.

Seeding the Great Field.

ABOVE: Plowing the Great Field.   BELOW: Harrowing the Great Field.

"Asking pardon" of the oxen after tilling the Great Field.

Uprooting seedlings at the Great Field.

Cutting seedlings to proper size before transplanting.

Transplanting at the Great Field.

Threshing on the inclined table.

Carrying rice to the mill.

Cooling rice after steaming it. The triangular fan in the foreground is used to hasten cooling.

Weaving.

Temporary field house.

Village home.

M, in white shirt, suggesting joint purchase of a tractor.

in order to maintain a close relationship with the recipient of their labor.[1] Villagers are quite outspoken in their belief that "kinsmen should *coj* one another." But it would be wrong, and insulting to the villagers, to consider this form of help a matter of explicit one-for-one reciprocity. It is rather a variant of the easy fellowship that pervades the household. If A generally *coj*'s B, then B generally *coj*'s A.

By the reward of *exchange* is meant the return of farm labor for farm labor given. There are three forms: *lo, termkan,* and *aw haeng.* The first, *lo,* is cooperative farming. It occurs when two or more households agree to work together until all have completed the tasks stipulated in their agreement.[2] If households agree to *lo,* they keep no account of the number of days spent at each task and plot. *Termkan* and *aw haeng,* the other two forms of what I call exchange, are often merged in casual speech. "But in *termkan,*" says an articulate former headman, "there is no compulsion to return the same service that one has been given, nor need the return be immediate. . . . *Aw haeng,* on the other hand, is like a formal contract in which [for example] one must return a day of male reaping labor for a day of male reaping labor." If A comes to *term* (literally, "to add to") B, then B is expected to go to *term* A on some job fairly soon.[3] This is called *termkan,* "adding to one another." Alternatively, B may return a "gift" (*pan*) instead of labor. For such an exchange, the reciprocal (*kan*) is not used. One is told, instead, that "A did such-and-such to *term* B, so B *pan*'d such an amount to A." Labor contributions that villagers call *term* can thus be reciprocated by any of the rewards.

Pan is a form of *goods,* the third reward for labor. Goods may be either rice or cash. Whichever one is given, villagers distinguish between a "gift" (*pan*) and a "wage" (*kha-cang*). A distinctive feature of a wage is that it is agreed upon through haggling before it is paid, while the amount of a gift is determined solely by the generosity of its donor. The recipient of a gift must therefore claim not to know how much he will receive.

Though these three rewards farmers obtain the labor they need in order to grow rice. In deciding among them, farmers are influenced by agricultural, social, and economic considerations which apply differently to different types of workers. Ban Ping's prosperity makes for

---

[1] For example, B comes to *coj* "Mother" K at harvest time because she is his sister. Months later, Mother K goes to *coj* at B's house building because he is her brother.

[2] Carpenter S and his son, for example, worked together with K and his wife to reap, shock, thresh, winnow, and cart the crop from K's 2 rai of home rainfall field, S's 6 rai of semi-irrigated field, and K's 3.5 rai of Great Field.

[3] My data suggest, but are insufficient to prove, that one difference between *coj* and *term* is that *coj* is usually initiated by the doner, while *term* starts with a request from its recipient.

an absence of full-time professional farm workers,[4] and thereby creates other categories of laborers.

Tillage-season laborers.—Table 10 records all contributions of extrahousehold tillage-season labor on the home fields. In 1960, eleven men (in addition to the one full-time professional farm worker) irrigated, seeded, tilled, and planted for households in which they did not reside. All these men were close kinsmen of the landowner, but not all were rewarded in the same way.

In the thirteen cases listed in table 10, the landowner's household labor force was insufficient to farm his field. In the first ten, younger kinsmen were said to be "helping" (*term*) an elder kinsman. In two of these (1 and 2), fellowship was the reward, for the young household still eats the rice of the parental field. They, like cases 3–8, were referred to as instances of "children giving sustenance to their parents." In cases 3–8, however, the child no longer eats his parents' rice. Rather, he is rewarded with a "gift" (*pan*) the size of which is determined solely by "how much his parents love him." That is, even though in every case the gift turned out to be approximately the same as the going wage for tillage-season labor (see cases 11–13), both parties claimed that they would not know its size until after the harvest. Tillage-season labor is "something with a price"; when such labor is donated, it must therefore be rewarded. But children (and the kin types of cases 9 and 10)[5] participate in too intimate a relationship for the villagers to call their reward "a wage."

When Maj M's son, U, worked for his father (case 11), the other villagers recognized, and criticized, a new and ugly development in the mobilization of labor, for Maj M "hired his son for a wage." Although it has been my policy to relegate illustrative examples to footnotes, this innovation should be described in some detail because to the villagers, and therefore to us, it is not minor.

---

[4] Only one of Ban Ping's 120 households normally bases its livelihood on working for the full year on the farms of others, although, for exceptional reasons, a second household came to depend upon the occasional earnings of its young members during 1960. No one from outside the village was hired to work the full year in Ban Ping, despite one abortive attempt to do so. This absence of landless laborers is in striking contrast to the situation in central Thailand where, in various places, such workers have been reported as constituting 13 percent (Janlekha 1955:table 10), 20 percent (Kaufman 1960:64), or even 46 percent (Dobby 1956:277) of the rural population.

Ban Ping's only professional agricultural laborer received 65 hap (approximately 26 hectoliters) of unmilled rice. Both employer and employee refer to this payment as a "wage" which was formally agreed upon before cultivation began. The distinction between the tillage and the harvest seasons is so pronounced that villagers spoke of the 65 hap as being half for one season and half for the other.

[5] Case 9 was a last-minute arrangement made by "Father" L after his hired hand left him before the end of the tillage season. Since little plowing remained to be done, Father L expected his nephew to help with the harvest also. In case 10, the worker was a prosperous trader with a large holding of distant flood field. This arrangement between brother and sister was quite close to pure fellowship, with the 10-hap gift a recognition that tillage-season labor is "something with a price."

TABLE 10
Rewards for Labor in Tillage Season on Home Fields

	REWARDED WITH GIFT (*pan*)	
Case	Worker's kinship to employer	Reward
1	"Son-in-law"	Fellowship
2	"Son"	"
3	"	30 hap
4	"	"
5	"	"
6	"Son-in-law"	"
7	"Son"	40 hap
8	"	Depends on size of crop
9	"Nephew"	30 hap
10	"Younger brother"	10 hap

	REWARDED WITH WAGE (*kha-cang*)		
Case	Worker's kinship to employer	Reward	Employer
11	"Son"	30 hap	Maj M
12	"Distant"	"	"
13	"Nonkin" from another village	"	"Father" L (Transaction not completed; replaced by case 9)

SOURCE: Survey of all households.

Maj M owns more Great Field than any other villager. "Mother" N, his wife's sister, the landowner of case 3, has the next-largest holding. Her son worked for her just as U did for Maj M. When Mother N's daughter-in-law was asked about the transaction, she replied at first, "What do you mean? My husband made his own fields this year, not his mother's." Upon further questioning, she added that her husband had "helped" (*term*) his mother to irrigate, seed, till, and transplant. She explained that "he was given a gift of 30 hap. He might have been given nothing, but his mother loves him. No wage had been agreed upon, he merely wanted to help." When, on the other hand, U's wife was asked about case 11, the reply was quite different although the reward of 30 hap was the same. "My husband hired out to work for his father. The wage was agreed upon before plowing started. Had Maj M offered less than 30 hap, 20 or 10 for instance, my husband would not have taken the job."

On the distant irrigated field it is difficult to discern patterns of tillage-season labor contributions, in part because only twenty-eight households farm there rather than the sixty who farm home fields.

The distant irrigated plots are new and, in some ways, experimental. They are bought and sold quite frequently and villagers vary their techniques of labor mobilization almost as much as they do their agricultural operations (see chap. iii, techniques on other fields). In 1960 there were six instances of contributions of seasonal tillage labor, all listed in table 11.[6]

TABLE 11

REWARDS FOR LABOR IN TILLAGE SEASON ON DISTANT FIELDS

Case	Sex of worker	Worker's relationship to employer	Reward
1	F	"None"	25–30 hap, as wage
2	F	"None"	25 + 2 hap, as wage
3	M	"Elder brother-in-law"	30 hap, as gift
4	M	"Son"	30 hap, as gift
5	M	"Friend"	30 hap, as gift, + 5 hap, as wage
6	M	"Kinsman"	20 hap, as mutual aid

SOURCE: Survey of all households.

Operators of distant irrigated fields, and those who work for them, live away from home for about a month from the beginning of the tillage season until the fields have been transplanted (see fig. 9, p. 167). Although they return to the village from time to time, they sleep in their field houses and eat there. For this reason, some laborers are retained to fill out the temporary distant-field household unit with tasks appropriate to their sex and age. Households with no women in their field-house group begin by getting a tillage-season female worker from a poor household. Cases 1 and 2 (table 11) are women who cooked for the men while they were plowing and who remained at the field house to guard it. Once the plowing was finished, they planted the seedlings. Both these women were "hired for a wage." Although the agreements with women were made in advance, they were somewhat vague, perhaps because work on irrigated fields was regarded as unpredictable and because there was little precedent for hiring women for the entire season. Moreover, the tasks of cooking, washing, and guarding made the employees seem almost like household members. In case 1, the needy worker was to be given "maybe 25, maybe 30 hap." In case 2, the employer was prepared to pay 25 hap "and maybe 2 more out of affection." The commercial flavor of these two arrangements is minimized by the vagueness of the reward.

The male kinsmen and the close male friend in cases 3, 4, and 5

---

[6] Although it may seem redundant to elaborate on quantitative data summarized in a table, it is necessary in order to suggest some of the differences between "objective" analysis and village categorizations of rewards for labor.

LABOR MOBILIZATION   121

were each rewarded with 30 hap; the rewards were called "gifts." The
difference in size between the rewards for men and those for women
suggests that the tillage-season labor of women, since they do not plow
and harrow, is not considered as valuable as that of men. The extra
5 hap of case 5 are "wages" paid for the friend's carabao.

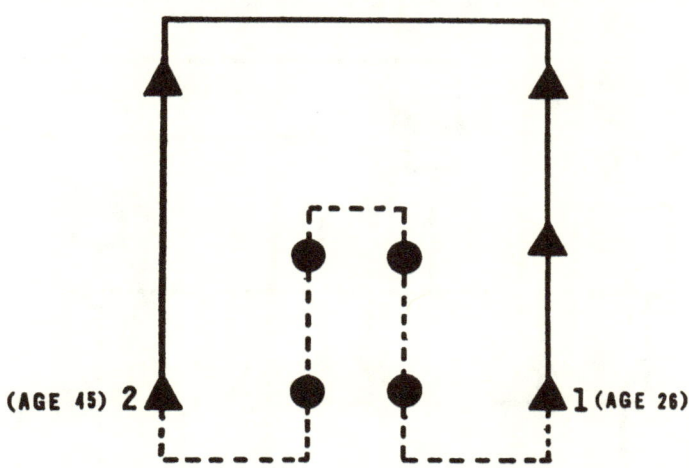

Fig. 4. Schematic genealogy: kinship manipulated to obtain labor. Dotted
lines show kinship relation traced during tillage season; solid lines, that
traced at other seasons.
KEY: 1 = landowner, table 11, case 6; 2 = worker, table 11, case 6.

The last case represents the most interesting compromise between
commerce and kinship. The worker, aged forty-five, is a generation
older than the twenty-six-year-old field owner. It would be embarass-
ing for a junior to employ his senior or to make him a "gift." Moreover, kinship between the two is too distant for close fellowship to
exist between them. Their arrangement was always referred to as
"mutual aid" (*termkan*), although the worker received 20 hap, which
was almost certainly agreed upon in advance. In addition, throughout
the tillage season, but rarely at other times, the worker continually
referred to and acted out his somewhat distant kinship relation with
the field owner. In doing so he traced a distant genealogical connection (WMSdH) [7] which placed him in the young landowner's generation, as an "elder brother" rather than a closer connection (FFBs) by
which he is his young partner's "uncle." Figure 4 presents a schematic
genealogy.

Tillage task laborers.—Seeding the bed takes little time, requires
few persons, and occurs when labor is not otherwise engaged. It is
accomplished by a casually organized group of household members,
together with kinsmen and neighbors most of whom come to *coj.*

[7] See the Explanatory Notes for the meanings of these abbreviated kin types.

Little attention is given to exact exchanges of labor. A young person often accompanies his friends or works for their households when there is no possibility of direct reciprocation. Seeding groups are structured through personal kindreds and other bonds of fellowship. This means that, although A works B's seedbed along with many persons who will soon come to A's bed, there are no discrete groups that exchange labor

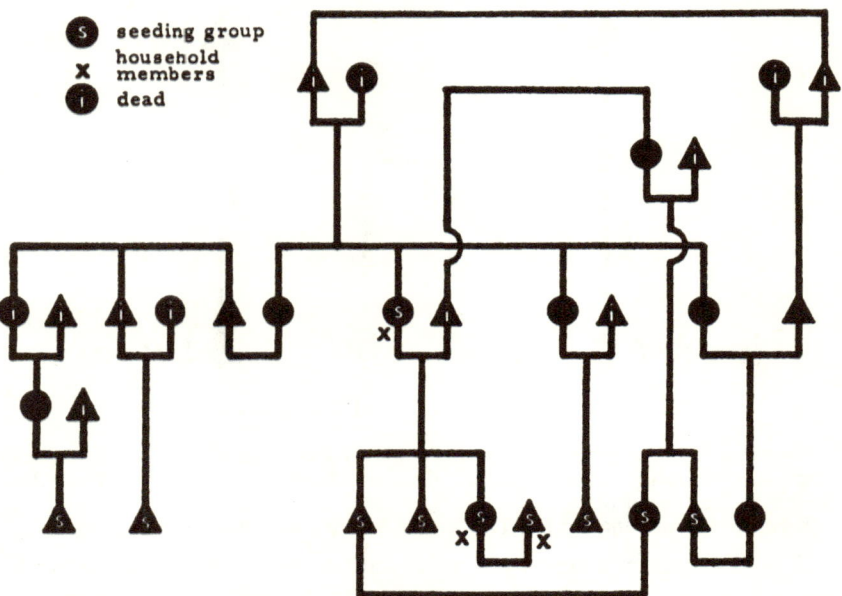

Fig. 5. Schematic genealogy of a representative large seeding group.

exclusively with each other. A wide range of kinsmen come "merely to *coj*," as can be seen in Figure 5 which records the kinship basis of a representative large seeding group. Those who came to *coj* included kinsmen as distant genealogically as a sister's husband's sister's daughter's son.

Other than household members themselves, the only men who plow and harrow are those working for the full tillage season. No one tills on a task basis.

Once the harrowing is finished, transplanting can begin. Labor for the first task, that of uprooting the seedlings, is provided by household members and through fellowship and exchange. No one, except for tillage-season workers, is rewarded with goods for the task of uprooting.

The second day of transplanting starts with male household members carrying seedlings to the fields. Villagers, however, view this day as dominated by the women who plant, although according to my sample they provide only 47 percent [8] of the labor expended. Households can themselves provide only about one-quarter of the labor that planting requires. On the home irrigated field more than half (58 percent), and on the distant irrigated field, all extrahousehold labor was rewarded with goods in 1960. Even when hiring is the only source of extrahousehold labor, the organization of the planting group is quite casual.[9] At the Great Field, the wage was 4 baht daily or 3.50 baht plus food.[10] About one-third (31 percent) of those who farmed there obtained all extrahousehold planting labor exclusively through fellowship or exchange. Another quarter (23 percent) relied on wages; most (46 percent) made use of all three rewards.

At planting time, unlike seeding time, only a few of a household's closest kinsmen "come merely to *coj*."[11] Nevertheless, the labor contributions can be quite significant. Not only do they work themselves, but through indirect exchanges they obtain the services of others for their kinsmen. Two ways in which this is accomplished are shown in figure 6. In example 1, when farmer A transplants, C, with whom A exchanges labor, comes to help. When C transplants, B, who is A's close kinsmen but has no Great Field land, works for C and so repays A's labor debt. The other ordering of indirect exchange is for B first to donate labor to C who repays it by working for A, B's close kinsman.

On the distant irrigated field, there is neither labor exchange nor fellowship. The small groups, who leave their homes for a month of tilling and transplanting, are anxious to get back to the village as soon as they can. They do not have the time to help others once their own work is done; they cannot call on Yuan strangers to "come and *coj*." Hence, they are restricted either to hiring daily workers from

[8] All percentage figures in this chapter are derived from the random sample described in Appendix B.
[9] The farmer who decides to hire mentions his plan to the young girls he meets about the village a day or two before the transplanting is to begin. Word spreads in this manner and those who want to work contact him. Even on the morning of planting day, he frequently does not know how many people will be working his fields. It often happens that a girl meets a farmer on his way to the fields and offers to work for him that day.
[10] Only one exception to a daily wage occurred. A young man had been loaned some of his father's Great Field for farming "private" (*lork*) rice, but was prevented from supervising the planting because he had to work on his father's land (and because he was so young). In order to get the planting on his own field done, the youth announced a flat fee for 30 baht. Seven women arranged among themselves to do the job. In Ban Ping, unlike central Thailand, piecework is never the basis for computing either labor exchange or wages.
[11] One prosperous household, for example, received through *coj* only 19 percent of the forty-seven worker-days needed to transplant its 3.2 acres of Great Field. The household itself furnished 28 percent, hired 4 percent, and received 49 percent through exchange. Unlike the example (see fig. 5) of a seeding group, those who came to *coj* at transplanting time were all quite close kinsmen (children, sister, son-in-law's brother).

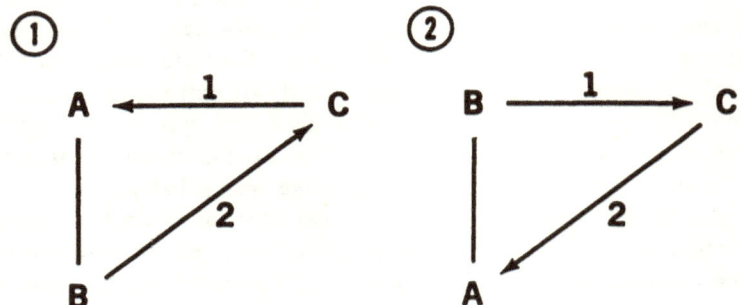

Fig. 6. Indirect exchanges of transplanting labor. Arrows show direction of labor contributions and numbers show their order. Vertical lines indicate close kinship.

nearby Yuan villages or to working for many days to transplant little by little. Most operators took the latter alternative and used the small household group to transplant for a week or even (in two cases sampled) more than two weeks. Slow transplanting, as a cash-saving alternative, is permitted by the newness of the distant irrigated field. Since the field is not uniformly cleared, parts of it are ready for planting while other parts are still under the plow.

Harvest laborers.—When the tedious work of the tillage season is at its peak, some six months earlier, villagers already begin to speak of the joys of harvest. "The harvest is fun, real fun," they say, "not like now when tears almost fall from one's eyes." Rice is abundant and harvesters are well fed. Another source of fun is that boys and girls work side by side. There is raillery, singing, courtship, and the chance for an assignation.[12]

The home rainfall field, where plots are usually small, is the first to be harvested. Operating households themselves provide about half (47 percent) of the labor required, with almost all (95 percent) of the rest furnished through fellowship and exchange.[13] The harvest is early, so young people are not yet called away to the distant flood field. It precedes the harvest on irrigated fields so people can come to help in order to gain exchange labor on the Great Field.

The semi-irrigated field is the next to be harvested. Holdings are larger than on the rainfall field, and the work is thus somewhat more arduous. Casual camaraderie is less characteristic of these fields than

[12] Large work parties are used for uprooting, planting, and reaping. The sample described in Appendix B indicates that the respective ratios of males to females are 4:3, 1:40, 1:1. During our stay in Ban Ping, one girl became pregnant out of wedlock. The affair was a harvest-season encounter.

[13] It was not untypical that a work party, which had finished reaping the rainfall field of one household, was observed to move casually to the adjoining plot of another household where a husband and wife had been working all alone.

it is of the preceding rainfall-field harvest. Nevertheless, fellowship is a somewhat more effective reward for mobilizing labor here than it is at the subsequent harvest on the Great Field.

On the Great and semi-irrigated fields, as on the rainfall field, operating households provided half (51 percent) of the harvest labor used. On these two fields, however, fellowship is a less effective reward and more (15 rather than 5 percent) of the extrahousehold labor was rewarded with wages. Three-quarters of such man-days were the work of harvest-season hands, most of whose labor was done on the distant fields also operated by their employers.[14]

The farmer who goes to harvest his distant irrigated field leaves behind him the intimates from whom he might obtain labor through fellowship. Those about him are anxious, just as he is, to harvest their own fields and so are unwilling to exchange labor with him. He must therefore hire most (60 percent) of the extrahousehold labor he needs to harvest his fields. To minimize the expense, and because workers are often difficult to find, each farmer tries to harvest as much by himself as he can. On the home fields, it will be recalled, farm operators provided about half of the harvest labor they needed. On the distant irrigated field, they provide 65 percent. Since work groups are smaller, the task takes longer than at the Great Field. For this reason, and because it is difficult to find hired harvesters for this isolated field, workers are hired not on a day-to-day basis, but for the whole season. For all of those hired, the season includes the farmer's Thunglor holdings as well as his distant irrigated land, and the wage is fixed on that basis.

Thunglor is far from the village and one's neighbors are young persons anxious to complete their own harvest. Just as at the distant irrigated field, each operating unit consequently provides most (63 percent) of the labor it needs, and must hire most (55 percent) of the

---

[14] Only three households of the twenty-four in the sample hired workers specifically for their home fields. Two of these three also operated large distant farms to which they were anxious to go. In one of them the hired hand, a young neighbor, remained at the home field to thresh for five days while the operating household went on to begin reaping their distant field. Only one farmer with no Thunglor land hired home field harvest help. He is the same commercially oriented individual who had arranged to serve as C's agent in 1961 (see chap. iv). By hiring four women to reap, he was able to complete in two days a task that would have taken his unaided household five days. (Reaping took fourteen man-days; Maj J's household has three members.) Maj J is a trader accustomed to cash; he knows how to use his time to earn it. He does not like to farm and would be even less willing to work on other people's fields than on his own. His wife's fits of insanity make her unreliable as a source of exchange labor for the household. Had he obtained needed reaping labor by exchange, his young daughter would probably have had to work for eight days to return it. She would thus have had to work for ten days to reap a plot that, with hired help, took her only two days.

rest. Half of those who farm distant flood fields must use some hired harvest labor.[15]

No Thunglor labor is obtained through the reward of fellowship. A significant amount (37 percent) comes through exchange, *aw haeng* and *termkan,* but almost half (46 percent) is obtained through *lo,* the cooperative farming arrangement that is less common on other fields. Cooperative farming is a binding, almost contractual, relationship made only among those whose landholdings are of approximately equal size. Whereas *lo* is commonly restricted to close intimates and even to members of the same household, one man in the sample made a cooperative agreement with a Lao stranger who farms the plot of land next to his own.

Fellow household members who have no Thunglor land provide another source (16 percent) of harvest help. Since Thunglor rice is "private" rice, and since farming labor is "something with a price," such help must be specifically rewarded. Usually, the farmer "gives" (*pan*) about the same amount that he would have to pay a stranger in wages. As on all fields, hired laborers are usually paid in rice at the end of the harvest season.[16]

At Thunglor, a negligible amount (3 percent) of hired labor is paid on a daily basis, always in cash. Two of the eighteen farmers in the sample who hired labor hired boys from other villages to work for 2 baht daily. For many (44 percent), the wage agreed upon was a reward for working the farmer's other fields, in addition to those at Thunglor. This wage reflects size of plot, the main determinant of how long and how hard the harvester will have to work. The standard that those who work harder should earn more is probably the reason that women are paid less than men.

Since rice merchants come to Thunglor at the harvest season, it is reasonable to express rice wages in cash value, and so make it apparent that workers paid in rice earn better wages than the few who are paid in cash at 2 baht a day. Although there is no evidence that villagers are aware of this, it is consistent with the high value that cash has in the local economy.

---

[15] "Forest farms" are an exception, for none of their owners hire harvesters. The low yields and high expense of virgin land at Thunglor discourage its owners from paying for the harvest. They rely instead on their own labor and on cooperative farming (*lo*).

[16] At the Great Field, the one lad hired to shock and thresh received 5 hap of rice and worked six days. Women hired to reap received a daily wage of 1 thang of rice or 2.50 baht, its approximate equivalent. They thus earned only half as much daily as did the young lad whose high wages probably reflect the common feeling that threshing is more arduous work than reaping.

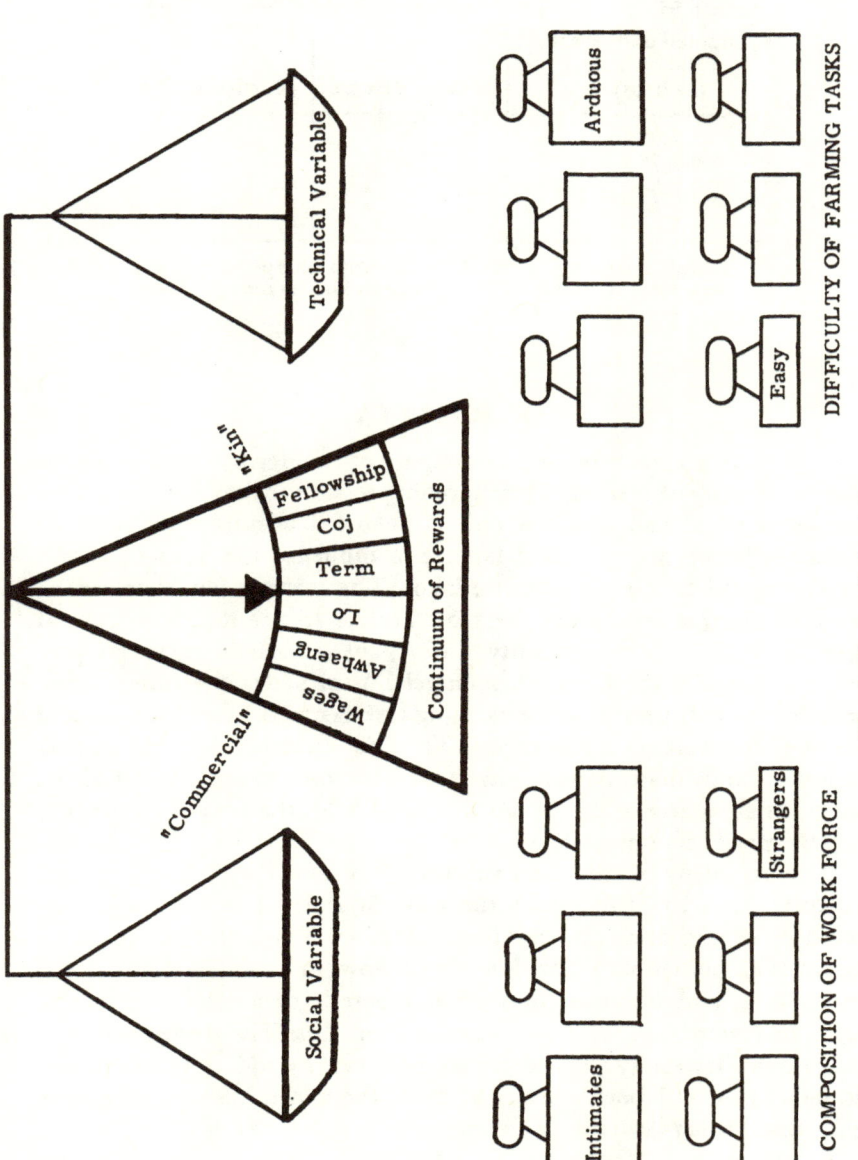

Fig. 7. Rewards for labor.

TABLE 12

FREQUENCY DISTRIBUTION OF THUNGLOR HARVEST WAGES

Computed daily wage per individual [a] (In baht)	Male	Female	Married couple
5.00	5	–	–
3.75	2	–	1
2.50	1	1	1
1.66	–	1	–

[a] Number of days worked taken from sample described in Appendix B. Cash value of rice wages taken at lowest current rate (5 baht/hap).

TECHNOLOGY

A farmer can mobilize any category of laborer by offering one of the three types of reward. The preceding section makes it evident that the physical difficulty of the task is balanced against the degree of intimacy between farmer and laborer to influence the farmer's choice of the reward he uses to mobilize labor. The rewards for labor can be arrayed along a scale from the most kinlike to the most commercial (see fig. 7). The easy mutuality ("kin") of household members provides one end and wages ("commercial") provides the other. Commercial rewards prevail as the farming task becomes more arduous and more of the workers are strangers. Thus, for example, because seeding is less arduous than planting, its reward is closer to the "kin" end. As kinsmen are scarce at the distant irrigated field, the reward for its harvest is more "commercial."

The balancing of two main variables, one social and the other agricultural, thus helps to depict the ways in which labor is usually rewarded for any particular farming operation. The influences upon an individual household's decision about how to mobilize labor for a given task, and upon an individual laborer's demand for a specific form of reward, are far more complex than this. The determinants of labor mobilization can be simplified, however, by adding to our earlier statement—that laborers prefer working their own land—the observation that farmers usually pay wages only as a last resort.

Seasonal labor supply.—When labor is scarce, farmers are deprived of the intimates who may be given rewards at the "kin" end of the scale. This is quite apparent during the harvest season. Although the peak of Thunglor operations follows the Great Field harvest, there is a significant overlap between the two (see fig. 9, p. 167). Toward the end of the Great Field harvest, the "private" rice at Thunglor beckons its young owners and, as private property that will be sold for cash, provides wages even to those who own no land there. The excitement of the distant fields and the lure of cash are felt by all the village. More and more young men leave for Thunglor and the distant irrigated field. The demands of household fields are always met, but, as the Thunglor harvest approaches, exchanges with increasingly distant "kinsmen" become progressively more grudging and calculated.[17] The resultant variation in labor supply, rather than the slight differences in the difficulty of harvesting various fields,[18] makes the reward of fellowship less effective as the harvest season progresses.

During planting time, too, one may observe the consequences of subtle variations in labor supply. Those who farm the home rainfall field obtain all their extrahousehold labor through fellowship and exchange, because early timing requires labor when others are free to donate it and frees the farmers' labor when donors need it most. Similarly, households with higher land on the Great Field may avoid hiring people to do their planting because water reaches their plots only after most other farmers have already planted. They can donate labor when others need it and collect labor after well-watered plots have been planted.

Resources in labor.—In the West, where labor is almost fully marketable, an economist need usually consider only cash and contract to describe an employer's claims on his laborers. In Ban Ping, cash is but one of a farmer's resources for mobilizing labor. Close kinship, distant kin ties, neighborhood, and ethnic membership may also be quite valuable. It is more important that an employer fulfill his social obligations than that he meet a payroll.

As can be seen most clearly at tillage time, a farmer's primary claim is upon the members of his household. Households that own land but have no young men to till it rent their land to others. A landowning household that has workers, but not enough of them to farm a plot sufficient to support the household, hires additional laborers. At plant-

[17] One household, which operates a semi-irrigated plot planted to a middle-maturing rice and an irrigated plot planted to a late-maturing rice, provides a convenient example. Its 1.6-acre semi-irrigated plot was reaped in less than a day by a work party composed of three household members, six persons with whom labor was exchanged, and five intimates who "merely came to help." Five days later, when the Thunglor harvest had begun in earnest, the household began to harvest its 3.6 acres at the Great Field. Although this holding is more than twice as large, only nine persons, rather than the fourteen who had worked on the semi-irrigated field, reaped on the first day. Of these, three were members of the household and the rest those with whom labor was exchanged. No one "merely came to help." The household had to work an additional three days in order to complete the reaping. During this time the two young men of the household expressed great frustration at being unable to get away to their "private" rice at Thunglor.

[18] Modal plot size at the Great Field is somewhat larger than at the semi-irrigated field where, in turn, it is larger than at the home rainfall field.

ing time, as well, the number of young household members relative to the area farmed influences a farmer's decision about hiring workers. Generally, those with the largest holdings hire most of their extra-household labor, those with middle-sized holdings hire about half of their nonhousehold workers, those with the smallest holdings supplement household labor with a few close friends and relatives.

In plow agriculture, then, the household is the basic unit of production. Marriage and rules of residence, birth and adoption, death and dissolution determine its composition. Villagers are fully aware of the farming significance of the household and of the processes by which it is formed. Only couples without sons adopt boys; only couples without daughters adopt girls. Thus, in fact as in popular explanation, adoption occurs when a couple "needs a girl to carry water or a boy to plow the fields." Marriage is similarly recognized as a claim upon labor. Parental approval, normally required before marriage, is based in part on wealth and even more on the prospective mate's reputation as a worker. Buddhism, as the villagers understand it, forbids weddings during the three rainy-season months of Phansa, the so-called Buddhist Lent. Productivity, as the villagers understand it, requires that all marriages take place either just before plowing or just before the harvest. As a young bachelor explained, the "old people won't permit marriages at any other time. They say that the son-in-law would then be coming just in order to eat their cooked rice."

Marriage is significant for rice production because it determines who will live in the household. The Lue rules of residence require that the young couple spend, first, three years with one set of parents, then three years with the other. The rule is explained and often labeled as "sustaining the old people." The parents most in need of labor might "go and beg" for the services and the residence of a young couple when the normal three-year rotation did not entitle them to it.[19] In the past, this was rarely necessary, however, since the productivity of an old longhouse composed of three or four or, in at least one instance, seven families would rarely be threatened by the loss of one young member. Like virgin lands, private *(lork)* rice, and alienable inheritances, the old residence rule provided a convenient and egalitarian fluidity in the factors of rice production. It sustained the

---

[19] The plasticity of the rule may be the origin of a custom, said to be recent, which, without knowledge of traditional residence rules, one might call "bride-price." In 1960, two Ban Ping households each paid an annual share of rice to the parents of their son's wife. Both are households with only one son and with a large amount of land. In both instances the wife left behind her numerous sisters in a poor household. Neither wife comes from Ban Ping, which perhaps accounts for the formality with which the parents of each husband have agreed to "sustain the parents of the bride" by means of rice payments for the three years in which residence would normally be with the wife's parents had they any need for labor.

old and made the young secure while they slowly accumulated the money, wood, and farmland to found their own household.[20] A quarrelsome couple who left parents prematurely would find no kinsmen willing to help them build a new house.

Now the young have Thunglor lands of their own. The market for rice furnishes cash that can buy, from fellow and from stranger, house-building labor previously furnished only by kinsmen. Households are much smaller than they were and often include no more than aged parents and a single young family. Marriage and change in residence therefore disrupt the production of a household much more than they used to. Neolocality forces farmers to make use of more distant claims on labor than coresidence. The way in which this is done has already been summarized in table 10. In the old days, a labor-short household would hire someone for the full farm year. Now, many households rely on tillage-season labor contributions from neolocal children and so replace the unity of the longhouse.

The first seven laborers of table 10 are prematurely independent householders who till their parents' fields and are rewarded for it.[21] The use of close kinship with nonresidents as a claim on labor can also be seen in case 10, in which a brother helped his sister for such a small "gift." It is even more apparent in cases 5 and 8, for the donor household in one case is the recipient household in the other. Maj S of household 47 (see fig. 8), an acute, prosperous, and conservative old man, has a rather dissolute son who, with his wife and children, lives in a house (number 112) of his own. In case 5, table 10, this son tills his father's fields for a "gift" of 30 hap of rice, and so "each helps the other." Living with Maj S, and married to his daughter, is the son of "Father" K, who lives alone with his old wife in household 44. To "sustain his old father and mother," Father K's son, Maj S's son-in-law, helps them in case 8 in return for whatever gift their meager harvest permits them to make. These transactions are represented genealogically in figure 8.

The young men who help their parents with tillage-season labor can live alone because they have distant flood land. During the harvest season, they are willing to help their elders on a day-to-day, task-to-

---

[20] There is some slight evidence, which I should prefer to discount, that the residence rule may once have been adhered to with surprising rigidity. An excellent old informant reports that around 1907, at the end of a three-year term, he and his young wife left her parents to return to his own parents' household. His parents-in-law, left alone, had to rent out their fields. He denies both that his own parents needed him greatly or that he had quarreled with his wife's parents.

[21] In cases 1 and 2 the children still "eat the rice of their father and mother." Although now under separate roofs, parent and child are a single household of production in which the young couple farms its "private" rice as well as the parental field. The "nephew" of case 9 would, in the old days, also have resided with the landowner who now makes him a "gift" in return for his "help."

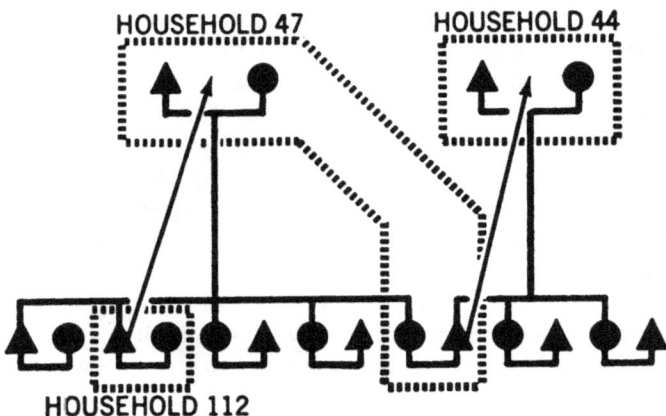

Fig. 8. Schematic genealogy: donation of tillage-season labor. Dotted lines enclose household members. Arrows indicate direction of labor contributions.

task basis. Their own Thunglor holdings, however, make them unwilling to accept responsibility for seasonal harvest work on the parental home irrigated field.

Thunglor holdings are large, too large for their young owners to harvest alone. Additional labor must be obtained, often through kinship ties less direct than those used on the Great Field. As the Great Field harvest proceeds, more and more young kinsmen are freed for work at Thunglor. Their donations of "help" in anticipation of an unknown "gift" may be seen as a shrewd compromise between kinship and commerce. One lad "helped" his "uncle" and was "offered a choice between 10 hap of rice or 4 baht for each day I had worked. I had worked about eleven days. There was no haggling about the amounts of money or of rice and I had no idea in advance how much he would give me. I took the rice because I figure that it's worth more —maybe 50 or 60 baht." The laborer can evaluate working for a kinsman in terms of his own material advantage. Even a man who is far less deeply enmeshed in the market economy than are many of his fellows, can report, "My son will *term* Maj K after our own fields are harvested. He'll probably be given something for it, but we can't say how much. Whatever Maj K wants to give. We can't say how much because we are kinsmen. If we ask for a lot, Maj K will say, 'Too dear.' If we ask for a little, we'll do ourselves in."

However well he pays them, the Thunglor landowner's resources in kinsmen are limited. Too many young villagers are themselves landowners for Ban Ping to furnish all the labor necessary for harvesting the distant flood field. More than two-thirds of the hired laborers come from other villages. Similarly, it will be recalled that the harvest at the distant irrigated fields nearly coincides with that at the Great Field where even relatively poor Yuan villages have subsistence holdings. It is therefore extremely difficult to find workers and almost as difficult to keep them. At both distant fields, the demand for harvest workers is quite substantial. Since valuables are the only reward and thus the only claim that a villager has on a Yuan employee, it often happens that agreements are broken when the worker is offered a better price by someone else.

When the supply of labor is limited and the demand for it is pressing, purely commercial relationships are unreliable. Coresidents, kinsmen, and other intimates thus constitute a productive resource although the "gift" one pays them is no smaller than the "wage" one has to pay outsiders. There were no instances of a kinsman, a neighbor, or even a fellow Lue reneging on a harvest labor agreement. An employer's claim on his laborers is also, of course, the laborer's claim on their employer but, since labor is scarcer than employment, this is rarely relevant. Nevertheless, laborers can sometimes benefit even from tenuous claims upon their employer.[22]

The utility of cash.—Whether an operator will hire laborers obviously depends to some extent on whether he can afford to. At planting time, for example, absence of cash clearly dominated the labor budget of one poor household which operated a rented plot of 6 acres. Despite its large farm, the household hired no labor. A farmer with little cash is unwilling to spend much, but some farmers are eager to buy services that they could obtain through other rewards. We have heretofore assumed that operators pay wages only as a last resort when other resources fail. This is the premise of most villagers in most situations. Nevertheless it would be misleading not to recognize the fact that some villagers—the young, those who have lived elsewhere, those experienced in trade—prefer the "commercial" end of the scale in rewarding labor. This choice is most conscious when laborers are mobilized for planting, since to reward with goods is neither as common nor as necessary then as it is for harvesting. For those who hire labor, the individual, not the household and certainly not the village, is the effective unit of production. Labor, when exchanged, is earned and returned by a household. Wages, when labor is hired, are received and owned by an individual. A farmer pays 80 baht of his

---

[22] One man, for example, hired three Yuan boys to help harvest his rainfall, home flood, and distant flood land. After ten days they left to work for someone else who was willing to pay the same price for less work. Although sufficiently distant (in kinship) to break their agreement with their employer, they probably regarded themselves as sufficiently close to him to be able to collect wages for the work they had done. The employer, who once sired a daughter by a woman in their village, described the incident in this way: "My hired boys deserted me. If I were like other people, I would refuse to pay them anything and even accuse them of stealing things. But if they are well spoken I won't say anything and maybe I'll give them something for the work they did. I have kinsmen in their village and would be ashamed not to."

household money to hire planters. His daughter, who thus is not obligated to return any labor for her parents, works for others in order to earn 4 baht daily toward a new blouse or a hot-iron permanent wave. The use of goods as the reward for transplanting thus represents the increasing influence of young people on village technology and the increasing importance of personal, as against household, goals. It also indicates that money, which can now be exchanged for many things, is, for some villagers, more valuable than labor which can be exchanged only for other labor. Some villagers now prefer to hire and be hired.

Those who do so justify the use of wages as a means for increasing "leisure." This justification must be understood in terms of the new uses that Ban Ping has found for money. Farmers who plan to hire transplanters commonly say, "It used to cost money anyway to feed those who came to help.[23] Now, if I hire, I needn't keep working every day [to return labor obligations]. Once my own fields are done, everything is finished." It would be a mistake to interpret this point of view as a preference for leisure gained over money lost. At least one villager was sufficiently articulate to express the entire choice: "If one hires planters, then one has time to do nothing. One can then hire oneself out to others." By rewarding planters with cash, one can earn cash. Those who spoke of wanting "leisure" were soon observed working the fields of others for pay. As soon as their own transplanting was completed, some of the men, who spoke of paying others in order to "finish" the work on their own fields, were employed almost constantly in making arduous carting trips to Phayao. The cart, the Phayao rice market, and the fact that the road is impassable to trucks have given the villagers of Ban Ping alternative employment during the rainy season. More people want more things that can be bought with the money which there are now more ways to earn. The wages paid to planters really buy, not leisure, but release from community obligations that would interfere with the pursuit of money.

EXTRACOMMUNITY RELATIONS

The farmers of Ban Ping have always participated in commerce, have always been party to trade, have always had relations with other communities. Nevertheless, the tractor and the rice market have increased the importance of commercial resources and rewards, and have made the mobilization of labor more dependent on other communities.

---

[23] The cost of feeding exchange laborers is, even by village standards, extremely low. Rarely does one buy meat, never liquor. Perhaps reference to the costs of hospitality reflects a new cognizance of ability to sell the rice and even the vegetables with which planters are fed.

It is therefore essential neither to exaggerate nor to minimize continuity.

Commerce.—The innovation of tillage-season labor is consistent with the traditions of the longhouse. It maintains those traditions, however, on the basis of the nuclear family and not the kindred, on the basis of two households instead of one, and on the basis of an explicit exchange of labor for "a gift" instead of on the basis of fellowship. Tillage-season labor is thus a pattern that conforms to the unity of the old household and, also, as in the case of Maj M and his son, permits purely commercial transactions to penetrate the close circle of kinsmen. In the specificity of its transactions and the discreteness of the parties to them, the new pattern of labor mobilization is commercial.

Intimacy is a more binding claim on labor than mere wages. Even at its most commercial, the mobilization of labor in Ban Ping is far more kinlike than in central Thailand. When he worked for Maj M, the only professional laborer in Ban Ping seemed to feel somewhat subordinate to the members of his employer's household, and somewhat resentful of Maj M. It was the laborer, B, rather than Maj M's sons, who represented the household at the communal irrigation work. Nevertheless, B, as a fellow villager and distant "kinsman," was no mere hired hand. He lived at home and remained a full member of his own household, able to farm its small plot of rainfall land and to earn extra wages at Thunglor once Maj M's harvest was completed. B deferred to his employer no more than Maj M's age and prominence required. The young people of his employer's household treated B like an equal and he felt free to exchange pleasantries with Maj M's unmarried daughter.

In Ban Ping where land is plentiful, kinsmen precious, labor scarce, and commerce little developed, employee relations are far less rapacious than those found in central Thailand (cf. Janlekha 1955:86 f.; Kaufman 1960:66). Moreover, since households with no young workers rent their land to others, persons are hired only to work *with* a household, never to work for it. Every hired laborer works side by side with his employers. Villagers express the hiring of workers in the idiom of cooperation, not exploitation. "In the old days, just as now," says an elderly farmer, "people worked for hire. In this way, those with land helped those without land. The wage every year was 30 hap of rice to a man and 15 hap of rice to a woman for working the entire year. Some would hire themselves out after their own small holdings were worked; some had no land." The current "gift" of 30 hap for the tillage-season labor of prematurely independent households probably derives from this traditional payment. Certainly, its amount is never fixed by haggling.

At Thunglor, on the other hand, distance from the village and Ban Ping's prosperity make many farmers dependent upon strangers who must be rewarded with wages. Persons are sometimes hired for particular tasks, such as shocking or threshing. Wages vary widely and are determined by haggling over their form, as well as their amount.[24] Wages, haggling, consideration of immediate profit, task specificity, and tit-for-tat reciprocity—even within the village and household—indicate the extent to which labor shortage and private (*lork*) rice have commercialized the Thunglor harvest.[25]

At transplanting time, hiring is a comparative novelty which informants claim began about 1956. Villagers often complain that even exchange labor has become more selfish and calculating. Some justify their use of wages by claiming that people nowadays shirk their labor obligations even though everyone keeps a much more accurate record of the labor he gives than was necessary in the past and demands its return more exactly and immediately. Although no villager was ever observed to criticize another for failure to fulfill labor obligations (even when I pointed out such failures to them), nonetheless they correctly characterized the contemporary mobilization of transplanting labor as "calculating" and as "requiring wages"; for transplanting had become demonstrably more individualized and commercial, even for those who exchanged labor.

Men in their fifties could still remember the time when the village was the unit for the exchange of transplanting labor. Huge work parties that ensured prompt transplanting were composed of everyone in Ban Ping and everyone in the next village. Each household head would inform the village headman of the days on which he wanted to uproot and plant. The headman would then send a messenger to announce the dates on the main streets of Ban Ping and the neighboring village. Ideally, every household in both villages sent representatives to all transplantings. They were gay occasions for which the farmer would provide good food, drink, and entertainment. With growing population, with an increasing number of farmers, and with smaller households, the old system disappeared to be replaced by a more carefully calculated exchange of labor among separate households, usually within the same village. Elaborate hospitality disappeared. To this household exchange, villagers claim, fewer kinsmen came "merely to *coj.*" Exchange replaced fellowship; household organization replaced village organization; inexpensive food replaced elaborate hospitality;

---

[24] One young stranger was hired for 180 baht, a sum that most people thought would be worth 18 hap of rice. The harvest-season price of rice, however, was unusually low. When paid, the 180 baht was worth 36 hap.

[25] Although it would be improper for close intimates to haggle, the commercialization of Thunglor or harvesting affects even them, or so the situation of the lad who had to choose between cash and rice from his "uncle" would indicate.

efficiency replaced fun; calculated reciprocity—and ultimately wages —came to dominate the work groups.[26] Nevertheless, noncommercial claims on labor are still far more basic to transplanting in Ban Ping than they are in central Thailand. In Ban Ping indirect exchange is used to cement fellowship between close kinsmen. In central Thailand, it is a device whereby "professional piece-workers" earn cash when farmers hire them to repay their labor debts (Janlekha 1955:113 f.). Completely unknown in Ban Ping is the exploitative *"khaurang* system" (which conceivably functions to keep interest and rental cheaper than they would otherwise be), whereby a wealthy landowner may conscript labor from his tenants, debtors, and other dependents (Kaufman 1960:104, 69, 77).

Dependence.—Prosperity resulting from tractor agriculture has made it difficult to obtain harvest laborers from among fellow villagers. The consequent dependence on other communities is, of itself, no innovation. The rice of Chiengkham has always been plentiful. Reginald Le May (1926:188), when he visited the district shortly after it came under direct Siamese administration, received confirmation of its prosperity.

In 1960, as in every year for as long as villagers can remember, a few young Lue men from Myang Khawp in the contiguous part of Laos came through Chiengkham seeking farm work. In 1960, as in every year since the development of full-scale tractor agriculture, there were new economic purposes and new social consequences from hiring these men.

Before the use of Thunglor land made for seasonal variation in the supply of labor, all workers, including those from Myang Khawp, were hired for the entire farm year. In 1960, since tillage-season labor is provided by prematurely independent households, lads from Myang Khawp were hired only to harvest. Their work, then, had become oriented more exclusively toward the rewarded completion of particular tasks. Moreover, they, and all harvest hands—whether they worked by the season, by the day, or by the task—were hired only by households that had distant fields. Sometimes they were hired sufficiently early in the season to work a household's home fields. But their main job—the reason they were hired—was to harvest the "selling" rice (*xaw xaj*) of Thunglor. This hiring is also a device by which parents retain their children's labor. In every case where a seasonal worker harvested home irrigated fields, he was also sent to harvest—for no additional pay—the Thunglor fields of his employer's children.

In the old days, workers from Myang Khawp were hired because marriage and other long-term arrangements had made the employing

---

[26] For a parallel case in Latin America, see Erasmus 1956.

household incomplete; that is, because the family lacked a male member. In 1960, Lue from Myang Khawp were hired when additional labor was needed for a specific task on a specific field. As fellow Lue, these lads from Myang Khawp formerly could, and sometimes did, become full members of the household and the village.[27]

It would be an exaggeration to claim that the new pattern of hiring solely for the harvest season has transformed the lads from Myang Khawp into anonymous factors of production. Their relationship with their employer is not purely commercial. They live in his house, use kinship terms as if they were his children, and are free to court the village girls. For purposes of fellowship and exchange, they count as household members. Under special circumstances,[28] it is still possible for lads from Myang Khawp to become kinsmen. Nevertheless, almost all of them now come at harvest time and go immediately after the harvest. No one knows or cares whether they will return next year or for whom they will work. In this respect, they are no different from the Yuan lads who come, work, and go, all for a negotiated price, the promise of which begins the relationship and the payment of which terminates it.

The ways in which Ban Ping bought labor in 1960 made for some changes in the village's dependence on other communities. The ways in which Ban Ping sold labor could make for far more basic changes.

Tractor owners, officials, and other townsmen sometimes own large plots of distant flood land. They never work their own fields, but hire village people even to sow them. Although no one in Ban Ping sows for hire, some do harvest for townsmen. For those who do so on a daily basis, the arrangement and the wage are no different than if they had worked for a villager. For a few villagers, however, harvesting for a townsman was a major source of income.

---

[27] The heads of two young families originally came to Ban Ping as laborers from Myang Khawp. The households they worked for took a liking to them, adopted them, and sponsored their marriages.

[28] Mai N, the son of C, is a rather young man who dabbles in trade. On a trading trip to Myang Khawp, he formed a *sio* relation with a Lue man there. The man later sent his son to Thailand to become educated, as there are no schools in Myang Khawp. The boy was entrusted to the care of Maj N with whom he stayed while in school. Maj N and C then sponsored the boy's ordination as a Buddhist novice. The young novice traveled fairly extensively about Chiengkham and nearby districts before settling into the temple of a village with which Ban Ping has numerous connections. At the beginning of the 1960 harvest season, the young novice left the order and came to stay with Maj N. He harvested the fields of Maj N, of C, and of S, Maj N's younger brother who lives with C. In return he was "given" 25 hap of rice, the same as the "wage" paid a young stranger from a Yuan village who also lived with and harvested for both households. By 1965 this young lad had become a full member of Ban Ping. He did so not, as was possible in the past, merely through having come to work there, but on the strength of preexisting ties between his father and Maj N.

The following tale of Maj W illustrates more than lack of communication between villager and townsman. Since they themselves do not farm, townsmen need villagers if they are to benefit from Thunglor. Like the somewhat different tale of Maj J (who will solicit business for C's tractor), Maj W's story shows how townsmen must use middlemen in order to control villagers.

During the time that the Ministry of Education required no more than a fourth-grade education, the headman of Ban Ping served briefly as a schoolteacher. So did a Lue woman, who lives in Chiengkham Town and is married to a Yuan school principal who owns land at Thunglor. Shortly before the harvest, the principal came to Ban Ping to find laborers.

The principal probably chose Ban Ping to look for labor because its headman is reputed to know Thunglor well and had once been his wife's colleague. He also knew that strangers gain access to a tightly integrated community like Ban Ping through its headman. Moreover, the headman's good offices help to sanction an agreement that, as we have already seen, when the only claim is commercial, might otherwise be broken. So the principal asked the headman to help him find a harvest hand. The headman sent for his close friend (and wife's younger brother), Maj W. In order to establish a claim of suitably binding intimacy, or so it appeared, the principal immediately began to try to determine whether Maj W was born in the same year as he and hence his *sio;* Maj W agreed, or so it appeared, to harvest the principal's 16 acres of Thunglor land in return for a wage of 30 hap of rice for each 100 hap threshed. Before giving the principal the impression that he had committed himself, Maj W admitted that he was reluctant to agree to the offer until he found out what others would be paying for the Thunglor harvest. Although 30 hap for each 100 threshed was the rate paid the year before, Maj W thought it possible that some might pay other rates in 1960, "and would not want to disappoint you by having to take another job merely because it paid more."

As it turned out, Maj W was able to harvest fields of a tractor owner in return for 50 hap per 100. He did not, however, tell the principal this. A few weeks after the original agreement was made, the angry principal reappeared at the headman's, muttering that Maj W had lied to him. "An adult shouldn't behave in this manner," he cried. Maj W had agreed to meet the principal at Thunglor, but had never appeared. The headman, whose own harvest prospects looked bleak, agreed to take the job for the same wage that the principal had offered Maj W. In accepting the middleman's role, the headman also became a subcontractor or straw boss of labor and his finances came to depend entirely upon subordinate relations with a townsman.

To everyone's surprise, that same year the headman hired full-season harvest hands for his own badly managed and unproductive fields. As a result, he and his children were called "lazy." He set these workers, together with his children, to work at no extra pay on the principal's Thunglor harvest. The headman did not have sufficient cash to pay his plowing fees of 2,620 baht. To help meet his obligations, he borrowed the temple treasury as well as money that had been collected for the village school. When the headman had to return this money, the tractor owner took away his cart and oxen to help pay for the plowing. This left the headman more than 3,665 baht in debt, 2,270 baht to townsmen. Although his wages from the school principal (333 hap of rice) were more than twice the amount of rice produced by his own fields, the headman remained so much more deeply in debt than any of his fellows that his plight seemed ludicrous to them. Were he forced to sell all his rice (worth 1,410 baht), he would still owe money to townsmen. His creditors would never force him to do that, however. Instead, he will always have enough rice to eat and will probably be able to sell small amounts when the price is high and his creditors are unobservant. His financial survival, like his financial plight, depends upon arrangements made with powerful townsmen.

The headman, while certainly not a typical villager, probably represents the promise and the danger inherent in increasing involvement in the outside world. In Ban Ping sudden and swift economic expansion usually must come from townsmen, upon whom the villager may thereby become excessively dependent. Tractor farming, even on a subsistence scale, requires the cooperation of townsmen; expanded production requires their active protection and support. In Ban Ping's economy, money comes from rice. If it becomes more common for rice to come from money, and if townsmen expand their Thunglor plots at the expense of smallholders, more and more villagers will have to sell their labor. Middlemen, like the headman, will profit from the arrangement and Ban Ping might come to resemble Bangchan (Sharp *et al.* 1953:31) or Bangkhuad (Kaufman 1960:64), where wide disparities of wealth have created a landless proletariat. Because the tractor is no longer much used in Ban Ping (see chap. viii), this prophecy remains unfulfilled. But because the implications of tractor farming are not peculiar to Ban Ping, it is worth pointing out what, it seemed, mechanized agriculture might lead to.

SUMMARY

Labor mobilization.—At the beginning of this chapter I showed that the abundance and the variety of Ban Ping's land affect the seasonal supply of and demand for workers and thereby complicate the ways in which labor is mobilized. I then distinguished among three rewards given for labor: fellowship, exchange, and goods. By describing each category of labor in terms of the social relations between farmer and worker, the number and sex of those in labor groups, and the attitudes toward the reward given and toward the task, I was able to isolate the principles—intimacy, task difficulty, and utility of cash—which underlie the farmer's choice of which reward to offer. The availability of intimates was related to the supply of labor available at the time that a task must be done on a given plot and to the changes in household composition which result from young men's ownership of Thunglor land. The laborer's estimate of task difficulty was seen to be related to the size and sex composition of work groups. The utility of cash was related to the market for rice and to opportunities for alternative employment. The farmer's claims on labor resources were shown to be successively less effective as he drew upon household members, close kin, distant relatives, co-villagers, fellow tribesmen, and non-Lue.

If one compares earlier times with 1960 and plow farming with tractor farming, one finds that wages, haggling, task specificity, tit-for-tat reciprocity, and the hope of immediate profit have become more important. Farming tasks have become less social occasions, the size of work groups has decreased, and the social range of contracting parties (i.e., village, kindred, nuclear family, individual) has diminished. Ban Ping's relations with other communities have shown parallel changes. Although neither a landless proletariat nor professional labor brokers characterized Ban Ping, there was a danger that village weakness, when confronted with the tractor owners' strong control, might bring them into existence.

Resource components and economic development.—A common course of social analysis is to start from the position that there are institutions and other discrete units of society whose interrelations are problematic. In order to make farming in Ban Ping understandable, on the other hand, I have traced detailed relationships among the components of farming behavior regardless of which components would conventionally be called natural environment, social organization, or ideology. For example, we have seen how a cash market, coupled with the tradition of "private" rice within the longhouse, stimulated neolocality and thereby changed the ways in which kinsmen were rewarded for their labor. To understand the history of Ban Ping's land use, we had to consider the socioeconomic factors that made population pressure an incentive (cf. Boserup 1965:105) rather than a source of despair, and interposed between a farmer's need for land and his resources for converting forests into fields and fragmented estates into efficient holdings. Ban Ping's rising population impelled young farmers to search at Thunglor for new land, which traditions permitted them to own and which the tractor enabled them to clear. If we are to understand a productive system and its potential for growth, we cannot regard land or labor as "disembodied . . . explanatory variables" (Schultz 1964:7). If we are to analyze—and thereby gain the capacity for influencing—technological decisions, we must learn how those who make the decisions understand their costs, incentives, and rewards (cf. *ibid.*, p. 112).

One way the field ethnographer serves the development planner is by discovering the properties and interrelations of native categories relevant to subjects of economic concern (e.g., production, saving, investment). It is sometimes difficult, however, to maintain the dedicated simplemindedness that this purpose requires. So, for example, Firth (Firth and Yamey 1964:18) defines capital as "a stock of goods and services . . . operated to increase the volume of consumption in future periods." Then, presumably because Western economists are concerned largely with measuring and pricing material goods at home, he says that "such resources are largely material" and proceeds to limit his discussion almost exclusively to items of material culture. Now, if we take the notion of resources for future production and consumption with the naïve seriousness which I suggest, favors as well as food (cf. *ibid.*, p. 19), kinship as well as contracts must be counted as capital if members use or understand them as "resources capable of yielding goods and services in a future period." It is obviously no part of the proper business of anthropologists to tell people that what they use as capital is really their social organization. That land in Ban Ping "has a price" or that tenants pay rent influences land acquisition fully as much as edaphic features. The relative reliability of fellow villagers influences labor mobilization fully as much as do the agricultural requirements of a task. This is not merely to say that natural and social resources are mutually dependent. When the villager chooses how and where to farm, his natural and social resources appear equally unalterable. He can no more expect aid without giving it or paying for it than he can move Thunglor to the Great Field.

My insistence upon intracultural simplemindedness does not mean that we should be unaware of the intercultural relevance of observations. Consider the incidence of purchase as a technique of acquiring land in Ban Ping. Table 5 shows that villagers rarely buy uncleared land at Thunglor. To cultivate a rai of "forest farm" and be secure in possessing it, one must first clear the land and then pay 50 baht to have it plowed. If, on the other hand, one buys a rai of "stubble farm," as developed land is called, his tenure is secure, his labor minimized, his yield far higher, and his plowing cost reduced by half. It is surprising, then, not that so few forest farms were purchased when in

1958 reasonably good areas could be claimed at no cost, but that any were purchased at all. Some chose to buy promising forest fields rather than to save money by claiming marginal land; some, as early as 1957, chose to buy stubble farms. (The plots villagers consider worth buying are comparatively level, lightly wooded, near the well and tractor shed, and adjacent to stubble farms that have already proved fertile.) Wolf's dichotomy between farmers and peasants is relevant here: "The aim of the peasant is subsistence. The aim of the farmer is reinvestment" (1955:454). Men who choose to invest money in good land rather than claim less promising land that would have cost them nothing are acting like farmers. Whatever the adequacy of the labels "peasant" and "farmer" (Firth and Yamey 1964:17), even in modern economies (Emery and Oeser 1958:84) it is quite useful to distinguish between those who think of their welfare as lying in increased production and those who think of it as lying in decreased expenditure.

The villagers of Ban Ping, Thai farmers, and probably peasant producers throughout the underdeveloped world show "a strong tendency to make the most of economic opportunities" (Bauer and Yamey 1957:92). Siam was opened to Western trade by the Bowring Treaty of 1855 which preceded a significant increase in world demand for Thai rice. This demand was met through an enormous increase in the land planted to rice (Ingram 1955:43). The great preponderance of new land was cleared in the basin of the lower Chao Phraya. This area was opened without money, machinery, or much direct government participation. Central Thai villagers, along with some from the other parts of the kingdom, felled forests, built homes, made fields, and dug irrigation facilities in response to the purely economic incentives of cheap land and good prices. In the last few years, the government has sponsored dams, credit unions, and agricultural extension in order to help maintain rice as Thailand's major export. During the fifty years in which Thailand became a modern nation, however, the burden of its agricultural development was carried almost exclusively by the Thai peasantry, eager to expand production in order to gain financially. Within the last five years, the peasants of northeastern Thailand seem to have responded just as clearly to purely market incentives with increased production which has raised maize from miniscule importance to stand above teak as a source of foreign exchange (Muscat 1966:82).[29] In Thailand, it is sometimes the villager who acts the classic entrepreneur by expanding his production, while the urban offi-

---

[29] As peasants are not the sole producers of maize in northeast Thailand, one cannot be completely sure that it is they whose response to improved roads and markets has so dramatically increased the production of maize. Nevertheless, there is no evidence either in the economic history of Thailand or in studies of its contemporary rural communities suggesting that price elasticity represents a *change* in peasant behavior (cf. Ayal 1966:7).

cial restricts the supply of strategic goods and services in order to increase his political control over their disposition.

The conditions of peasant life are usually such that economic ambitions born within the community must be fulfilled outside it. In Ban Ping, as Dalena, India (Epstein 1962), collecting crops, granting credit, and hiring laborers for townsmen form a significant route toward personal economic advancement. In the south Indian village (*ibid.*, p. 200), "a contractor, they say, must be strict and not be swayed by kinship or other obligations." Because they must apply the townsman's standards when performing their brokerage tasks, such local agents are frequently unpopular. In my opinion, this unpopularity is not a trivial matter.

In Ban Ping, some villagers perceive and respond to economic opportunities more acutely than others. Generally, those who save, invest, expand their production, and use the market more efficiently than their neighbors are the villagers who, for these and other reasons, are criticized as calculating, aggressive, and selfish. Studies of village economies in India and Latin America support the observation that successful village entrepreneurs frequently fail to maintain the common peasant values of equanimity, generosity, loyalty to kinsmen, and conspicuous piety. They choose workers by effectiveness, not affection; save for investment instead of spending for prestige; devote their leisure to increasing private income and not to community activities. To put the matter baldly, it is not uncommon that villagers who are ambitious, enterprising, or successful are, in the eyes of their fellows, "sons of bitches." Peasant communities frequently value generosity, regard one man's gain as another's loss (Foster 1965), and lack the social resources for communal saving, pooled risks, and community-wide cooperative production. It should therefore not surprise us, first, that the individual—or household—is the usual unit of economic development and, second, that in the course of such development "nice guys" (as judged by the standards of village culture) often finish last (as judged by the standards of Western economics). In Ban Ping, it was the nice guys—the gentle, conservative, polite, and traditional villagers —whom I liked the most. I expect that most field anthropologists and community development workers share this preference. But we must nevertheless recognize the possibility that our best friends—the dutiful son, the quiet-spoken woman, the gentle, wise old man—are unlikely agents of economic expansion. It may be that national programs should concentrate on rural ambitiousness, not cooperation, and on developing not communities, but aggressive individuals. Perhaps the state's unpleasant role in encouraging economic development should be to train and reward the ambitious, while providing compensatory social services for those whom they outdistance.

PART FOUR: *CHOICE AND CHANGE*

We have examined the different techniques available for getting land and labor and for operating rice farms in Ban Ping. We have analyzed the factors that influence such minor farming decisions as how to seed or whether to hire transplanters. In Part Four, we turn to two major farming decisions—distant fields versus fields near home, the plow versus the tractor. In chapter vii I begin with the ways in which villagers themselves seem to view their farming decisions, and then examine these choices from the external viewpoint of their costs and returns. The costs are land, cash, labor, and capital investment. In discussing the returns that villagers receive for them, I use "yield" to refer to the amount of rice harvested per unit area of land, "productivity" for the harvest per unit of labor, and "dividend" for the harvest in terms of cash currently expended to achieve it. I apologize for the crudity of these terms and hope that the reader will not be confused by their divergence from correct economic usage. In order to understand farming decisions made in Ban Ping it is essential to distinguish among these three returns, and I can think of no better labels.

In the final chapter I review in general some of the ground covered, describe Ban Ping's farming in 1965, and discuss the forms of significant change.

VII.
Choice in Farming

THE VILLAGERS' PERSPECTIVE

Some households could probably own land on each of Ban Ping's six fields, but none do. If a household did own a plot on each of the six fields, it could not farm all of them. Of Ban Ping's 120 households, none managed five or six farms, and only 2 percent managed four. Twenty percent of the households were able to manage three farms, 40 percent managed two, and 29 percent, one. To some extent, this constraint is the voluntary result of villagers' economic calculations. Most households do not have, and no household is willing to expend, all the resources needed to farm all fields. The farmer's main limitation is the labor required by different fields. The tasks and timing required by one field may make it extremely difficult to cultivate some other field.

Not all farmers react to this difficulty in the same way; one man's challenge is another's despair. In part, these differing responses can be ascribed to household composition. Bachelors planning marriage exert extra efforts; parents with many young mouths to feed must work hard; a pregnant or nursing wife limits a family's effective labor force. Differences in personality, however, are also quite important. Although work is valued, a lazy or foolish man is punished only by his own penury. Often, differences in household composition and personality so merge that it is impossible to say which is paramount.[1]

Choice required.—There are severe limitations upon the number of plots that a household can farm with the plow. The dependable water supply for irrigated and semi-irrigated fields obviates the use of trac-

---

[1] For example, one young man with two children, both less than two years old, lives with the families of his wife's parents and his wife's sister. In addition to farming on the Great Field and the semi-irrigated field, he works distant irrigated land of his own. "First the home fields are worked. Then I go to the distant field where [although spending a night alone is frightening to villagers] I stay alone with no one to help me plow or transplant, with no one to cook my food." Another villager, whose household is composed of his wife and their daughters of two, seven, and nine years, says "I will farm only at Thunglor and will rent out my Great Field land. I'm only one man alone, and I can't farm at two places."

tors, which villagers—fond of cash, afraid of debt, and expecting lower yields—use only when they feel they must. Furthermore, the low dikes, which enable the farmer to keep the water level even, would either be destroyed by a tractor or, if left standing, would make tractor operation inefficient. All irrigated and semi-irrigated fields thus require intensive plowing labor, the timing of which is set by the monsoon which strikes all of Chiengkham on the same date. Transplanting, the date for which is set by plowing and the rains, also requires intensive labor during the tillage season. This task is performed wherever possible both because it is customary and because farmers believe that transplanting produces more rice. These technological considerations, along with the shortage of labor which results from the availability of land, make it all but impossible to farm every plowed field, but some combinations are easier and more efficient than others. In view of Schultz's hypothesis (1964:37) that "there are comparatively few inefficiencies in the allocation of the factors of production in traditional agriculture," it should come as no surprise that these combinations are also the most common.

Semi-irrigated, home flood, and home rainfall fields are not all watered at the same time. After the Great Field is inundated, its spill-off goes to the semi-irrigated field. When this occurs, not enough rainfall has yet accumulated for the cultivation of either the home flood or rainfall fields. By using rices that mature at different rates, it is possible, but difficult, for a household to accommodate its labor supply to the successive demands of Great Field, semi-irrigated, home flood,[2] and rainfall land. This difficulty is reflected in table 13, which records the frequencies with which home fields were combined. No household farms all four fields, and more than half (58 percent) of those who farm home fields limit themselves to only one farm. Nevertheless, almost half (43 percent) of those who farm home fields are able to cultivate more than one type of land near the village. The timing requirements of Great Field and home rainfall land make this combination the least difficult and the one that accounts for most (65 percent) cases in which two home fields are farmed.

The differing maturity dates of the rices known to Ban Ping facilitate combining the various plow-cultivated home fields. It is far more difficult to combine any of these fields with the distant irrigated field. For the reasons indicated (chap. iii), irrigation, seedbed preparation,

---

[2] The home flood field is omitted from most of the subsequent discussion because only seven Ban Ping households farm there. Three of these hire tractors and so do not till. Of the remaining four households, three also operate irrigated fields. These are the three households that dry-plow with a buffalo and broadcast seed on the home flood field before the time for intensive labor on irrigated fields. The one household that transplants on the home flood field operates only one other plot, a small one at Thunglor.

plowing, harrowing, and transplanting follow upon each other quite closely. Since the same water regime governs the home and the distant irrigated fields, their tillage-season tasks ideally are simultaneous. In addition, distant field tillage requires farmers to absent themselves from home for long periods. For these reasons, of the seventy-five households that farmed either irrigated field in 1959–60, very few (8

TABLE 13

FREQUENCY DISTRIBUTION OF HOME FIELD COMBINATIONS

Home fields farmed	Number of households
Farming one field	
Great Field	18
Semi-irrigated	5
Rainfall	13
Flood	3
Total	39
Farming two fields	
Great Field and semi-irrigated	7
Great Field and rainfall	17
Rainfall and flood	3
Total	27
Farming three fields	2
Grand total	68

SOURCE: Survey of all households.

percent) farmed both. Since home and distant irrigated fields are so difficult to combine, it is of some interest to determine how villagers choose between them.

The agronomic demands of Thunglor, unlike those of the distant irrigated field, rarely conflict with the demands of other fields, since Thunglor requires no tillage labor. Because its water regime is uniform, no one has to harvest his rice early so as not to obstruct his neighbor. All plant the slowest-growing rice; all are willing to let their ripe rice dry until it is convenient to harvest it. Thunglor is thus compatible with all other types of field: 75 percent of the seventy-nine households that farmed at Thunglor in 1959–60 also operated other fields.

Choice permitted.—The need to choose which fields to farm, while primarily ecological, involves values and social structure. A farmer's ability to choose, although also ecological, similarly involves more general considerations.

In the agriculture of Ban Ping, there are few traditional checks on productive activity. There are no hereditary occupational castes, few religious prohibitions that concern farming techniques, hardly any agricultural rituals. Moreover, although villagers are loath to recognize it, the factors of agricultural production can often be bought and sold for cash. Labor can be paid; land and animals can be bought, sold, and rented; the tractor can be hired; seed can be obtained by purchase and exchange; tools can be acquired by buying them. But the factor markets are not perfectly elastic, and villagers view cash as an independent factor rather than as a mere medium for calculating and exchanging the values of other factors. Labor may be in short supply and no one can buy another man's son. Customers for valuable land may be hard to find when the owner wants to sell. The water regime prevents any number of carabao from being the equivalent of a tractor at Thunglor. Such constraints preclude assigning cash values to all productive inputs. Nevertheless, within the limits described earlier, the villager is free to translate money into other factors of production and so choose which land to farm and how to farm it.

By using varieties of rice which mature at different rates Ban Ping farmers can stagger the dates of planting and harvesting at their various fields, thereby gaining a "labor adjustive device" (Janlekha 1955: 111) which is second in importance only to the tractor. Field records, which are probably incomplete, record the names of thirty varieties of rice used in Ban Ping.[3] Villagers subject these varieties to a twofold classification: grain type and rate of maturation. In terms of grain type, twenty-three of the thirty recorded varieties are glutinous, the rest ordinary. As is common in Asia, three maturation categories, which I translate as "late," "middle," and "early," are recognized by villagers. Of these, late-maturing rice has the largest number of varieties. Table 14 presents the number of recorded varieties in each of these categories.

Of the twenty-three glutinous rices, sample households (see App. B for description of sample) planted fourteen: eleven of them late maturing, two middle, and one early. Presumably, additional varieties

---

[3] Since varietal names vary so much from region to region, even within the northern Tai area, it would make little sense to list them here. Some varieties are called by proper names, others by names that seem to refer to the characteristics of the plant or grain. Examples of the latter are "short-stem," "black," and "fragrant." Some have place-names, presumably their source, such as Myang Tung (Chiengtung), Myang Pae (Phrae), Myang Phan.

Gourou (1940:298) reports the existence in the Tonkinese delta of 300 local varieties of rice. Since Tonkinese farmers grow two or even three crops annually, it is not surprising for them to have developed many more varieties than are known in Ban Ping. Nevertheless, it is unlikely that every Tonkinese farmer knows ten times as many varieties of rice as the Ban Ping farmer does. Gourou's figure is a total for many villages, and he does not seem to have been aware of the difficulty of determining whether or not the local names used in different villages refer to the same varieties.

CHOICE IN FARMING   151

were planted by households not in the sample, but the sampled distribution within the categories is probably representative.

As is explained below, late-maturing rices are planted wherever conditions of growth and the demands of other fields permit. This policy partially accounts for the rich variety of late-maturing rices since they occupy more land area and are thus subject to more varied conditions. Among the many rices within the late-maturing category, farmers

TABLE 14

VARIETIES OF RICE PLANTED IN BAN PING, 1960

Maturity	Glutinous	Ordinary	Total
Late	17 [a]	4	21
Middle	4	2	6
Early	2	1	3
Total	23	7	30

[a] It is possible that only fifteen varieties are named on the same level of specificity, as two names may be merely optionally distinguished subvarieties of the same variety. The three kinds in question are *khwang*, broken-flower *khwang*, and great *khwang*.

select those whose minor varietal peculiarities best accord with their plots and harvesting schedules. One weak-stemmed variety ("Chiengtung"), for example, is planted in depressions because it grows tall. Another variety ("Perennial") is shorter, but has a strong stem that recommends it on plots where lodging is a danger.

Plot quality and labor resources vary from household to household, even when households cultivate the same field. Maturity dates and plant characteristics differ from variety to variety even within the same category of rice.[4] No variety is perfect for all fields. The farmer may have to sacrifice strength of straw to gain height, sacrifice eating quality so that the rice is resistant to cracking in the sun, or give up some yield for a convenient harvest. The good qualities of some varieties, however, are sufficiently impressive for them to have achieved general popularity. A single variety accounts for slightly more than 60 percent of all (77) plantings of late-maturing glutinous rice. A second variety accounts for another 14 percent. A single variety of middle-maturing

[4] Early-maturing, or "three-month," rices are ready for harvesting within a few days of each other. There is more significant variation among late-maturing rices; one popular variety is ideally reaped during the first half of the second lunar month (roughly corresponding to late November–early December), while another is not ready until the second half of the month, and a third is reaped still later.

glutinous rice accounts for almost all sampled plantings (21 out of 22) of that category.

The choice of which category to plant is determined rather straightforwardly by the water regime of the field where it is planted and by the harvesting demands of a farmer's other fields. Table 15 records the percentage distribution of the different kinds of rice planted by sample households.

TABLE 15

VARIETIES OF RICE PLANTED ON DIFFERENT FIELDS, 1960
(In percentages)

Field	Variety of rice			
	Late glutinous	Middle glutinous	Early glutinous	Nonglutinous
Home irrigated and semi-irrigated (N = 37)	49	43	8	—
Distant flood (N = 53)	95	—	—	6
Distant irrigated (N = 7)	100	—	—	—
Home rainfall (N = 16)	6	31	56	6

SOURCE: Sample described in Appendix B.

Table 15 suggests a number of observations about the ways in which Ban Ping farmers choose their rice seed. Ordinary rice, a commercial product, is never used on fields that are animal plowed and transplanted. Of the four sample plots on which ordinary rice was sown, three were at Thunglor and the other was a tractor-plowed plot of home rainfall field. At the Great Field almost half of all plantings are middle-maturing rices and about another 10 percent are "three-month" rices. Planting these rices is an innovation made in response to tractor plowing on Thunglor. In the past, all Great Field plantings were of late-maturing rices and the modern middle-maturing rices were used only on rainfall fields. When "Myang Han three-month" rice was introduced on the rainfall field about 1930,[5] it replaced middle-maturing varieties which farmers then began to use on high and irregular plots of irrigated fields. Their use was excep-

[5] Evidence for the recent introduction of three-month rice is furnished by a detailed account from a reliable informant. Nevertheless, it is surprising and perhaps doubtful that early rice was introduced only in the 1930's. Adams (1948:264) reports that sixty- and hundred-day varieties are mentioned in the *Shou-shi T'ung-Kao*, a Chinese agricultural encyclopedia compiled in 1742. In the nineteenth century, the first Christian convert in northern Thailand seems to have made a rhetorical reference to early rice in his deathbed speech: "You plant the rice fields in the water and in the rain, but three months from now you will gather the harvest" (Presbyterian Board 1884:458).

tional, however, until the development of Thunglor placed a new demand on household labor resources.

It may be remarked that these two shifts—early rice to the rainfall field and then middle-maturing rice to the Great Field—indicate that the farmers of Ban Ping would probably be quite willing to accept new improved seeds if any were offered to them. The willingness to innovate, the careful choice made among varieties, and the correlation of category with land type all indicate that the farmers of Ban Ping, like those of Tonkin (Gourou 1936:388 f.) and Japan (Matsuo 1954: 27), make expert and objective use of rational criteria in deciding which rice to plant. Perhaps it would not be necessary to point out the technological astuteness of these elaborately interlocking decisions had not other studies of Thai farming ascribed them to "ancient tradition" (Pendleton 1962:160) or "the dictates of custom" (Sharp et al. 1953:139; cf. Barton 1960:156).

Criteria of choice.—When the people of Ban Ping are pressed to explain their actions, they, like most Americans, are content merely to point out, "This is the way we do things," or "This is how things have always been done here." The difficulty of explanation and the inappropriateness of questionnaires is increased by the high value that Thai villagers place on polite and facile answers, on "answering easy, easy." In attempting to discover the criteria of choice presented below, I deliberately avoided highly structured interviews and continual repetitions of, "Why do you do this instead of that?" The criteria emerge from a large number of fairly casual conversations, in many of which I was merely a quiet observer. All the decisions, criteria, and relationships presented here are known and expressed by village farmers. Their combination and organization, however, is mine.

Without exception each villager wants to farm in the way that gains him the most rice. All villagers recognize that the rice in their granaries represents a return for the resources and operations of farming. Everyone reckons this return in terms of the volume of rice he harvests. Most speak of bung or hap; a few, especially among the young, reckon in terms of the official thang,[6] or approximations to it. I hardly ever heard villagers speak of yields or fields in terms of the weight of the grain produced, although it is by weight that townsmen pay for rice.

All villagers recognize the same productive inputs and are prepared to reckon their return in terms of them. These inputs are land, cash, labor, and capital investment. All villagers agree that some fields and

[6] The thang is an official unit of volume equal to 20 liters. In Ban Ping, "bung" refers to a large basket which usually holds about 1 thang, and the noun "hap" always means a shoulderload of two such baskets. In central Thailand, "hap" sometimes refers to the official picul, a unit of weight equivalent to 100 catties or 60 kilograms.

farming techniques offer a better return in terms of certain inputs than other fields and techniques. Most villagers are in agreement about which field is best for which input. Depending on their age, their wealth, and the size of their household, however, villagers evaluate the inputs differently. Different groups thus have different standards of maximum gain. Some, hampered by limited resources, may not be able to farm in the way that seems best to them, but all are conscious of costs and returns, whether social or monetary, and are prepared to evaluate their farming accordingly.

Choice among home fields.—The choice among plowed home fields is straightforward, made according to the single criterion of yield per rai. Yield is the criterion by which villagers most commonly discuss and evaluate fields and farming systems. Other things being equal, every villager prefers the land and techniques that produce the highest yields. It is often true, however, that other things are not equal. The value of other inputs may then override the importance of land; however, irrigated, semi-irrigated, and rainfall fields all have approximately the same requirements of seed, labor, and cash. Since the necessary amounts of seed, labor, and cash are equal on all home plowland, these inputs are irrelevant for deciding which to farm.

All villagers agree that the Great Field yields more than the semi-irrigated field which, in turn, yields far more than the rainfall field.[7] To the villager, the variety of rice planted is a major explanation for these differences in yield. Water availability and harvesting convenience make farmers plant fast-maturing rices on the rainfall field and middle-maturing rices on the semi-irrigated field; only on the Great Field can the slowest-growing rices be planted. The rainfall and semi-irrigated fields do not have water long enough for the slowest-maturing rices to survive, while early rice would be ready for harvest when the Great Field is still inundated. In addition, rainfall and then semi-irrigated farms must be cleared of their crop and their water before farmers can bring their draft animals to the Great Field harvest. For these reasons, the type of field dictates the category of rice to be planted (see table 15). The category of rice, in turn, influences the yield. Villagers are agreed that a rice's yield varies with the time required for maturing. Although not all agronomists are convinced of this relationship between yield and maturation rate (see Grist

---

[7] These preferences affect land prices which, in turn, exert some influence on farming choice. Pelzer (1958:130) points out that "land that can be kept inundated . . . always brings a higher price" because of "the amount of labor that has had to be invested in order to alter [its] topography." His argument is true as far as it goes, but it should be emphasized that farmers would not invest in labor to get higher prices if they did not expect the land to produce more rice. This expectation is thus the basic standard of choice, and the one emphasized in the present study.

1959:67 f.; cf. Gourou 1936:388), it has long been given extensive credence in Asia. In the seventeenth century, Robert Knox (1681:12) recorded the Sinhalese conviction that rice "which is soonest ripe, is most savoury to the taste; but yieldeth the least increase."

Despite the conviction that they produce the best yields, late-maturing rices are becoming less popular in Ban Ping as a result of tractor agriculture. Table 15 indicates that 8 percent of the Great Field farmers (in the sample) planted "three-month" rice. As one of these farmers explained, "I am planting three-month rice on the Great Field as well as on the rainfall field. This way, my home harvest will be over by the time that I go to Thunglor where I have broadcast the slowest-growing rice."[8] The "household" (*hern*) farms of the Great Field are dependent on the harvesting labor of young men. Because the reward of goods at Thunglor is extremely attractive to these young men, even those households without distant flood land of their own are being forced to plant faster-maturing rices at the Great Field.

The variety of rice planted is the villager's main explanation for the differential yields of home irrigated, semi-irrigated, and rainfall land in any one season. Of even more importance for evaluating these fields is the relative dependability of yield from year to year. All villagers agree that irrigated fields are preferable because they afford better protection against drought and flood. The Great Field irrigation system is an established one in which "rain anywhere benefits land everywhere." Some reckon that the constant fertility comes about "because the water comes straight from the mountains, bringing the manure and fertilizer of the hills with it." On the Great Field itself, land is valued according to its proximity to a major irrigation ditch. Similarly, the semi-irrigated field's comparative immunity to flood and drought makes it more dependable than the rainfall field and thus more desirable.[9]

Choice among irrigated fields.—Most villagers agree that yields are better at the distant irrigated field than at the Great Field. They maintain that this superiority can be verified merely by inspection, since the richness of a harvest and of a field is reflected by the height

---

[8] Even farmers whose reactions to Thunglor are not so extreme as the one expressed by this farmer often shift to faster-ripening and less productive varieties. Maj M, to whom yield and profit are particularly important, says: "I planted very little of the slowest-maturing rice. My children wanted to plant rice no slower than [the earliest variety of the late-maturing class of rices] and very little even of that. Otherwise, the Great Field harvest wouldn't be over in time for them to go to Thunglor."

[9] A further, albeit minor, source of flood protection comes from the kinds of rice which may be planted on fully irrigated fields. Slow-maturing rices do not sprout so readily as the fast-growing varieties planted on the home rainfall field. There is, therefore, less chance of losing slow-growing rices through unseasonable harvest-time rains.

to which the rice grows. At the Great Field, the rice stands only waist high; at the distant irrigated field, it often is taller than a man. Old men claim that the rice at the Great Field is far shorter than it was in their youth. Some ascribe this to the "land being old and tired" from generations of uninterrupted cultivation, and recommend the use of manure or ash on the home irrigated field and seedbeds. Those who farm the distant field and champion it, like those who seriously contemplate farming there, compare yields as well as height. Rarely, however, is this comparison more than a vague approximation; all were intrigued by the more accurate figures I computed. In the absence of accurate computations of yield, villagers demonstrate the fertility of the distant irrigated field by the small amount of seed rice they say it requires. On the Great Field, rice is usually said to be transplanted at intervals of about a handspan. At the distant irrigated field the conventional distance is a *sork,* the length of an arm from fingertip to elbow.[10]

Distant irrigated land is cheap as well as fertile; it sells for about half the Great Field price. Even farmers who inherited their Great Field land, thus paying nothing for it, recognize that the proceeds from its sale could buy twice as much land, and thus more than twice as much rice each year, at the distant irrigated field. If villagers agree that land at the distant irrigated field is cheaper and more fertile, why do not more of them farm there? The most basic criticism of the distant irrigated field is its unreliability. As a farmer who owns land both there and on the Great Field explains, "Distant irrigated land is cheap because it has an inadequate irrigation system. Its yield is far less certain than at the Great Field. Some years there's a lot of rice, some years very little. At the Great Field the yield is fairly constant." [11]

An even more common explanation of relatively low prices at the distant field is, "The Great Field is closer to home. It's a lot of trouble to go to the distant irrigated field." Villagers enlarge upon this reason and say that it is "inconvenient" and "lonely" at the distant field.

---

[10] These folk measurements correspond quite closely to the planting distances observed by a Thai agronomist who writes of 20-inch intervals on good land and 8-inch intervals on bad (Santiwongse 1913:4). For Cochin China as well, Gourou (1940:289) reports planting distances of about 8 inches on poor soil and about 20 inches on good soil. If the agronomists who believe that Asian cultivators lower their yields by planting rice too densely, thus reducing the sunlight and nutrition received by individual plants, are correct, it is possible that the planting distances at the distant irrigated field may partly cause, rather than reflect, its supposedly greater fertility.

[11] Some farmers, in fact, are critical of the superior irrigation system of the Great Field. They complain that its local dams and canals require much more work than is necessary on the distant irrigated field. It is quite unlikely that this criticism has much real weight when villagers decide where to farm. Nevertheless, it provides an example of how difficult it sometimes is to evaluate villagers' explanations of their own behavior.

Some who cultivate the distant irrigated field accept this explanation and ascribe the reluctance of others to farm there to "laziness."

An occasional farmer voiced a further criticism of the distant irrigated field. "I don't have a cart, and would forever be hiring people and so would lose any advantage of having fields there." Since harvest-time carting is a substantial cost, it is surprising that so few farmers mentioned it in objecting to fields away from home.

Although it is probably relevant to their decisions, no one pointed out that the choice is not really between the distant irrigated field and the Great Field but, rather, between the distant irrigated field and all the home fields that could also be operated if the distant field did not force those who farm it to leave the village for so long. In Ban Ping, the main technological specification of distant fields is not the price, the difficulty, or the fact that one meets strangers there (cf. Epstein 1962:206). The relevant specification is simply that, given the local perceptions and the local need for living near the farm during tillage and harvest tasks, the distant irrigated field is distant from the village.

Choice between plow and tractor.—All villagers agree that plow agriculture produces higher yields. The conventional expression of this agreement is that animal plowing and transplanting yield 40 hap for each rai farmed, while tractor plowing and broadcasting yield only 20. Although aware of the phenomenon of tillering and the danger of lodging, villagers do not ascribe higher yields to transplanting per se (cf. Grist 1959:66, 119 f., 122). Instead, they speak of the grass that "eats" the young rice on broadcast fields. The least desirable sections of distant flood field are victimized by especially long and hardy grasses. Throughout the distant flood field, and on all broadcast land, there are grasses that survive inundation. Such grasses, say the villagers, are rarely important on traditionally farmed land where they are controlled by harrowing, particularly by the *kaw-tyt* sequence: "This kills the grass which [then] turns into green manure and so helps the rice rather than competing with it." [12]

Low reliability is felt to be another shortcoming of tractor agriculture which, unlike plow agriculture, is never practiced on irrigated land. On tractor-tilled land the harvest is considered a windfall. One young man, who has land at Thunglor, expressed his viewpoint: "Broadcast fields aren't really rice fields [*na*]. They're not like the Great Field which always gives rice because neither floods nor drought bothers it."

[12] Villagers also believe that grass can be controlled on animal-plowed land by burning the rice stalks after harvest and say that it is especially desirable to do so on field seedbeds. During the seeding season, villagers are able to distinguish by the grass growing on them those seedbeds that had not been burned during the preceding year from those that had. The ashes from the burning, it is claimed, also provide a valuable fertilizer.

Tractor farming has two compensating advantages. First, and most important, it permits the cultivation and consequent owning of land that otherwise could not be farmed. Second, it requires much less work to hire a tractor and to broadcast seeds than it does to plow and transplant. Since the tractor is thought to produce far less rice, those who use it on the home rainfall and flood fields, where villagers do not consider the tractor necessary, are sometimes criticized as "lazy." Some, however, concede that the use of tractors on these fields might permit these plots to be cultivated during years when late rainfall did not allow sufficient time for traditional techniques of plowing and transplanting.

As villagers view it, the basis of this labor productivity is also the main shortcoming of tractor farming. Hiring tractors is expensive, and this fact, together with the risk of a bad harvest, makes tractor agriculture seem to pay less dividend. "Thunglor fields are money fields," says a villager, "and one has to buy them back from the tractor owners year after year." One or two villagers, in addition to Maj M, vaguely considered buying a tractor (see illus.), but soon rejected the idea because, conscious of their ignorance relative to townsmen, they feared that drivers, suppliers, and mechanics would take advantage of them.

COSTS AND RETURNS: THE OUTSIDER'S PERSPECTIVE

Responses to a schedule of questions asked of forty farming households, a random sample, make it possible to compare farming in Ban Ping with agriculture elsewhere [13] and to evaluate how accurately villagers estimate their criteria of farming choice. Despite these advantages, formal, quantitative, and objective research techniques also have inherent shortcomings in a small and unsophisticated community. Some of the shortcomings are discussed in Appendix B, which also presents the schedule of questions. Although the data analyzed in this chapter are probably no less accurate than most quantitative information found in ethnographic studies, it would be a mistake to equate them with econometric data from modern societies where people are accustomed to keeping books and to answering questionnaires. The only difficulty of quantification which need concern us here, however, is the ethnographic necessity for using incommensurable standards, for adding apples and elephants.

When agricultural economists study the costs and returns of farming, they assign cash values to all factors of production. They impute a price to family labor, for example, in terms of the usual wage paid to outsiders or in terms of the market prices of the goods that family members consume. A precise statement of profit and loss can then be

[13] Comparative information irrelevant to Ban Ping's technological decisions is concentrated in footnotes and in Appendix C.

formulated by comparing the sum of such costs with the market value of the farm's produce. Such a procedure seems inappropriate to peasant choice in Ban Ping. Economically, it would make little sense because there are no jobs alternative to working within the household, few nonfarm investments, little income not based on rice. Since family members have not made an economic decision when they work for their household, there is little theoretical justification for imputing a "wage" to them. Assigning cash value to all the factors in rice farming would be misleading socially and offensive morally to villagers who do not live in a world where everything and everybody has a price. They would find it repugnant to evaluate a child's service in terms of his meals or of wages paid to outsiders.[14] Technologically, assigning cash value to all productive inputs would totally distort farming decisions in Ban Ping. It is precisely those qualitative differences between family and hired labor, or between land and money, which present the villagers with the need and the criteria for choosing how to farm. Equating inputs by inputing a cash cost to all of them would confuse the mechanisms and standards of technological choice. To judge from Epstein's report (1962:222), Ban Ping is clearly not unique in this respect.

Yields.—Yield per unit area is Ban Ping's main criterion for deciding which field to farm and how to farm it. Table 16 presents these yields in the unit by which villagers speak of them, hap per rai. In general, it may be said that the table confirms the direction but not the extent of the differences in yields which guide village decisions of how and where to farm. Just as villagers claimed, the distant irrigated field proved the most fertile; in 1960 farmers harvested 5 hap there for every 4 grown on the Great Field. To people for whom rice is the staff of life and the source of cash, this difference is important. If villagers are correct in their belief that slow-maturing rices produce the highest yields, this relationship, while presumably less important than soil fertility, may account for some of the superiority of the distant irrigated field. However, the close association of rice category with land type precludes testing the villager's supposition. The slowest-growing rices are always planted on the best lands, so that one cannot discriminate between the influence of these two variables on yield.

Whatever its explanation, the difference between home and distant irrigated fields is less pronounced than I had anticipated [15] on the

---

[14] Janlekha (1955:84) quotes a Bangchan farmer's estimate that "hired labor is usually more expensive than family labor except in good years, for you can't help giving generous gifts to the faimly in a good year." The farmers of Ban Pang, although they contrast hired with exchange labor for transplanting, simply do not make such comparisons.

[15] It may seem somewhat incautious to base this comparison upon a sample that includes only seven distant irrigated farms, but further evidence is provided by

basis of the villagers' eloquent contrasts between the tall growth of the distant irrigated field and the stunted waist-high plants at home. Nevertheless, the distant irrigated field does seem to be significantly superior to the Great Field unless, as its critics maintain, yields there are less dependable.

Just as villagers claimed, the yield of Thunglor was smaller than that obtained from the Great Field. As with their claims for the superiority of the distant irrigated field, however, the order of dif-

TABLE 16

MEAN YIELDS IN HAP PER RAI BY FIELD, 1959 AND 1960

Field	1959		1960	
	Area (In rai)	Yield	Area (In rai)	Yield
1. Great Field	141	25.2	197	22.5
2. Distant irrigated	39	34.0 [a]	83	27.5
3. Thunglor, overall	403	16.4	559	17.4
4. Thunglor, established	—	—	473	19.0
5. Thunglor, virgin land	—	—	86	8.0
6. Rainfall, overall	—	—	62	11.0
7. Rainfall, tractor	No tractor used		17	11.8
8. Rainfall, animal	19	12.0 [b]	45	10.8
9. Home flood, overall	—	—	16	14.8
10. Home flood, tractor	No tractor used		8	12.5
11. Home flood, animal	16	17.2	8	17.0
12. All fields	618	19.8	917	19.0

[a] Based on only three plots.
[b] Based on only four plots.

ference is less than anticipated. Many villagers, it will be recalled, maintain the convention that transplanting at the Great Field produces twice as much rice as broadcasting does at Thunglor. This contention is somewhat exaggerated. Yields from the untamed "forest farms" (*na pa*) at the distant flood field are quite low (8 hap per rai). After its first year of use, however, Thunglor produces harvests scarcely

an independent sample of the 1959 harvest which resulted in a yield (19.8 hap per rai) of roughly the same size as that obtained in 1960 (19.0 hap). The independent sample, although not statistically random, was selected without known bias. It includes six distant irrigated farms (a total of 60 rai) and fourteen home irrigated and semi-irrigated farms (a total of 150 rai) not included in the random sample on which table 16 is based. The independent sample for 1959 confirms the order of difference found by the random sample of 1960. The mean yield of its fourteen Great Field farms was 20.5 hap per rai, while its six distant irrigated farms produced 27.5 hap.

[16] In 1959, when the Great Field harvest was quite good and the Thunglor sample included a high proportion of forest farms, the ratio was 20:13.

smaller (11:13 is the ratio) than those obtained from the home irrigated and semi-irrigated fields.[16] This difference, or rather, the lack of difference, is of more than local significance.

The consequences of transplanting are a matter of some dispute and must therefore be given somewhat more attention than my strictly ethnographic purposes warrant. Most specialists (Adams 1948:258 f.) would probably agree with Grist's comment: "One can but emphasize the fact that the weight of evidence throughout the paddy areas of the world is that transplanting . . . results in increased yields" (1959:122). Some minimize the advantages of transplanting itself and ascribe increased yields solely to water conservation, weed control, the potential for double-cropping, and the concentrated attention that young plants can receive in a small seedbed (Jones 1947:268; Matsuo 1954:78).[17] This analysis makes Wickizer and Bennett (1941:244) conclude: "On lands where at present only one rice crop and no other crop is grown each year, some of the chief potential advantages of transplanting cannot be realized." Grist, on the other hand (1959:222), "emphasizes the fact . . . that transplanting is beneficial to the plant" itself. He cites evidence (from Ceylon) that with late-maturing rice "transplanting increased the crop by 30 to 46 percent" (*ibid.*, p. 121). Janlekha (1955:93) reports a "general belief among leading [Thai] agricultural officials that the broadcasting method . . . gives only half the yield of the transplanting method." Gourou (1936:389) accepts this ratio for Tonkin, but Janlekha himself "reserves . . . judgment on this, for no systematic comparison between these two methods of growing rice has yet been made" (1955:93).

Because Thai farmers usually transplant where they can and broadcast only when they must, the national yield ratio of 4:1 (for 1962, the most recent year for which figures are available [Thailand 1965:8]) tells little about the consequences of the techniques themselves. Data from Ban Ping, however, provide a basis for systematic comparisons between transplanting and broadcasting the same varieties of rice during a single year by the same farmers in similar environments and sometimes on the same field. However narrow their source, the data therefore may have general relevance. Comparison among all fields cultivated in 1960 (excluding the forest farms of Thunglor) reveals that transplanting produced a mean yield of 22 hap per rai and broadcasting a yield of 20.5 hap, a ratio of only 14:13 in favor of transplanting. Although differences in soil fertility complicate this comparison, the chemical composition of soil is remarkably unimportant for the yields of inundated rice (see Grist 1959:11 f.). Nevertheless, the disparity between the distant and home irrigated fields shows that

---

[17] On the issue of concentrated seedbed cultivation, see also Gourou 1940:301.

soil fertility is not irrelevant. Although villagers rarely make this comparison themselves, it might therefore be more appropriate to compare the new land at Thunglor with the equally new distant irrigated field rather than with the Great Field.

From table 17 it can be seen that on fields of comparable fertility, transplanting is superior to broadcasting by a ratio of only 8:7. This sample of 12,262 rai (253.6 acres; 54.4 transplanted, 199.2 broadcast) indicates that the inferiority of broadcasting is less pronounced than one would suppose from Grist's argument that transplanting benefits

TABLE 17

Yields Obtained from Transplanting and from Broadcasting on Fields of Equivalent Fertility
(In hap per rai)

Transplanting		Broadcasting	
Field	Yield	Field	Yield
Distant irrigated	27.5	Distant flood (Thunglor) [a]	19.0
Rainfall	10.8	Rainfall	11.8
Home flood	17.0	Home flood	12.5
All three fields	21.3	All three fields	18.7

[a] Established farms (*na ferng*) only.

the plant itself as well as helping to control weeds. In Ban Ping, the benefit of weed control is recognized by the villagers when they attribute the superior yields of transplanted fields to the absence of grass. Since neither type of field is weeded, and since both are inundated, superior weed control probably results not from transplanting itself but from the tillage techniques that accompany it. Making furrows, plowing the grass under and allowing it to rot, and using the Great Field as grazing land may control weeds well enough to account for the rather slight differences in yield between transplanted and broadcast fields.[18]

To both villager and outsider, the main recommendation of broadcasting is that it clearly increases Ban Ping's production of rice by permitting the cultivation of land that would otherwise lie idle. Before

[18] If the same technique of seeding were used on animal- and tractor-tilled fields, one might expect higher yields from the latter. Experiments, admittedly out of date, conducted in 1933–34 compared yields from tractor- and animal-plowed fields. With early varieties of rice the tractor yield was 8.5 percent better; with late-maturing varieties, like those used in Ban Ping, the tractor yield was 17.9 percent better. The superiority of the tractor is in its greater ability to destroy weeds, which accords most benefit to late-maturing varieties because they get off to a slower start (Thailand 1947:33).

the development of tractor agriculture the farmers of Chiengkham were unable to make effective use of the huge plain of Thunglor. On Ban Ping's home rainfall field—which can be farmed by traditional techniques—late rainfall in 1959 discouraged 87 percent of those who have land there from farming it.[19] Had the tractor owners made their machines available to home rainfall farmers in 1959, most of them would probably have tried to farm their land there.

It will be recalled that the dependability of yields, as well as their size, is an important standard for farming choices. In addition to producing lower annual yields, broadcast and distant fields are supposed to be less reliable than the Great Field. The verification of this belief is not a matter of finding the standard deviation from the mean, which is a measure of variations in yield among different plots on the same field. The farmer's concern is with variations in yield from the same plot in different years.[20]

I have such data only for the years 1959 and 1960, and even these are not sufficient to indicate the relative stability of distant irrigated yields, a matter of some interest. To determine the comparative reliability of Thunglor and the Great Field, on the other hand, there were sufficient distant flood (27) and home irrigated (23) plots from which the yields for both years could be determined. Table 18 records the sum of the differences between yields in the two years for both fields. Just as farmers claimed, the yields from tractor farming were (25 percent) less reliable than those from traditional agriculture. The meager figures from the distant irrigated field also support the villagers' claim, but a sample of only three farms is too small to rely on.

Productivity.—For agronomists and national planners, yield per unit area is sometimes the only standard of farming effectiveness. This concentration probably arises from the circumstances of industrialized nations in which cultivable land is usually quite scarce and expensive while complex machines and advanced techniques make labor seem capable of almost infinite expansion. Anthropologists (e.g., Conklin

---

[19] Of thirty-one rainfall plots sampled in 1960, only four were cultivated in 1959. This unreliability, as well as their low yields (table 16, lines 6–8), amply justifies the villagers' low regard for the home rainfall field and their interest in planting crops other than rice there.

[20] For this reason, neither the variance nor the standard deviation of yields from different fields has been computed. Those statistics, like other measures of the spread of a distribution, have two main purposes. First, the "spread of a distribution may be of interest . . . as it aids in gauging the precision with which a sample mean estimates the corresponding population mean" (McCarthy 1957:150). For a sample as small as the present one, however, a useful gauge is furnished by Appendix B and by table 27, which presents the frequency distributions of all yields used for computing means. The second purpose of such statistics is that the "spread of a distribution may be of direct interest" (*ibid.*). For the present argument, however, the only spread of direct interest to the farmer is that between past years' and this year's yield from a given plot.

1957:152; Geddes 1954:64 f.; Lewis 1951:154 ff.), on the other hand, since they deal with a wide range of technological systems, frequently consider labor productivity when they compare and evaluate alternate ways of farming. In Ban Ping, labor productivity is clearly a prime consideration. In traditional farming, labor, as a major resource for acquiring land, is the most basic and often the scarcest factor in production. It is often, still, the only productive resource a young man has to convert into rice or land or money. Furthermore, labor

TABLE 18

MEAN DIFFERENCES PER PLOT BETWEEN 1959 AND 1960 YIELDS

Field	Number of plots	Sum of the differences between 1959 and 1960 yields	Mean difference per plot
Home irrigated	23	75.9	± 3.3 hap per rai
Distant irrigated	3	11.5	± 3.8 hap per rai
Distant flood	27	106.5	± 4.0 hap per rai

is the productive input that reaches most deeply into the fabric of village life. What has been called "the mobilization of labor" is, from another point of view, the human relations, social organization, and warm camaraderie of Ban Ping. In addition, the modernization of agriculture generally (Schultz 1964:117), as well as its specific form in Ban Ping, is a matter of increasing the productivity of farm labor. For the present study, moreover, labor is the factor of production most amenable to technological choice. If a villager has inherited some land, it is likely to be on the Great Field and he will till it with the plow. If a villager has Thunglor land, he will hire a tractor for it. The mobilization of labor, however, is constantly subject to choice and to change. Wages or exchange, intimates or outsiders, *lo* or *term* or *aw haeng*—the technology of Ban Ping always permits and sometimes forces villagers to exercise choice when they mobilize labor for the production of rice.

In this section on productivity, I attempt to quantify the amount of labor expended in farming. After reviewing the annual farming cycle, I consider how much labor is needed for the successive operations of plow and of tractor agriculture, and then show how slight variations of land use affect these labor requirements. Finally, I discuss the relative productivity of the various fields and farming systems used in Ban Ping.

Except for the tractor men, who plow Thunglor during March, farming begins in May. During the hot dry month of April, the seventh month in Lue reckoning, villagers are free for ceremonies and

CHOICE IN FARMING 165

for repairing the ropes, harnesses, plows, harrows, and baskets they will need for tillage. In May the dams and canals of the home and distant irrigated fields are repaired and the seedbeds are prepared and seeded. The semi-irrigated seedbed is prepared, the home flood plow field is tilled and Thunglor is sown (fig. 9). In June the irrigated fields are tilled, the semi-irrigated bed is seeded, and the home rainfall seedbed is prepared. In early June some farmers are still seeding at the distant irrigated field, whereas at the Great Field transplanting begins toward the end of the month. Also during June, tractors arrive to plow the home flood and rainfall fields. During July, the semi-irrigated and rainfall fields are tilled. July is also the time for transplanting all except the home rainfall field. During July and also during June, Thunglor farmers occasionally go to inspect their fields. By August the pace of work has sharply diminished; transplanting takes place on the home rainfall field, and other home fields are inspected occasionally. At Thunglor the water level is already too high for farmers to visit their holdings. During the heavy rains of August, September, and early October, villagers are hired to cart loads to Phayao or else they stay indoors to gossip and gamble.

During October preparation is made for the harvest. Flails and tables are prepared, and mats are woven. By the end of October it is possible to begin reaping the three-month rice of the home rainfall field. During November, first the rainfall, then the home flood, and finally the semi-irrigated fields are harvested completely. Harvesting at other fields also begins in November but, depending largely on the variety of rice planted, continues through December at the distant irrigated field, and into January at Thunglor when the last rice is carted to the farmers' granaries.[21]

[21] Even casual inspection of the farming cycle represented in figure 9 demonstrates again that the noninvolution of Ban Ping's agriculture results not from a lack of ambition but from the size and variety of landholdings. Another way of indicating how hard villagers work is through presenting the farming timetables of representative households. Consider, for example, "Mother" K, whose daughter and two sons farm 3.6 acres of Great Field and 1.6 acres of semi-irrigated field. The sons, in addition, farm 10 acres of "private" land at Thunglor. Since half of those who farm at home operate more than one field there, and since four-fifths of Thunglor farmers also operate other fields, Mother K's household is not untypical.

On May 6, four days after the first head-of-the-year rains, the boys brought coconut fronds to burn on the Great Field seedbed. On May 18 they began to cultivate the bed which, by May 23, was seeded with a late-maturing rice. After seeding the field bed, the boys began to burn and clear a forest seedbed for the semi-irrigated field. By mid-July this bed had been seeded with a middle-maturing rice. On June 15 the boys began to build a field shelter and to prepare equipment for tilling the Great Field. Plowing and harrowing took them from the 1st to the 12th of July. On July 13 the field was transplanted so that on July 15 they could begin to till the semi-irrigated field which was transplanted on July 24.

Had the household any home rainfall land, they would now have begun im-

The successive tasks of the farming cycle (fig. 9), their ordering, staggering, and duration, are, of course, all known to villagers who incorporate them in their plans. Villagers are also aware of the relative difficulty and amount of work required by their farming operations, but their view does not correspond perfectly to the quantitative analysis that follows. Since manure is used so casually and by so few

TABLE 19

Labor Expended per Task for Plow-farming Great Field and for Tractor-farming Thunglor

Great Field			Thunglor		
Task	Number of man-days	Percentage of man-days	Task	Number of man-days	Percentage of man-days
Irrigation		13	Pointing	42	
Wood preparation	120		Broadcasting	42	
Great Dam	48		Tillage tasks		3
Local dams	240				
Seedbed		5			
Preparation	125				
Seeding	24				
Tillage	566	18			
Transplanting		22	Growing-season		
Uprooting	267		tasks	42	2
Planting	417				
Harvesting	1,311	42	Harvesting	2,697	95
Total	3,118	100		2,823	100

households, irrigation is the first significant task for plow farming at the Great Field. The schedule of questions administered at harvest time, however, did not inquire about irrigation or other pretillage operations because respondents would not have been able to remember how many man-days they had expended a half year earlier. Instead, the figures for irrigation, seedbed preparation, and pointing given in table 19 are estimates (see App. B); man-days for other operations are computed from the schedule administered to the sample. The table shows that Great Field irrigation is a rather time-consuming task, one

mediately to till it. Operators of home rainfall farms were observed transplanting from the 3d to the 17th of August. Its harvest began on November 10. Mother K's household began to reap its semi-irrigated field on November 17, 116 days after planting. A week later the rice was ready for threshing. On November 21, immediately after the completion of shocking on the semi-irrigated field, they began to reap the Great Field. By December 12 all rice from the home fields had been threshed, winnowed, and carted to the granary. The distant flood harvest could begin.

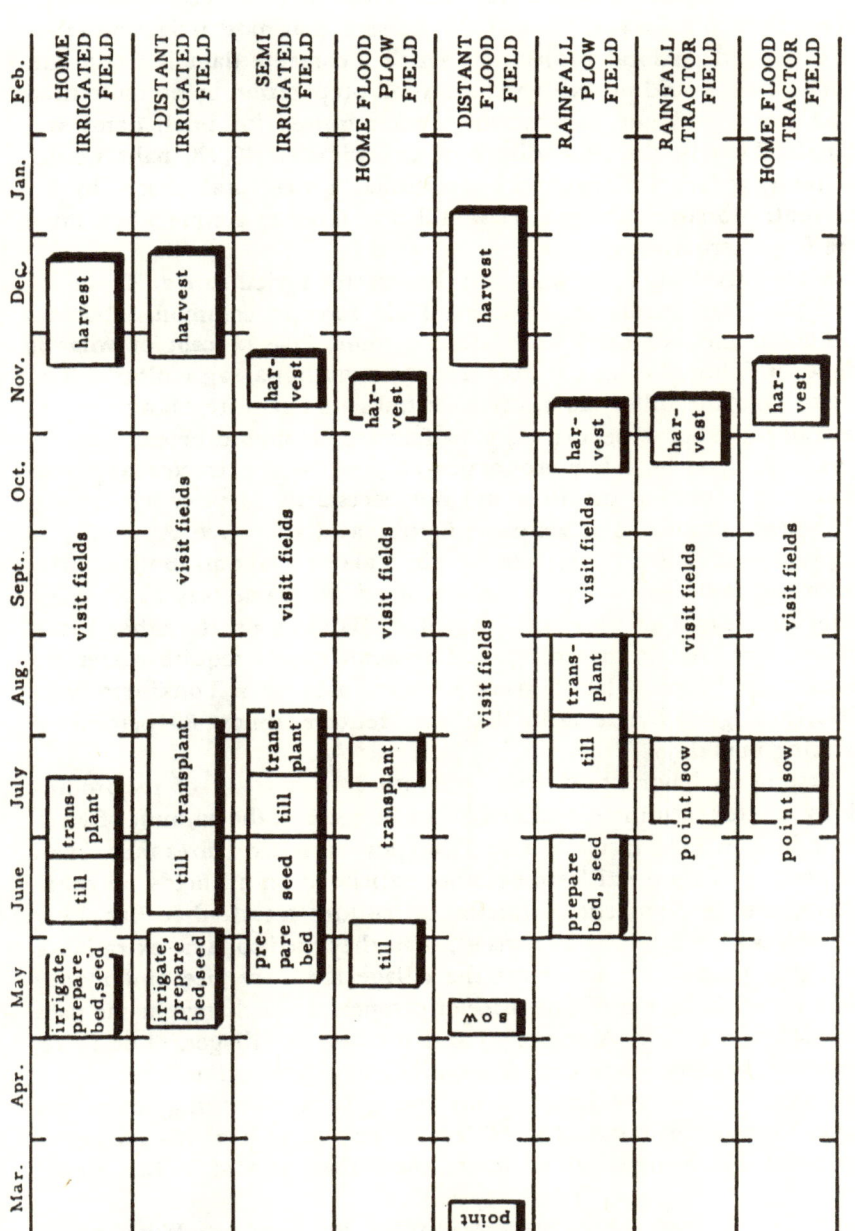

Fig. 9. Annual farming cycle.

that accounts for 13 percent of the man-days.[22] The main argument of the government officials who propose erecting the concrete dam mentioned in chapter iii is the time and labor such a dam would save. From the table, however, it can also be seen that most irrigation labor is expended on local projects to which a concrete dam is irrelevant. Such a dam would probably reduce wood preparation by no more than half and would not decrease the work required for small dams and canals. That is, the expenditure of an estimated 40,000 baht would, at most, reduce Chiengkham's traditional agricultural chores by 3.5 percent. Moreover, the project would save labor at a time when there are few alternative uses for it.

Since harvesting is the only task that tractor agriculture at Thunglor and plow agriculture at the Great Field have in common, labor demands at the two fields are quite different. Five percent of what is done at Thunglor is not required by traditional agriculture. The tractor, on the other hand, obviates tasks that require about 60 percent of the labor expended on plow farming. It should be emphasized, however, that the labor economies effected by the tractor apply to Ban Ping's farming practices and not necessarily to plow agriculture elsewhere. From the incomplete figures available (see App. C), it appears that central Thai farmers (in Nakorn Pathom) budget their labor on land plowed by animals in much the same way as do their compatriots in Ban Ping. In "involuted" Tonkin, on the other hand, painstaking tillage, manuring, and postcultivation require a tremendous expenditure of labor. Were a tractor used on a Tonkinese flood field, it might obviate tasks that now require almost 80 percent of farming man-days.

Despite its labor productivity or, rather, as a result of its productivity, tractor farming has caused a vast increase in the amount of work done by Ban Ping farmers. The Thunglor harvest requires more than 35 percent of the total farming labor expended on all fields. In other words, the development of tractor agriculture means that Ban Ping farmers work harder, by 35 percent, than they used to. The extra labor is highly productive and earns the village far more rice and money than it ever had before. One price of prosperity is a change in the pace of work and of life. A respected and prosperous villager, close to retirement, acknowledges the community's new wealth but laments the fact that "life is now frentic, with young people running to harvest here, running to harvest there." The objective basis of his lament is apparent, for, as figure 10 indicates, more than a third of Ban Ping's

---

[22] In his preliminary report about a small village near Chiengmai, Wijeyewardene (1965:258 f.) estimates that irrigation takes each farmer twenty to thirty days each season, and concludes that "the maintenance of the irrigation system is one of the major tasks, if not *the* major task, in the agricultural cycle."

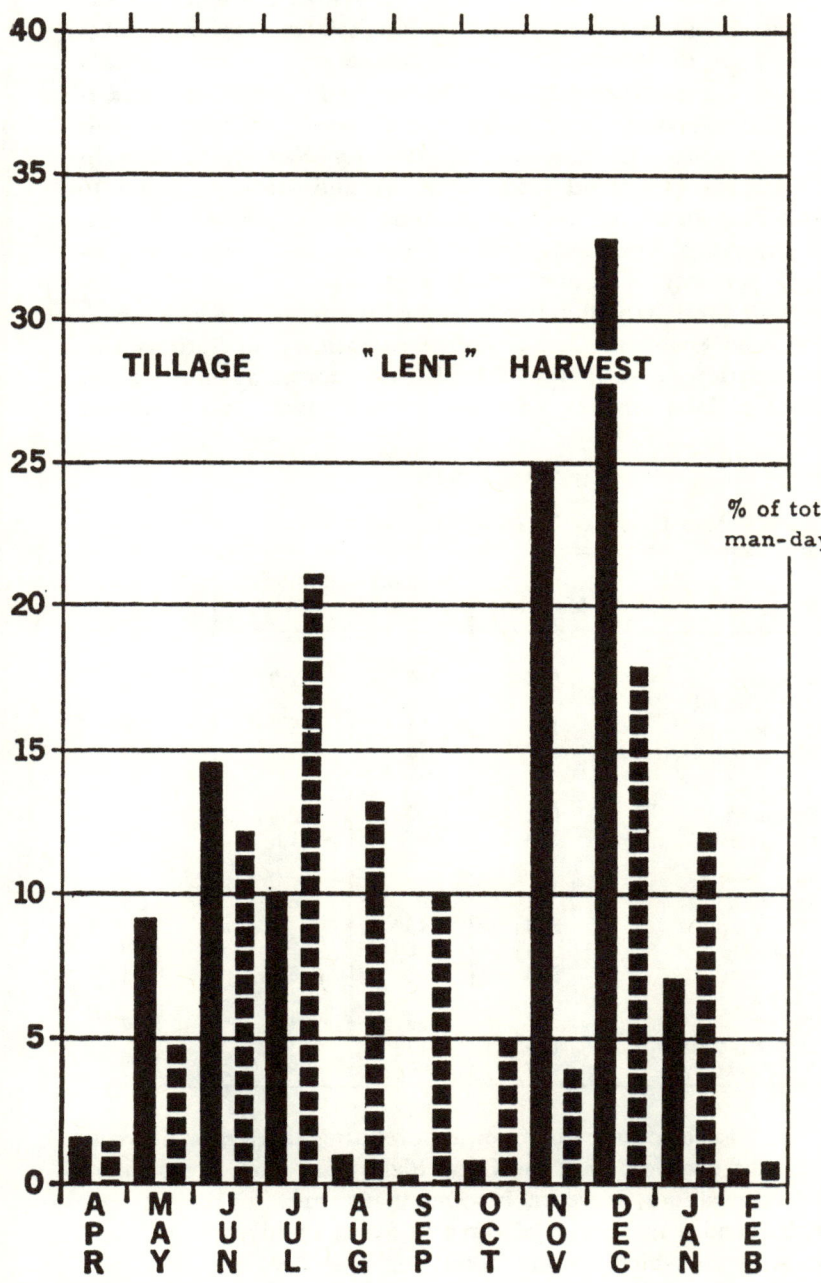

Fig. 10. Seasonal labor use in Ban Ping and in central Thailand. Solid bars represent percentages of total man-days (7,640) expended by farms sampled in Ban Ping. Broken bars represent percentages of total man-days expended by an "average" central Thai farming family (Thailand 1959. table 10).

farm work is now crowded into the busy harvest of November; more than 60 percent (62.5 percent) of Ban Ping's farm work now takes place during the three-month harvest season. Since this schedule is a direct result of tractor farming, in which the only significant work is the harvest, it is reasonable to suppose that Ban Ping's former labor schedule was rather like the one reported for Nakorn Pathom in central Thailand (Thailand 1959: table 44) and shown in figure 10 In Nakorn Pathom no month requires more than one-fifth (22.0 percent) of the year's total labor, and the harvest takes less than one-third (29.5 percent) of annual family man-days.

Previous chapters have indicated some of the ways in which physical, social, and economic factors influence farming operations and labor mobilization on each type of field. These forces obviously affect the amount of labor required for agricultural tasks. At the distant

TABLE 20

MAN-DAYS PER TASK ON DIFFERENT FIELDS

Task and field	Man-days	Number of rai	Man-days per rai	Man-days per hectare
Tillage				
Home irrigated	566	197	2.9	18.1
Home rainfall and home flood	137	51	2.7	16.9
Distant irrigated	307	73	4.2	26.2
Transplanting				
Home irrigated	684	197	2.1	13.1
Distant irrigated	118	66	1.8	11.3
Harvesting				
Home irrigated	1,311	197	6.7	41.8
Home rainfall, plow	208 ⎱	45 ⎱	4.8	30.0
Home flood, plow	44 ⎰	8 ⎰		
Distant irrigated	545	83	6.6	41.3
Distant flood (Thunglor)	2,697	559	4.8	30.0
Home rainfall, tractor	176 ⎱	17 ⎱	8.8	56.0
Home flood, tractor	47 ⎰	8 ⎰		

irrigated field, for example, the main dam requires three days of work rather than the two needed at the Great Field main dam. From interviews and observations, however, it seems that farmers of distant irrigated fields spend a maximum of three to five man-days on the local irrigation projects which require about ten man-days on the Great Field. At the distant irrigated field, then, net irrigation labor is reduced by half. On the home flood and rainfall fields, where plow farming is also practiced, irrigation, of course, takes no time at all.

The relative difficulty of plowing and harrowing also varies from field to field. The estimate made by villagers, that it takes a day of labor to plow a rai of field, seems to be conventional in Thailand (Kaufman 1960:64). According to the sample, the mean tillage time on the home irrigated (Great Field) was close to three days per rai and at the distant irrigated field it took four days. Since tillage involves numerous postplowing operations (see chap. iii), the conventional estimate of one rai plowed in a day may be rather accurate.

When local conditions require the farmer to plow on dry land, tillage becomes more difficult and time consuming. Some Ban Ping households, none of them in the sample, use animals to plow the still-dry home flood field before broadcasting seed there. One hard-working farmer was observed to take a full day to dry-plow one-quarter of a *rai*.

The number of man-days it takes to transplant on the home and distant irrigated fields is approximately equal. Nevertheless, the task is more arduous at the distant field because work parties are smaller and, consequently, more man-days must be provided by the farmer himself. The same situation prevails at harvest time. At the Great Field, just as at the distant irrigated field, it takes about six and one-half man-days to harvest a rai. The distant field, however, is not completely cleared and this, together with its partially voluntary (see chap. vi) shortage of extrahousehold labor, makes the harvest there a time-consuming and somewhat inefficient task. On the home fields, households are aided by large groups of workers and so can reap about an acre (1.08 acre) each day. On the distant irrigated field, it takes a household and its few helpers three days to reap a single acre.

It was found that villagers exaggerated the differences between yields from plow and those from tractor farming. When they speak of the productivity of labor at Thunglor, on the other hand, they do not exaggerate. Sample households farmed 197 rai of Great Field with an expenditure of 3,118 man-days; it took 2,823 man-days to farm 559 rai at Thunglor. Traditional plow farming thus required 15.8 man-days per rai (98.5 per ha), while tractor farming required only about one-third as much.

Productivity, as I have been using the term, refers to a relationship between labor expended and rice gained. Table 21 records the productivity of all fields farmed by Ban Ping except for the home flood field, which was cultivated by only two farmers in the sample. Although a Thunglor farm requires only one-third as much labor as one at the Great Field, each workday at Thunglor produces two and a half times as much rice. Even forest farms are almost 50 percent more productive than Ban Ping's most fertile animal-plowed land, the distant irrigated field. A further, and surpassing, advantage of tractor agriculture is that its product is a clear addition to village farming. Carabao were ineffective at Thunglor and, ideally, the tractor is used on the rainfall field only when there is insufficient water for plowing. In terms of total product, the only disadvantage of tractor agriculture is that it has encouraged the planting of lower-yielding varieties of rice at home.

TABLE 21

MEAN LABOR PRODUCTIVITY BY FIELD

Field	Task	Man-days	Harvest in hap	Hap per man-day	Kilograms per man-day
Home irrigated	All	3,118	4,442	1.41	31.0
Distant flood, virgin	Harvest	232			
	Other	19	690	2.75	60.5
Distant flood, established	All	2,572	9,056	3.50	77.0
Distant irrigated	Wood prep.	35			
	Irrigation	49			
	Seeding	7			
	Seedbed and tillage	307			
	Transplant	118			
	Harvest	545	2,152 [a]	2.03	14.7
Home rainfall, tractor	Harvest	176			
	Other	5	200	1.10	24.2
Home rainfall, plow	Tillage	113			
	Seeding	11			
	Transplant	90			
	Harvest	208	485	1.15	25.3
All plowed fields [b]		4,694	7,215	1.54	33.9
All tractor fields [b]		3,051	10,046	3.32	73.0

[a] The actual harvest from the distant irrigated farms sampled was 2,285 hap. The figure has been reduced here to compensate for the failure of two respondents to report on man-days spent in tillage and transplanting.
[b] Includes home flood field.

Dividend.—In most transactions—whether among villagers, with outsiders, or with the supernatural—cash and rice can be substituted for each other. When substituted for factors of production, they affect the cost and returns of farming. Although cash and rice are useful in production only because farming occurs within a larger economic system which permits them to be exchanged for other goods and for each other, the present inquiry does not extend into where the villager gets his money or how he spends it, other than for production. "Dividend" refers to the relationship between the amount of cash (or its rice equivalent) villagers expend for farming and the amount of rice they receive from farming. Since this relationship can be expressed by means of tables, it is not discussed at a length commensurate with its importance.

The preceding section demonstrates the high labor productivity of Thunglor. Tractor agriculture is productive because it requires neither transplanting nor plowing by animals. The first convenience, as was seen earlier, results in somewhat lower yields. The second convenience certainly results in higher costs. Villagers say that "Thunglor fields are money fields." We shall now learn what that money bought.

The payment of tractor fees is the first occasion on which the villager substitutes cash for labor.[23] When the villager speaks of "money fields" it is to these fees that he refers. Table 22 records them, along with the amounts of land plowed and rice harvested.

TABLE 22

Tractor Fees as a Cost of Production

Field	Rai	Harvest in hap	Fee in baht	Cost in baht per rai	Cost in baht per hap
Thunglor, "forest"	86	690	4,850	56.50	7.05
Thunglor, established	473	9,056	10,080	21.50	1.12
Rainfall	14 [a]	160 [a]	305	21.50	1.88

[a] Reduced because one household did not report its tractor fee.

Plowing is not the only cash cost at Thunglor, for carters must also be hired. In 1960 the usual cartage fee was 7 baht for each 10 hap carried (see App. B). This and other cash costs are recorded in Table 23.

Table 23 indicates that villagers are clearly correct in their claim that even the poorest man can farm by plow. Plow farming, including the relatively expensive operation of the distant irrigated field, costs less than one-quarter as much per rai and less than one-sixth as much per hap as tractor farming. Before Thunglor was farmed, plow agriculture need have cost no cash at all. Cash payments in plow agriculture have developed concurrently with tractor agriculture and, to a large extent, are dependent upon the competition of tractor agriculture.

Services that can be bought with cash can also be bought with rice. Households sometimes give rice in return for tillage-season labor on the Great Field. Five households in the sample did so, at a total cost of 170 hap. A large amount of rice is also expended for tillage-season labor at the distant irrigated field and for the harvest at other fields.

[23] This analysis excludes unusual expenditures, like those made by one man for seed rice and tree felling or those made by a household, not in the sample, for extra seedlings at the distant irrigated field.

TABLE 23
Cash Cost of Farming in Ban Ping

Field	Rai	Harvest in hap	Cost in baht	Baht per rai	Baht per hap
1. Home irrigated	197	4,442	731.50	3.75	.16
2. Distant irrigated	83	2,285	1,598.00	19.20	.70
3. Distant flood, established	473	9,056	15,549.60	33.00	1.72
4. Distant flood, virgin	86	690	5,264.00	61.00	7.65
5. Irrigated (lines 1 and 2)	280	6,727	2,329.50	8.32	.35
6. Thunglor (lines 3 and 4)	559	9,746	20,813.60	37.25	2.13

Table 24 records how much rice the sample households spent for labor. Payments made for work on more than one field have been prorated according to the number of days spent on each field.[24]

TABLE 24
Rice Paid for Labor

Field	Harvest in hap	Pay in hap	Net harvest	Percentage of harvest paid to laborers
Home irrigated	4,442	228	4,214	5.0
Distant irrigated	2,285	118	2,167	5.2
Thunglor, established	9,389 [a]	320	9,069	3.5

[a] Includes rice headman received from school principal (see chap. vi).

NET APPARENT ADVANTAGE

The first part of this chapter was concerned with farming information available to villagers; the second with survey data available to me. We shall now attempt to reconcile the two.

Information available to villagers.[25]—Of all the criteria by which villagers evaluate their fields, comparative yield is the most important. Yet, as has been indicated, there is often surprisingly little difference

[24] Rice can buy land as well as labor. Sampled households farmed ten of the fourteen Great Field plots (see table 8) rented within Ban Ping in 1960. For these plots they paid 337 hap as rental, thus reducing the gross sampled Great Field harvest (of 4,442 hap) by 7.6 percent.

[25] As I failed to ask farmers how they obtained their information, this section is based on observation of what villagers say to one another, but also, to some extent, on guesswork.

among the mean yields of various fields and farming systems. This raises two questions: How can villagers make a clear-cut choice on the basis of yields that differ little from each other? Why did villagers express themselves in such a way as to make me anticipate there being greater differences among yields than actually exist? An obvious, although partial, answer to the second question is that I took too literally the casual conventions of village speech, of which the most important here is that transplanting yields 40 hap per rai and broadcasting only 20. Before considering the ways in which Ban Ping farmers seem to collect and evaluate information about relative yields, let us briefly consider some of the ways in which they formulate relevant quantitative statements.

The comparison that villagers express most often concerns height of plant at harvest. The conventional units are knee high, waist high, shoulder level, and over one's head. The usual assumption is: the better the soil, the higher the plant and the larger the yield. Occasionally it is said of rare specific fields, rice varieties, or techniques that great height is the result of fast growth, which produces empty heads and consequent small yields.

Older farmers, when they evaluate fields, sometimes compare the ratio of seed to harvest, a convention that is usual among Yuan swidden farmers in Nan (Judd 1964:63-64). Thus, one is told that long ago Ban Ping farmers stopped growing dry rice because "a bung of seed produced only 20 bung of rice, while in the mountains of Myang Khawp two bung of seed make 100 to 200 bung." Or a traditional account of agriculture may refer to how much wood must be brought to the dam for each basket of rice a farmer drills into his seedbed. Conventionally, villagers consider that fields require about one bung of seed for each rai farmed. Thus the ratio of seed to harvest is probably no more than an expression of yield per unit area made by men whose fields, whether cleared or inherited, have never been measured accurately for government registration. Although the ratio of seed to harvest is essentially an expression of yield, it has intrinsic interest for two reasons. First, villagers speak of this ratio fairly frequently and read of it in their farmers' almanacs. To emphasize how disappointed he was at the harvest from his virgin fields at Thunglor, the headman pointed out that he had sowed more rice than he harvested. The ratio of seed to harvest is also used in village metaphor, as in the words of the village sage: "We make offerings [to the priests] in order to gain merit to get things in the next life. It's not as some people think, that for each 50 cents offered one gets 50 cents in return. It's like planting the seedbed. One gets far more than one gives."

A second reason for interest in the ratio of seed to harvest is that the ratio might be used to record comparable information from the numerous places where, for reasons as varied as taboo and topography, it is difficult to measure land areas with any accuracy. Among the Iban of Borneo, for example, Freeman (1955:95) found a dry-farming ratio of seed to harvest of 1:60. Since this figure was based on a single plot, and one "well above the normal average for an Iban farm," the ratio must not be taken as representative of dry farming. In Nan, Judd (1964:63–64) reports swidden ratios between 1:14 and 1:44, with an average of 1:31. In Ban Ping the ratios of seed to rice harvested are 1:40 for broadcasting on developed land, 1:38 on Great Field and semi-irrigated land, and 1:127 at the distant irrigated field. I list them in order to elicit comparable figures from other students of rice farming. Although Freeman's ratio is admittedly unrepresentative and Judd's wide-ranging, comparing them to Ban Ping's ratios does make one suspicious of the easy assumption that the cultivation of inundated rice always produces higher yields than swidden farming.[26]

In addition to comparing ratios of seed to harvest, villagers sometimes speak of farms in terms of the volume of rice used to seed them. In doing this, they rarely state (but one must assume that they know) the ratio of seed to area and never formulate it as a quotient. Nevertheless, determining the amount of rice seeded per unit area of field permits verification of the villagers' observation that transplanting is far denser at the Great Field than at the distant irrigated field; provides a further, indirect check on yields from broadcasting; and furnishes a rough index of the comparative success (see App. C) of farming in Ban Ping.

The farmers of Ban Ping use 1.25 bung of seed for each rai of Great Field land and less than half a bung (0.44) on the distant irrigated field. On Thunglor, villagers use 1 bung per rai.[27] Broadcasting, commonly assumed to require more seed than transplanting, requires less seed than is used on the Great Field. Further evidence of the comparative infertility of the Great Field is furnished by the lower rate of seeding required by the distant irrigated field. My computation of 0.50 bung versus 1.50 bung confirms the villagers' estimate that transplanting is about two and a half times denser at the Great Field than it is at the distant irrigated field. Villagers interpret this difference as a sign of soil fertility. Western specialists would probably agree with this interpretation; as Grist (1959:120) points out, "The quantity of seed required to transplant an acre varies, rich land requiring fewer seedlings per 'hill' and wider spacing than poorer land."

We may now return to considering how villagers seem to collect the

[26] In addition, the ratios illustrate the comparative fertility of the distant irrigated field whose ratio of 1:127 is far better than that of 1:50 suggested by Rajadhon (1961:28) for good yields of transplanted rice in Thailand.

[27] It is likely that the broadcasting ratio of 1 bung to 1 rai has been distorted by the ideal of "answer easy, easy." Those who were observed sowing at Thunglor broadcast about 20 percent less than this ratio.

CHOICE IN FARMING

"hard" information about comparative yields upon which they base their technological decisions. These yields differ from those that produced table 16 in at least three ways. A villager does not accurately calculate his own yield or randomly sample the yields of his fellows; nor does he compute a mean yield for each type of farm. Rather, he makes a rough reckoning and comparison of the yields obtained from the various farms he himself cultivates, and may also do the same with the yields of a few friends and neighbors. Insofar as this procedure can be likened to any statistic, it is more like comparing frequency distributions than it is like comparing means. A comparison of frequency distributions exaggerates differences among mean yields and so corresponds more closely to the estimates made by villagers and to the ideal technological choices described in the first part of this chapter.

TABLE 25

YIELDS IN HAP PER RAI OBTAINED BY HOUSEHOLDS
FARMING BOTH GREAT FIELD AND THUNGLOR

	1959 yields		1960 yields	
Household	Great Field	Thunglor	Great Field	Thunglor
A	17.2 [a]	14.0	18.5 [a]	17.5
B	21.3	20.0	23.0	20.0
C	20.5	28.0	26.5	21.7 [b]
D	39.5	16.8	31.0	22.0
E			37.5	17.0
F	32.5	16.3 [b]	28.0	18.1 [b]
G	45.0	14.9 [b]	40.0	15.8 [b]
H			24.0	17.2
I	33.4 [a]	17.1 [b]	36.0 [a]	19.0 [b]
J			25.5 [a]	22.0
K	20.0	17.5 [b]	20.0	16.5 [a]
L			17.2	18.5
M			20.0	20.0
Mean	28.7	18.1	26.7	18.9

[a] Average of three plots.
[b] Average of two plots.

The main datum for understanding these comparisons is the likelihood that a farmer will learn about a field of one type which produced a yield markedly different from that produced by some field of another type about which he also knows. The comparison which it is most reasonable to suppose a villager will make (and the comparison observed most frequently) is among plots that he himself farms. It will be recalled that 75 percent of those who farm Thunglor will be able to make such comparisons.

Table 25 lists the yields obtained by sample households that farmed both Thunglor and the Great Field in years for which I have data. Of thirteen such households in 1960, eleven obtained superior yields at the home irrigated field and only one obtained a superior yield at Thunglor. The mean yields obtained on the two fields differ by a ratio of about 7:5, a far greater difference than between the mean harvests of the two fields for the entire sample. In an absolute sense, this difference is quite large for matched dependent samples. Since the same households are involved in each comparison, variables other than soil quality and farming technique have probably been eliminated. For 1959, as well, the means of these matched dependent samples differ far more widely (by a ratio of about 5:8) than do those of the total sam-

TABLE 26

CUMULATIVE DISTRIBUTIONS AND COMPARISONS OF GREAT FIELD AND THUNGLOR YIELDS

Yield in hap per rai	Thunglor			Great Field	
	Number of farms	Cumulative percentages of farms		Number of farms	Cumulative percentages of farms
12–13	4	100	11	5	100	17
14–15	5	89	26	1	83	21
16–17	2	75	32	1	80	24
18–19	7	69	60	1	76	28
	[D] ᵃ					
20–21	6	49	69	4	73	42
		[B]				
22–23	8	32	92	4	59	55
	[C]			ᵃ		
24–25	2	8.6	98	3	45	66
26–27	1	3	100	1	35	69
	[A]					
28–29	–			3	31	80
30–31	–			2	21	88
32–39	–			1	14	90
40	–			3	10	100

ᵃ Median.

KEY:

[A] Thirty-one percent of Great Field farmers will hear of no Thunglor farms that produced a yield superior to the one they obtained from the Great Field.

[B] Almost all (92 percent) Thunglor farmers will discover that well above half (59 percent) of the Great Field farms they hear about produced a yield superior to the one they obtained from Thunglor.

[C] For about half of those who farm on the Great Field, the probability of learning about superior plots at Thunglor in only .086.

[D] For the corresponding half of those who farm at Thunglor, the probability of learning about superior plots at the Great Field is .73.

ple. Although only eight households are represented in 1959, they are of interest because comparative yields in 1959 presumably influenced 1960 farming decisions.

In addition to comparing the yields obtained from his own farms, the villager inquires about the farms of those about him. It is reasonable to suppose that the sum of such inquiries is fairly random with respect to the frequency distribution of yields. If the percentage of

TABLE 27

FREQUENCY DISTRIBUTIONS OF YIELDS, 1960

Yield in hap per rai	Tractor broadcast Fields				Animal-plowed transplanted Fields				
	DF	HR	HF	Total	HI and SI	DI	HF	HR	Total
6–11	–	2	–	2	–	–	–	6	6
12–13	4	1	1	6	5	–	–	2	7
14–15	5	–	–	5	1	1	–	1	3
16–17	2	1	–	3	1	–	1	1	3
18–19	7	–	–	7	1	1	–	–	2
20–21	6	1	–	7	4	–	–	–	4
22–23	8	–	–	8	4	–	–	–	4
24–25	2	–	–	2	3	1	–	1	5
26–27	1	–	–	1	1	1	–	–	2
28–29					3	–	–	–	3
30–31					2	1	–	–	3
32–39					1	2	–	–	3
40					3	–	–	–	3

NOTE: DF = distant flood (Thunglor); HR = home rainfall; HF = home flood; HI and SI = home irrigated (Great Field) and semi-irrigated; DI = distant irrigated.

Great Field plots with high yields exceeds the percentage of Thunglor plots with high yields, there is a greater probability that Thunglor farmers will come to believe that Great Field farms are superior than that Great Field farmers will come to believe that Thunglor farms are superior. Table 26 indicates that the distribution of yields obtained from the two fields in 1960 would support the villagers' conviction that the Great Field is superior to Thunglor. (See the numbered comparisons, indicated by broken horizontal lines, in the table.) Table 26 is unusual in form and, I fear, rather difficult to read. I must beg the reader's indulgence on the grounds that, as far as I know, it is one of the first attempts systematically to compare quantitative information available to natives with the corresponding data available to the ethnographer. Table 27, which presents the frequency distributions of yields obtained from all transplanted and all broadcast fields sampled in 1960, shows that a fourth ($12/48$) of those who transplanted on any field would find that their yields are better than those obtained by anyone who broadcast. The convention that transplanting produces twice as much rice as broadcasting also appears more reasonable in the light of comparative frequency distributions than it does from the ratio of 14:13 for the mean yields of these two techniques. Table 27 shows that it is possible to get 40 hap per rai from the home irrigated field and that 10 percent do so. It is common (69 percent of Thunglor plots in 1960) to get only 21 hap per rai, or less, at Thunglor. Since no broadcast field yielded more than 27 hap per rai, only those transplanting farmers whose plots yielded less than 14 hap would be able to discover a broadcast field with a yield twice as good as theirs. Since no transplanted field yielded more than 42 hap, all broadcasting farmers whose plots yielded less than 21 hap would be able to discover a transplanted field with yields twice as good as theirs. From table 27 it can be seen that about a fourth (27 percent) of transplanting farmers might discover broadcast fields that double their yield, while fully half (51.5 percent) of the broadcast farmers might learn of transplanted plots that produced twice as much rice as theirs did. The matched dependent samples in table 25 suggest similar conclusions. In 1960, two farmers doubled their broadcast yield at the home irrigated field. In 1959, four farmers (half of the very small sample) had done so. In neither year did any farmer double his transplanted yield at Thunglor. Once comparisons like those made in table 26 have prejudiced the villager in favor of the Great Field, it is not surprising for him to claim that 20 versus 40 is the usual ratio of yields between the two fields. It must also be borne in mind that villagers, although aware that forest farms do not indicate the true potential of a Thunglor plot, probably are further prejudiced against Thunglor because of the forest farms they cultivate or hear about.

It seems plausible that comparisons like those for which tables 25–27 have been used, rather than comparisons of mean yields, influence a villager's decision of how and where to farm and color his estimates of differential soil fertility. The primary purpose of these tables is to suggest what villagers themselves are likely to know about the yields of farming in Ban Ping. Regardless of the accuracy of my specific model, I am convinced that one can judge the reasonableness of native technological decisions only if he is aware of how natives collect information and of what kinds of data are available to them.

We have already seen (tables 19–21) that my statistics confirm the villagers' judgment that tractor farming requires much less work than plow farming. Just as in comparing yields, however, they probably perceive a larger difference than the one I measured. Two factors affect the villagers' belief that tractor farming is so easy: the pleasantness of the tasks and the incidence of hired labor at Thunglor. When villagers complain, as they often do, about the difficulty of plow agriculture, their complaints are almost invariably directed at the tillage and local irrigation tasks which together account for only one-quarter of Great Field labor. They never complain about harvesting and rarely about transplanting, although these chores together account for about 45 percent of man-days. Harvesting and transplanting require far more work, but they are "lots of people, lots of fun." The ease of Thunglor farming is accentuated for villagers because almost all labor (95 percent) there occurs at the harvest. For the village farmer, apparent differences in productivity are even greater because many of the Thunglor man-days are not his own, but hired. Sample households who farmed the Great Field hired 93 days of harvesting labor and 204 man-days of transplanting labor. Except for 124 days of tillage labor, all other Great Field work was performed by household members, either on their own field or in reciprocating those who came to *term*. Farmers themselves thus had to work 14.3 days on each rai of home irrigated field. At Thunglor, sample operators hired 549 man-days of harvest labor, thus reducing their own work to 4.1 man-days per rai.

There is no need to reconcile our external view of dividends with the villagers' except to repeat that, as may be typical of peasants (cf. Epstein 1962:222), they regard cash as an independent and scarce factor of production. It should perhaps be pointed out, as well, that the tractor fees recorded in table 22 are the cash prices reported by respondents, although (see chap. iv) farmers who cannot give cash in advance often pay more. In 1960 credit was actually quite cheap, for the postharvest price of rice was extroardinarily low. At about 5 baht per hap, it was the same as tractor owners had credited for "green rice" months earlier. The low price was a hardship for everyone, but especially for those who owed money or who were owed rice. Its main technological significance is that for many months the harvest from Thunglor forest farms was worth less than it had cost to have the fields plowed. This is not as unprofitable as it might seem, since by plowing a forest farm the villager obtains land as well as rice (cf. Epstein 1962:60).

Relative advantages of various fields.—Costs in cash and rice slightly alter the returns from farming presented previously. In table 28, rice costs have been deducted from gross harvests and hired labor from gross man-days in order to compute the net apparent advantages of various fields.

We can now summarize Ban Ping's major farming alternatives and their implications. Although some higher plots are still being expanded slightly by clearing new forest seedbeds, the ownership of home irrigated land depends on having bought it or inherited it. Villagers generally think of themselves as farmers and, indeed; operate farms unless they lack some factor of production. An owner of home irrigated land farms it if household labor, or the labor of nonresident children, is available to him. If such labor is available but insufficient, he obtains a tillage-season worker, preferably through giving a gift to a "son," less preferably by paying a wage to a stranger. Otherwise, he rents his Great Field land to someone with a household labor supply, but no land of his own, or to someone who is farming a contiguous plot.

The location and height of a Great Field plot influence seedbed cultivation, rice type, tillage technique, and other details already

TABLE 28

NET APPARENT ADVANTAGES OF VARIOUS FIELDS

Field	Net yield in hap per rai	Net productivity in hap per man-day	Net cost in baht per hap
Home irrigated	19.6	1.44	0.19
Home rainfall, plow	10.8	1.15	Nil
Distant irrigated	26.2	2.35	0.74
Home rainfall, tractor	11.8	1.16	1.88
Distant flood, established	18.5	4.33	1.77
Distant flood, virgin	8.0	2.75	7.65

sufficiently described for our purposes (see chap. iii). In the present context, we need remember only that the Great Field is regarded by villagers as preferable to and compatible with Thunglor. Its cultivation, however, conflicts with the distant irrigated field whose farms are larger, less dependable, and farther from the comforts of the village with its helping kinsmen. That is, for the apparently higher yields of the untamed distant irrigated field, villagers must leave their relatives, work harder, spend more, and risk uncertain harvests.

Within the narrow range of economic possibilities available to villagers, it is only a slight exaggeration to regard distant field farming as adventurous in spirit and entrepreneurial in motive, while Great Field farming is conservative and subsistence minded. While these implications are imputed, choice itself is not, since Great Field land is freely acquired, maintained, or alienated by purchase and sale. In 1960 a few ambitious villagers of early middle age were selling their inherited Great Field farms in order to buy distant irrigated land. The buyers were the landless from other villages or older men who wanted home irrigated land so that its rental would guarantee their independence when they were no longer able to manage a farm and their children had left them.

One can usually acquire distant irrigated land only by purchase. One farms such land if, and only if, one owns it. Aside from trying to minimize cash expenses (e.g., transplant and reap in small parties), techniques of cultivation (e.g., use of roller, seeding style) are set by one's understanding of microenvironmental requirements. The decision to purchase distant irrigated land in the first place, however, was influenced by whether one already owned land at Thunglor, for the fields are fairly close to each other and both were discovered and developed by adventurous young men. By 1960 the distant irrigated field had demonstrated its relative dependability, high yield, and low cost. Since, also by 1960, any Thunglor plot, even a forest farm, was salable, the distant irrigated field had, in a limited and nonexclusive way, become an alternative to Thunglor. Some men in their thirties and early forties had begun to sell small parcels at Thunglor to still-younger men, and to use the proceeds for expanding their holdings at the distant irrigated field. There was thus a tendency for Thunglor to remain young man's land, for the distant irrigated fields to belong to middle-aged men, and for the Great Field to stay with the aged.

However much they may complain about the high costs and low yields, those who farm at Thunglor have no choice but to hire tractors and to broadcast. Although, by commenting upon the comparative ease of farming there, villagers show that they recognize Thunglor's labor productivity, we must not presume that they interpret this productivity as an agricultural economist might. First, for the village as a whole and for most individuals who farm there (since they also farm other fields), Thunglor represents a net addition to labor expended in farming. Old men comment on how frenetic the pace of work has become; young men take pride in their ability to farm many types of field. The tractor, although a laborsaving device from the macroeconomic perspective, supports Boserup's suggestion (1965:53) that "we may view the changes in agricultural employment brought about by population growth and intensification of land use in a given region as a gradual lengthening of working hours in agriculture." The villagers' willingness to work harder, however, is more a matter of Lue pride in hard work and self-sufficiency and of the incentives furnished by the institutions of "selling rice" and private (*lork*) land than it is a direct response to "the compulsion of increasing population or the compulsion of a social hierarchy" (*ibid.*, p. 54).

Second, the villagers' evaluation of labor productivity is more subjective than ours. Table 28 indicates that use of the tractor on home rainfall land made for no significant increase in labor productivity, largely because its harvest was so inefficient (see table 21). Villagers, however, seemed unaware of this inefficiency, probably because it results from the home rainfall harvest being pleasant (see chap. vi) and so enlisting more labor than it requires.[28] This inefficiency may, in fact, mislead the villager because he does not compute productivity

---

[28] A further reason for inefficiency in 1960 was the unusual harvest-season rains which made it difficult to thresh and winnow the somewhat sprouted three-month rice of the rainfall field.

in man-days per hap. Instead, he remembers the arduous task of tillage and the painstaking work of transplanting, and compares this hard work with the joy of harvesting. If he rejects the tractor at the rainfall field it is not because he recognizes that the tractor fails to make farming more productive, but because he considers its apparent productivity not worth its cash price. Since the Lue villager takes pride in working hard and spending little, leisure has little allure for him unless it offers alternative employment. At the time of tilling and transplanting the home rainfall field, there is little profit in leisure, and those who now find tractor farming most appealing are often traders. Unless the economy of Chiengkham develops lucrative alternatives to farming, it is likely that few villagers who are not also traders will use the tractors on the rainfall field in order to take advantage of its illusory productivity. Owners of home rainfall land may let it lie fallow, plow it, or hire a tractor. (Rental is not a possibility for them so long as the far more productive Great Field is available.[29]) Those who plowed rainfall field in 1960 said that they might hire a tractor if its yields were good. Although yields from tractor agriculture were only slightly less than those obtained by animal plowing and transplanting, it is unlikely that many more villagers will begin to hire tractors for the home rainfall field. Tractor farming is much more expensive; cash is scarce in Ban Ping and highly prized. Its expenditure on the home rainfall field resulted in no increase in yields. The compelling advantage of the tractor at home is that it might permit the rainfall or flood field to be cultivated when the monsoon is insufficient, too late, or too unpredictable for plow farming (see chap. iv). Should the demands of distant fields become more constraining, it is also possible that use of the tractor on the home fields might be recommended because the tractor permits owners of home rainfall and home flood fields to add (or maintain) distant fields in their operations.

These observations suggest the third, and most important, way in which the villagers' notion of tractor productivity differs from our own. At Thunglor, and wherever the tractor is used, its contribution is the clearing and maintaining of land uncultivable without it. In the villager's view, labor productivity is epiphenomenal to this benefit; for the use of Thunglor land he is willing to sacrifice the lower cash costs, the higher yields, and the greater personal autonomy he associates with plow farming.

[29] For an individual renter, the difference in net productivity between the two fields would be .16 hap per man-day, assuming a rental of two-fifths of the crop and assuming that the renter has a sufficient labor force to obviate hiring tillers and harvesters (see table 21).

VIII.
Change in Farming

Change and economic development.—When I returned to Ban Ping in July 1965 after an absence of more than four years, villagers were no longer using tractors or broadcasting at Thunglor. It would be false to say that I had predicted this change, and dishonest not to confess that it surprised me. To the villagers, however, it was neither striking nor surprising. It was hardly a change at all. The perceptions, understandings, rules, and criteria that constitute a culture are generative not only of the present behavior of its members, but also of the kinds of actions they are likely to take should their culturally significant environment change. Insofar as truly understanding a culture implies being no more surprised than its members by what that culture becomes (cf. Goodenough 1957:168), my understanding of Ban Ping was a faulty one.

In response to my questions, farmers pointed out that they no longer needed the tractor because flooding was no longer a danger; all of Thunglor had been cleared and leveled. The villagers had always regarded broadcasting as a source of reduced yields and the tractor as an uncomfortable expense, so they dispensed with both as soon as the altered physical environment permitted them to. This reversion to traditional farming, more than any other single fact, convinces me of the practical importance of understanding the native's perception and cognition of his technological system. If we insist on viewing the tractor solely as a laborsaving device, reversion to the plow seems incredible. Had I paid due attention to the villagers' view of the tractor, I might have thought to wonder whether the tractor would be used once all land had been cleared and claimed; I might have asked agronomists if there was any chance that clearing and leveling the Ing plain might diminish flooding and thereby eliminate the villagers' main incentive for using tractors.

A culture consists not of customs and artifacts, but of the criteria, and rules for their application, which account for the native's ability to produce, recognize, and interpret culturally appropriate behavior. The tractor, to Western eyes a dramatic innovation in itself and significant as a cause of productivity, was to the Lue apparently little more than a larger ax for clearing land and a stronger carabao for tilling it. In accepting the tractor and evaluating its effectiveness, most farmers in Ban Ping employed criteria no different from any they had used before. When by those traditional standards—and because the physical environment had altered—the tractor was no longer worth its cost in cash, yields, and autonomy, it was no longer used except by a few people whose standards or whose circumstances had changed.

The *kamnan* broadcasts and uses tractors (he owns three) because he farms 730 rai. No villager broadcasts regularly; only one-third use tractors at all, and not even the largest village landowner uses tractors solely because of the size of his holdings.[1] The reasons villagers use tractors have changed somewhat since 1960, and have certainly become more complex. Just as in 1960, the few who still have "forest" land hire a tractor to prepare it for its first farming season. Maj M, and perhaps other landlords, tractor-plows before his tenants use their carabao and transplant because Thunglor tenants are unwilling to rent unless this work is done for them. Some villagers, not all of them owners of large plots, hire tractors to destroy the tough grass roots still found at Thunglor and then use carabao to plow. The largest village landowner (with 50 rai) plans to alternate between tractor/broadcasting and carabao/transplanting farming, depending upon soil and grass conditions and upon the availability of carabao and labor. The new sophistication of his economic reasoning is suggested by his argument: "Although one does get somewhat more rice from transplanting than from broadcasting, those who transplant solely for this reason have not really thought carefully, because hiring workers and carabao for traditional farming really costs more than hiring a tractor."

Schultz (1964:176) insists that agricultural growth depends on employing modern means of production. Boserup (1965), on the other hand, ascribes such growth to intensified use of present resources and longer working hours. To her, Java and Japan, archetypically different as they are to Geertz (1963), are equivalent in that both countries have intensified their farming in response to increased population and have thereby raised their production. What happened in Ban Ping, I think, permits us to reconcile our understanding of Java's increased production with its involution and to suggest a distinction between economic growth and economic change.

No man is immortal, and none spends his entire life locked in unblinking repetition of the same words to the same people. That is, social life is forever in flux; this truth is the source of the social scien-

---

[1] Quantitative information for 1965 is based on an opportunity sample of thirty-three farming households.

tist's difficulty in defining what he means by change. Structural change versus random variations, revolution versus the circulation of elites, role change versus the recruitment of new members—with such essentially undefined contrasts we have attempted to distinguish significant and analyzable social change from the constant flux epitomized in the observation that one never steps into the same river twice. To argue that a major change is one with many consequences and implications often only shifts the argument from the external data to the analyst's ingenuity in handling them. In contrasting two south Indian villages—one of which seems to have increased its production and so developed without changing very much, the other to have altered its economy and so changed without much adding to its overall income— Epstein (1962) argues that not all economic development is economic change. She suggests a distinction between "unilineal change," in which the same old things are done somewhat differently, and "non-unilineal," or real, change. The distinction, as one might suspect, is difficult to apply in any other than *ad hoc* fashion. It is here, I think, that decision-making models, however imperfectly fashioned, have utility, for they permit one to assert that basic cultural change consists of changes in the ways in which people view their activities and, most critically, of changes in the goals for which decisions are made, in the criteria by which they are made, and in the kinds of evidence taken into account in making them. Economic change occurs with the appearance of new standards for making economic decisions and not, as with Ban Ping's tractor, when the outcomes of decisions merely take a modified distribution (cf. Goodenough 1956).

Changes in rules and criteria for decision making are changes in how people view and assess their world. By this standard, there have been changes in Ban Ping's farming since 1960: changes less dramatic than the tractor, but also probably less ephemeral. At least one man claims to calculate tractor fees, his probable incremental yield from transplanting (taking soil conditions into account), and the costs of hiring laborers in deciding how to use his land each year. He, along with some other villagers, now annually plants half his Thunglor land to glutinous rice, half to nonglutinous. Statistically, this practice may represent no increase in the acreage planted to ordinary rice when averaged over a few years. As an economic decision, however, such hedging is a significant change for people who had formerly reserved their anticipated subsistence needs in glutinous rice and then planted only their guaranteed surplus in the variety that had sold better during the preceding year. The reason for the new policy is simple, wise, and frankly commercial: "We cannot tell what the price will be."

Another material change in farming is that many villagers are now willing to use chemical fertilizer on failing seedbed patches; some use it on the entire seedbed, even when the rice is coming up well. It would seem that only members of this latter category have begun to think differently about farming; at least one of them claims to calculate (however imperfectly) whether or not the net gain from using fertilizer is substantially greater than its cost.

Focusing on new standards, and not solely on new behavior, alerts us to the potential durability and generality of the changes we observe. It may also highlight the processes by which new ideas are learned, imitated, and maintained. In 1953 villagers learned to broadcast and to use tractors from private businessmen. Their current interest in fertilizers has a similar source. Although numerous government pronouncements extolled fertilizers and insecticides during 1959–1961, villagers ignored them. For that matter, I do not know of any innovation in production which the villagers of Ban Ping have knowingly received from government officials. What the government suggests is the government's way, the way of "men who eat a monthly salary" and who are not familiar with or sympathetic to village productive considerations. Businessmen painstakingly demonstrate new devices, supply them on a trial basis, and, above all, have a direct and material stake in their success. When the wealthy *kamnan*'s son, fresh from the National University of Agriculture, hires villagers to spread fertilizer on his own fields, and when his fields are sufficiently close for villagers to be able to compare the results with their own and to judge the relevance of the new technique to their own land and styles of farming, fertilizer begins to pertain to "men who works for a livng." Some Lue and Yuan from villages near town copied the *kamnan*'s son. When they observed the poor condition of Maj N's Thunglor seedbed, they recommended fertilizer and told him how to use it and where to buy it. Now Maj N tells those of his neighbors who ask him about fertilizer to use it every year on all of their seedbed regardless of how well the seedlings are doing without it. Other observers of Thai rural life seem to confirm my impression that businessmen and wealthy farmers are usually more effective as agents of agricultural improvements than are government officials. Schultz (1964:174) is probably correct in pointing out that "most farmers in poor agricultural communities are too small and too isolated to undertake a search for new agricultural factors." Such farmers are nonetheless often quite able to appreciate the advantages of the new factors when these are used by larger farmers with whom they can identify, and to understand reasonable recommendations made by salesmen. I do not share Schultz's (*ibid.*, pp. 153–156) pessimism about the unwillingness of profit-seeking firms to disseminate new information to small markets with high entry costs. No one who has seen the extraordinary variety of imported goods available in even the most isolated Thai market or who has witnessed

CHANGE IN FARMING   189

the elaborate efforts made to sell tiny packets of patent medicine can doubt the strong pull exerted by even the lowest profit margins. Merchants and firms in Thailand seem to have adapted to the small market for specific products by carrying a wide variety of goods; they hope that the man who buys fertilizer today will buy insecticide and spray guns tomorrow.

Technology.—We saw that villagers in 1960 were willing to work harder than they had in the past in order to farm both at home and at Thunglor. It is thus less surprising that they were willing to work still harder (and to complain about it still more) in 1965 in order to farm both areas by traditional means. The devices that permit them to do so are ones with which we are already familiar. Farmers of home irrigated fields now take account of subtler plot variations than they did in 1960 and plant only their deepest land in late-maturing varieties of rice. More of the Great Field is now planted to middle-maturing and even early-maturing varieties than formerly. In addition, the home field farming cycle now begins earlier than it used to. This change makes seedbeds more subject to drought, thereby increasing the frequency of artificially watering the seedbed and perhaps also partially accounting for the villagers' greater receptivity to chemical fertilizers. The great pressure of work upon the many men who farm both at Thunglor and at home [2] encourages them to hire tractors for preliminary (precarabao) plowing at Thunglor.

What farmers do in 1965 is intelligible and rational in terms of what we learned about their perception of their social and natural environments in 1960 and of the value they place on rice. Although the actual thoughts of Ban Ping villagers are locked away from us, we have been able to deal with locally relevant choices among fields, operations, techniques, and resources. That these alternatives have Lue names suggests that natives recognize them to be alternatives (Goodenough 1957:167 f.). I have tried to describe the attitudes and emotions aroused by some of those alternatives (e.g., success, rent, wages), but the standards of choice are those revealed by my analysis; my data rarely permit us to test whether they coincide with those consciously exercised by the farmer (cf. Goodenough 1951:11; 1964:186). Farming, as Evans-Pritchard (quoted by Bohannan 1963:320) said of magic, "is a learnt mode of technical behavior with concomitant speech forms." It was possible to specify the villager's farming alternatives,

[2] Consider the work schedule of one young man who first seeds his home nursery, then (after twenty days) plows his home field and plants its deepest portions with late-maturing rice. He then seeds his Thunglor nursery and returns home to plow higher land and plant part of it with the earliest of the late-maturing rices, the rest with three-month rice. During this time a tractor has plowed the Thunglor field which he then replows with carabao and plants with late rice. At harvest time, he reaps high portions of his home field, then lower portions, then Thunglor.

to analyze the criteria by which he chooses among them, to indicate how he obtains information about those criteria, and to suggest how the evaluation of farming alternatives is influenced by the resources and values that characterize the villager as he progresses through his career. Although I have thereby delineated the rationality of the villager's choices, even "rational behavior on the part of the 'economic man' may actually be habitual" (Katona 1951:230).

Ethnography.—In chapter ii, I suggested that ethnography suffers from inadequate demarcation of domains, inconsistent definition of criteria for classification, and confusion among native, Western, and analytic categories. It is only fair to inquire into the extent to which this study has avoided these faults.

I asserted that rice farming constitutes a domain of which very similar limits are recognized by agronomists, by the natives, and by myself. All the farming operations described in Part Two were listed by informants responding to the question, "What kinds of things do you do when you farm?" To make the steps of their narratives intelligible as choices and as articulated parts of a coherent technological system, it was necessary to add to these answers the results of numerous other conversations and observations (and also to examine the literature). Although I am convinced that nothing has been added which villagers would consider foreign to *het na* (or subsequent fieldworkers foreign to farming in Ban Ping), the assertion that their domain and mine coincide remains an assertion, demonstrated only by the plausibility and consistency with which the operations, resources, and alternatives of farming were discussed.

Since the agricultural operations and resource components discussed in earlier chapters are each contrastive, yet are all related to farming, it could be claimed that they thereby constitute a domain (cf. Colby 1966:7). Such a claim would be rather trivial without my also demonstrating both that nothing within the native domain has been excluded from my analysis and that the native domain, in its entirety, contrasts with the same domains with which the putatively equivalent American domain contrasts. Since I cannot honestly demonstrate either of these, the present study contributes by recognizing, but not by solving, the problem of demarcating ethnographic domains.

In regard to consistency of classification, my attempt was more successful. It proved possible to consider the things, activities, persons, groups, and ideas used in *het na* as means for producing rice and as sources of extracommunity relations. Items as substantively different as pride in handicrafts, the presence of forests, and ethnic identification were subjected to this consistent analysis, and even such traditional anthropological concerns as kinship, residence, inheritance, and landownership were viewed not as "sacrosanct" (Conklin 1964) compartments of our discipline, but solely as they concerned my analytic definitions of technology and "peasantness."

This study utilizes both native categories and my own, consistently distinguishes between them, and sometimes indicates the differential significance of these categories in varying contexts (e.g., "fellow Lue" is significant for hiring labor but not for renting land). But native categories (e.g., *term, lo, aw haeng*) are sometimes treated as variants of a single concept which has not been demonstrated (cf. Goodenough 1963:238 f.) to include them. This shortcoming is mentioned as a warning to other artisans of "decision-making models" (Howard 1963: 409). It may be especially difficult to avoid in studies of technology because the ethnographer easily assumes that he or some other Western scientist knows the "correct" solution to the technical problem and is thereby able to assign the "correct" and hence "significant" categories (Conklin 1962b:124 f.) without inquiry into native criteria of classification. The ethnographer who attempts retrospectively to translate (or "define" [Frake 1962:83]) categories into their presumed component native perceptions is trying to turn waffles back into batter.

Extracommunity relations.—Traditional rice farming, the apparent apotheosis of village self-sufficiency, is pervaded by the "part-ness" that defines the peasantry. Tools such as plows and sickles, techniques such as tillage and irrigation, materials such as land and fertilizer, are heavily influenced by the villagers' relations with other communities. With the introduction of the tractor, the goods and goals, tasks and timing, land and labor of farming in Ban Ping became more dependent on powerful forces beyond the villagers' control. For water, labor, land, and knowledge—for everything he needs for farming—the villager came to depend on the town and the nation and upon more purely commercial relationships with erstwhile "kinsmen." This dependence weakened the old social bonds that had been forged in the days of cleared land and the longhouse, when resources in people counted more than resources in money and when every person's well-being was tied to the well-being of someone else.

It is tempting to exaggerate these changes, to suggest that Ban Ping has progressed from insularity to dependence, from status to contract, from *Gemeinschaft* to *Gesellschaft*. But we have learned that even at the beginning of Ban Ping's history, to the extent that we can know about it, land was bought and rented, wages were paid and strangers employed; relations with other communities were important to the village. Although Ban Ping has indeed progressed toward increasing participation in the nation and in the world market, it is still a peasant village in which "the household and the local community remain the primary units" (Fallers 1961:108) on which to base an understanding of farming and of life. The tractor did not transform the village into a modern industrial society based upon economic classes and voluntary associations. Most villagers are still content to improve their lot, "little by little, as a small bird builds its nest." Most wealthy men loan rice to their close relatives without charging interest and help their children without hiring them. The crucial moves toward commercialization are difficult to document because they involve attitudes toward production and money and people. The frequency of innovation in Ban Ping and its "intermediacy" (Casagrande 1959) mean that each villager is presented with a variety of ways of life on which to model his own. By the same behavior, different villagers may aspire to different models. One inconvenience of the somewhat mentalistic concept of culture adopted in this study is that no two villagers have quite the same culture. If Ban Ping's prosperity persists, many of the younger generation will come to share the commercial attitudes now found among only a few. It will be easy for them to do so because Ban Ping has few traditional means for preventing its individual members from behaving commercially. Avoidance and withdrawal of reciprocity are the villager's only punishments for someone who is "selfish," "stingy," and "calculating." For ambitious individuals who prefer payment to exchange and for whom avoidance means only the absence of kinsmen who come to borrow, such punishments may, in fact, be rewards.

Like the lack of sanctions, traditional values facilitate change and make it nondisruptive. Trading ventures and "private" rice encouraged saving, a virtue that parents try to inculcate in their adolescent children. The Lue have long been proud of their frugality and hard work which they claim distinguish them from the Yuan. In addition to the values of saving and hard work, two other traditional ideas—reciprocity and commodity—predispose Ban Ping farmers toward the changes stimulated by the nation and the market.

Conscious reciprocity makes a community of Ban Ping's otherwise isolated individuals and households. Villagers articulate and value the self-interest of actions which we would justify in terms of compassion, generosity, public spirit, or pride in craftsmanship. Easily and without embarrassment, the villager explains his relations with his family, his friends, and his gods in terms of something received for something given. Aid for aid, sweetmeat for sweetmeat, visit for visit, the ideal and the fact of constant conscious reciprocity pervade Ban Ping and probably prepare its people for participation in the commercial world of goods for cash, labor for wages, land for rental.

The old concept of commodities, of "things with a price," furnishes an additional basis of continuity. Even in the "old days," goods and services for which there was a market, those items that had to be bought and could be sold, were supposed to be transacted with kins-

CHANGE IN FARMING

men at the same price that outsiders would pay for them. The existence of this ideal is not surprising, for some goods and services have always circulated beyond the kin-based reciprocity of the village. Although the Ban Ping villager sometimes mourns the loss of festive work bees and berates the frenetic pace of modern life, with its selfish neighbors and domineering officials, he perceives commercialization as a change in degree, not in kind; the concept of commodity is an old one which has merely come to cover more goods and services than it did in the past (Moerman 1966b).

Trucks spewing dust and noise have replaced the docile pack oxen with their melodious bells. A concrete wall has obviated propitiating the spirit of the dam. Landownership, once gained through kinsmen, now depends upon the town. Wage agreements with outsiders are beginning to mobilize labor, formerly an affair of fellowship among intimates. Yet, Ban Ping has not been destroyed; the tractor merely tilled the soil that the plow reclaimed.

APPENDIX A

Glutinous Rice: Its Distribution, Use, and Nature

Distribution.—Although glutinous rice helps to define and isolate a continuous culture area of about 200,000 square miles, its distribution cannot yet be explained. Adams' influential article (1948) barely mentions glutinous rice, and Terra mistakenly regards it as "the basic food of the 'Indonesians'" of mainland Southeast Asia (1953:444). Even the most authoritative sources dismiss it by saying that "in no country does glutinous rice replace hard rice" (Grist 1959:79) or that glutinous rices "invariably claim less of [man's] interest than the non-glutinous rices" (Burkill 1935:1596). Although no one knows why the Tai of northern and northeastern Thailand, Laos, and Yunnan eat glutinous rice as their staple, to explain it as simple dietary preference is not wholly satisfactory. Although it cannot be denied that Asian rice preferences are influenced by differences of flavor, aroma, and texture so subtle that they often escape the notice of Europeans, the method of preparing and the style of eating glutinous rice are so different from those for ordinary rice that the preference cannot be regarded as a minor variation within a cuisine. Furthermore, there may well have been environmental factors that helped to establish the two kinds of rice, each in its own homeland. This may have happened before the central and northern Tai came to their present locations. Although there has been little systematic comparison of the physical geography of north Thailand with that of central Thailand, the regions certainly seem to differ with respect to regularity of rainfall, range of seasonal and diurnal temperature, and hours of sunlight. It seems eminently possible that such environmental differences may at least have helped to continue regional preferences for different kinds of rice.

Before such a disorderly array of authorities, it would be presumptuous for an ethnographer to attempt an environmental analysis of the distribution of glutinous rice; far too many ecological and microecological influences may be involved. Varietal distributions in Japan, for example, involve photoperiod, back-cropping, labor variations, soil conditions, and pest resistance in addition to the obvious factors of temperature and water (Matsuo 1954:27 ff.). Nevertheless, those who are qualified to formulate an environmental analysis may find a basis suggested to them in the technology section of chapter iii and particularly in a study of Ban Ping's peculiarities of timing and seedbed preparation.

Use.—Unlike other Asians, the Lue—along with most other Tai of northern Thailand, Laos, and Yunnan—eat glutinous rice as their staple food. Where glutinous rice is the staple food, milled and winnowed grains are soaked overnight and then steamed, not boiled. Rice prepared in this way does not have the sweetish taste and viscous texture experienced by those who have eaten glutinous rice in regions where it is boiled or steamed in an airtight leaf container. Where ordinary rice is the staple, glutinous rice is often used as a special-purpose food and for sweetmeats; in the glutinous-rice region, ordinary rice is used as a special food and for making sweetmeats. When steamed to be eaten as a staple, glutinous rice forms a coherent mass in which individual grains can be seen and tasted separately. A small handful of rice is broken off the main lump and formed into a ball which is dipped, in much "the same way as a piece of bread in Europe" (Gouineau 1959:221), into the sauce, paste, flesh, or vegetable that accompanies the meal.

Although rice is the basis of Thailand's domestic economy and its main source of foreign exchange, the glutinous varieties to which the northeast devotes about 75 percent of its farmland and the north about 90 percent play little part in world commerce (Thailand 1958:12). The north's insulation from the vagaries of the world market is especially marked in that it usually plants and prefers a broad, short grain for which there are far fewer foreign customers than for the longer-grained glutinous rices of the northeast (Dasananda 1960). Rice sales are of great importance to the individual farmers of Chiengkham, but the rice of northern Thailand, as a region, is not sold abroad, except, perhaps, as part of the current United States program of import support for Laos.

As more and more Ban Ping farmers come to think of rice as a cash as well as a subsistence crop, planting large areas to glutinous rice reflects a market-oriented decision based in part on anticipated price and yield. Unfortunately, I cannot report in the present study on the differential productivity of the two kinds of rice. About 1956 the farmers of Ban Ping began to grow significant amounts of ordinary rice. As a result of the low price of ordinary rice in 1959, however, all the rice they grew in 1960 was glutinous.

Nature.—The glutinous character is inherited as a simple recessive to starchy (Rhind 1959:91; Nagai 1959:312), but cuts across the common distinctions made among rices for commercial purposes. As a class the "glutinous rices possess a dull and soft grain, the cut appearance being . . . paraffin-wax-like. . . . The main characteristic of glutinous rice is that when treated with iodine the starch stains a yellow or reddish brown color . . . instead of the usual blue reaction of starch" (Grist 1959:78 f.).

To this characteristic may be added lower specific gravity (Nagai 1959:312) and the greater sensitivity of its starch to chemical reagents (Saenz-Lascano-Ruiz 1950:22), especially to mineral acids (*ibid.*, p. 30). Grist (1959:79) claims that the protein content is lower and the fat content higher, but the chemical analyses presented by Saenz-Lascano-Ruiz do not seem to confirm this statement. The peculiar iodine reaction of glutinous rice is probably due less to dextrin (cf. Burkill 1935:1596) than to the structure of the starch in the endosperm (Wickizer and Bennett 1941:10 n. 4). Chemical analysis indicates that in glutinous rice, unlike ordinary rice, all the starch of the endosperm is composed of amylopectins which would account for the reaction to iodine (Saenz-Lascano-Ruiz 1950:13, 39) and for the stickiness. The same analysis, however, confirms Burkill's position that glutinous rices contain more dextrins than ordinary rices (*ibid.*, table 8), and so makes more plausible his belief that the special character of the endosperm may relate to "deferring of ripening" (Burkill 1935:1596).

My research suggests that standard sources are wrong about the crop characteristics of glutinous rice. Wickizer and Bennett (*op. cit.*) claim that it has a soft straw which subjects it to lodging in high winds or strong current. McHale (1960), then in contact with the Agricultural Experiment Station of the Federation of Malaya, denies this, as do the farmers of Chiengkham who, in fact, assert that the contrary is true. Terra (1953:444) states that glutinous rice ripens faster, an assumption shared by others (Dobby 1956:270; Fisher 1964:497 ff.; Pendleton 1962:160; deYoung 1955:78) who use it to explain the crop's distribution in Thailand. But the glutinous rice grown in Chienkham does not mature any more quickly than does the nonglutinous rice grown there or grown elsewhere in Thailand. The scientist in charge of rice breeding in Thailand says that there are no known differences between the needs of the two classes of rice in growing season, soil, climate, and rainfall (Dasananda 1960). Although some (Nagai 1959:312 f.) claim that the softer endosperm of glutinous rice makes it more subject to breakage when milled, Dasananda reports as the only significant difference that the opacity of glutinous rice may make it difficult to predict its milling qualities. My casual impressions—listening, watching, eating, and drinking—confirm Terra's (1953:444) claim that cooked glutinous rice keeps longer without turning sour and that it ferments better.

APPENDIX B
Obtaining Quantitative Data

Before describing some of the ways in which quantitative data were obtained for this study, it should be emphasized that I regard such data as less important for my analysis and understanding of farming in Ban Ping than nonquantitative data. Most of what I know about village agriculture comes from living in Ban Ping, from talking casually with and listening to its farmers, and from going with them to their fields and occasionally working there. In the course of my stay in Ban Ping, I made detailed—and occasionally verbatim—notes on the spot which I then typed and cross-indexed later the same day. Despite the importance I assign to these innumerable and subjective experiences, in this study (especially in chap. vii) I do make use of quantitative information obtained from a survey of the location, size, ownership, price, source, and use of all rice land owned or operated by the villagers of Ban Ping and from a schedule of questions asked of a random sample of village farmers. This appendix describes that sample survey.

Sample.—A sample is supposed to represent the universe from which it is selected. One of the difficulties I encountered was defining that universe. When we arrived in Ban Ping there were 114 physically distinct residential units. When we left, there were 121. My sample is composed of 40 "house roofs" of farmers but of only 39 units of consumption, as one household "still eats the rice of its father and mother." If the household is viewed as a unit of production, how to define it becomes even more difficult. Some of the young households in the sample are prematurely independent in that they provide their parents with tillage labor on the Great Field. On the other hand, members of many sample households farm private (*lork*) rice. Thus, a given sample household may be less than a unit of production on the Great Field, yet contain more than a unit of production at Thunglor. It would, of course, be possible to formulate a single arbitrary definition of the household. Such a definition, while consistent with quantitative methods, would be false ethnographically because it would ignore the great formal variability of the house-roof unit recognized by the villagers. Adequacy of sample size should perhaps be judged, not against the number of village households, but in terms of the proportion of village farms sampled. This information is presented in table 29. Because the sample includes only one of Ban Ping's nine semi-irrigated farms, data from that farm were combined with those from the Great Field. The sample also contains fewer distant irrigated farms than are required for comparing them confidently with home irrigated farms. The small size of my sample is one reason that only the most straightforward computations have been made.

Two further features of the sample should be mentioned. Because anthropologists sometimes use the word "random" for samples that are, at best, haphazard or desultory, it should be stated that my sampling procedure was random in the technical sense. Specifically, using a table of random numbers, I selected a starting point blindly. Groups of three digits above, below, right, or left of the starting point were then recorded; the direction in which these were read was arbitrarily determined by the position of the second hand of a watch. As every village house had been assigned

TABLE 29

SIZE OF 1960 SAMPLE

Field	Number of farms in sample	Number of farms not in sample	Percentage of farms in sample
Home irrigated	31	24	57
Semi-irrigated	1	8	11
Distant irrigated	7	18	28
Home rainfall	16	15	52
tractor	(5)	(3)	(63)
animal	(11)	(12)	(48)
Home flood	2	4	33
tractor	(1)	(1)	(50)
animal	(1)	(3)	(25)
Distant flood	42	61	41
Total	99	130	43

a number by the Thai government, my groups of three digits determined which houses fell into the sample, though I first had to renumber some houses (the official numbering was somewhat confused). Because Ban Ping has far fewer than 999 households, it was also necessary to reject most of the selected three-digit groups. Second, it should be noted that the "no response" or "not at home" returns which derandomize most sociological sample surveys did not occur in my work.

Interviewing.—Peasant farmers usually mistrust the outsiders upon whom, by definition, they are dependent. For this reason, it is rarely desirable to base all data upon records compiled by government officials. It is probably a mistake to suppose than an official, by virtue of his status, can readily obtain accurate information from peasants (cf. Sharp *et al.* 1953:113), unless he is an extraordinary individual willing to adopt a "nonofficial status" (Janlekha 1955:19) and to use his power soley for the benefit of his respondents. When I compiled quantitative information about Ban Ping, it was desirable, as well as convenient, to make use of local personnel. Most of our interviewing and recording of sample households was done by two village teen-agers: A, a girl who lived in our house as an "adopted daughter" and S, the son of our closest friend. Although neither of these assistants was educated beyond the fourth grade, both worked with extraordinary diligence and care. During the transplanting season, A went each day to the home fields of households in the sample. She counted the number of hired workers and recorded their pay, recorded the names of those who had come to *term* or to *coj*, and asked about the variety and amount of seed planted. During the harvesting season S went each night to every farmer who had completed harvesting a field that day. He recorded their answers to the questions on the schedule (see below) and immediately brought them to us. Whenever possible, questions about a given plot were directed to the individual who was responsible for farming it.

The results of the survey were subjected to a number of tests of internal consistency. It was possible to compare some of the information that S obtained with that gathered earlier by A. The size, type, and value of landholdings could be compared with an earlier survey of the entire village and also with a subsequent sample of individual histories of landownership. Information about the size of harvests could be compared with a subsequent stratified random sample of annual household budgets. Man-days reported could be compared with observations of the composition of work groups. Tractor fees and amounts of seed rice provided a rough check on landholdings, as did examination of land-tax records in the district office.

Although the data are far more accurate than those obtained by government officials, they are subject to some of the same bias. This fault pertains especially to information about landholdings. All plots at Thunglor, and some at the distant irrigated field, were measured accurately (see chap. v). Other holdings were the villagers' own approximations. For the objectivity and the representative quality of a random sample, the anthropologist sacrifices intimate rapport. While no respondent exaggerated his holdings, a few probably underreported them because they were careless or suspicious. Although our interviewers and other friends could usually correct such inaccuracies, Great Field acreages are probably somewhat underestimated.

Units of measurement.—Few peasants are acquainted with international standards of measurement; even those who are rarely keep accounts. The Ban Ping farmer who reports that he "tilled for half a month" is credited with half a lunar month, or fourteen days, of plowing and tilling although the time actually spent might be ten days or twenty. Amounts of rice, like units of time, are subject to errors which probably cancel each other. Villagers quantify rice in units of volume. The baskets used, however, vary somewhat. Although it was possible to eliminate gross errors by determining which informants used the old style "three-tang baskets," some minor errors do remain.

A further source of error is inconsistent units of measurement. Sometimes local units, such as rice prices in baht per hap, are used. It is in these terms that villagers make their farming decisions; translation into other units, like dollars per bushel, would be meaningless. Some measurements, like the yield of rice in thang per rai, are expressed in central Thai terms in order to facilitate comparisons with other studies and with national statistics. Some measurements are expressed in Western terms in order to facilitate wider comparisons. These comparisons are, for the most part, restricted to weight per unit area, a figure that conveys false precision because the density of rice is quite variable. I failed to weigh samples of Ban Ping's rice, and have therefore accepted the village estimate that one thang of their rice weighs 11 kilograms. Sharp uses the same figure for for Bangchan (1953:14).

Errors of estimation.—Where farmers do not keep accounts, but are almost compulsively polite, it would clearly be a mistake to ask for factual information which the respondent can be presumed to have forgotten. It is often better to make estimates based on observation. Our figures of tillage-season labor requirements, for example, are based on a combination of questioning, observation, and estimation. Questioning and observation during the early part of the farming cycle permits an estimate of man-days expended at pre-tillage tasks. A number of households were seen to be occupied with fashioning wood for irrigation dams and for seedbed fences for about two weeks, but this work was often interrupted for a day of carting or fence building or seedbed preparation. Even without these interruptions, household members rarely worked a full day at a time. To judge from our neighbors, whom we could observe most closely, it is fair to estimate that each household spends about five man-days preparing wood for the dams and fences used in plow agriculture. To this must be added time spent working on the dams. Each household that farms the Great Field spends two man-days at the Great Dam. Smaller dams and canals near their plots take even more time: the most common figure seems to be about ten man-days per household. Irrigation labor is a matter of the number and location of one's fields. Work on the seedbed, on the other hand, varies with its area which, in turn, is heavily influenced by the number of rai to which seedlings will be transplanted. In addition, the amount of time spent in seedbed preparation differs between field and forest beds. Since seedbed labor is a relatively minor component of plow agriculture, data rich enough to account for all this complexity were not collected. In two closely observed instances, it took two young household members three days to prepare a bed for transplanting ten rai (1.6 ha) and four days for a bed sufficient for twelve rai (1.9 ha). On this basis, an expenditure of seven man-days of seedbed preparation for each eleven rai (1.8 ha) of field has been estimated. The estimate for seeding itself is also an approximation. Normally, all able-bodied household members perform this task which lasts for only a few hours. Household members also seed on the beds of kinsmen and on the seedbeds of those who have helped them. As a convenient approximation, one man-day of seeding labor for each farm has been reckoned.

Thunglor farming begins with the task of pointing, that is, of marking plots and measuring them. The task of clearing virgin land, although sometimes quite time consuming, is omitted since it is difficult to quantify and since it is also required on animal-plowed land during *its* first year of use. Marking and measuring is estimated at a day for each plot. The next task—burning off the preceding year's stubble—is done either on the day of pointing or on the day of broadcasting, so has not been counted as a man-day. Broadcasting, like pointing, required a man-day of work from each farmer. Most villagers with land at Thunglor made at least one trip there to inspect and resow their plots. This task, too, has been estimated as one man-day for each farm.

For the distant irrigated field, time spent in preparing wood for irrigation and fencing has been estimated at five man-days for each plot, although the actual time may be somewhat less. Irrigation work itself, at both the major and the local dams, has been estimated at seven man-days per farm. Seeding has been estimated to take one day, the time required at the Great Field. Other figures are computed from responses to the schedule of questions (see below).

For the home rainfall field, seeding and transplanting have been estimated from the rates obtaining on the Great Field.

The cash cost of 7 baht per load for carting the Thunglor harvest is a somewhat arbitrary figure estimated on the basis of a price that ranged between 6 and 10 baht (the latter for a few farmers at the height of the season), with a clear mode of 7 baht, from which must be subtracted the cartload carried by the farmer himself and the rice sold at the field.

The cash cost of farming at the sampled distant flood fields includes cartage, tractor fees, and 16 baht paid to harvesters. The cash cost of distant irrigated farming includes cartage and 230 baht paid by sample households for harvesting, transplanting, and renting animals. The cash cost of farming the home irrigated fields includes 17.50 baht paid to harvesters by one household and the far larger amount (204 man-days @ 3.50) paid to transplanters.

Schedule of questions.—A two-page form was mimeographed in Thai for S to use in recording answers in the presence of his respondent. The following questions were asked separately about each plot of land farmed by members of the sampled household.

1. Respondent's name.
2. Location and name of field.
3. Varieties of rice planted.
4. Amount of rice planted of each variety.
5. Amount of fertilizer used on seedbed.
6. Amount of fertilizer used on field.
7. Number of carabao used in plowing.
8. Number of oxen used in plowing.
9. Number of household animals used.
10. Number and source of animals received through *coj* and exchange. If any, who sent them?
11. Number, price, and source of animals hired.
12. Tractor fee.
13. Number of household carts used for harvest.
14. Number and source of carts obtained through *coj, term,* and exchange.
15. Number of carts hired.
    From whom?
    Price paid to carters.
16. Size of this year's harvest.
17. Size of last year's harvest.

18. Variety of rice planted last year.
19. Size of plot farmed last year.
20. Present (asking) price of plot.
21. Number of days spent in reaping.
    For each reaping day: number of household workers of each sex, number of those of each sex who came to help or exchange labor, names of those who came to help or exchange, number of workers of each sex who were hired, names of hired workers, wages paid to hired workers.
22. Shocking. As for 21.
23. Threshing. As for 21.
24. Tilling. As for 21.
25. For distant irrigated field, transplanting as for 21. (Home irrigated transplanting labor collected separately.)

APPENDIX C

Quantitative Comparisons: Rice Farming in Ban Ping and Elsewhere

Thai yields.—Table 30 indicates that farmers in Ban Ping and the rest of northern Thailand obtain high yields from their glutinous rice, but the very accuracy of my figures for Ban Ping limits their usefulness for com-

TABLE 30

THAI RICE YIELDS IN KILOGRAMS PER RAI

Year	National [a]	Central plains [a]	Bangchan [b]	North [a]	Chiengkham [c]	Tambon Yuan [c]	Ban Ping [d]
1948	222	254	363	270			
1949	215	245	253	259			
1950	205	232	352	231			
1951	204	233	326	241			
1952	206	231	277	256			
1953	222	258		288			
1954	202	221		287			
1955	218	245		316	264	242	
1956	230	256		345	512	486	
1957	208	208		345	219	218	
1958	218	250		303	196	220	
1959	206	234		318	183	248	436
1960	222	255		310			418

SOURCES:
[a] Thailand 1965.
[b] Janlekha 1955.
[c] Rice reports compiled by the Chiengkham District Office under the direction of Assistant District Officer Khynyng Wongyai.
[d] Author's sample.

parative purposes. In an interview (Dasananda 1960), the then Deputy Director-General of the Thai Department of Rice expressed the belief that, although some provinces overestimate and some underestimate their yields, annual estimates of national production have been quite accurate. Official figures for the District of Chiengkham, however, seem to be grossly underestimated. In 1959, for example, the administrative borough (*tambon*) which Ban Ping forms, along with seventeen other hamlets, is credited with a mean yield of only 248 kg per rai, while my sample indicates a mean yield of 436 kg for Ban Ping. It is unlikely that the other hamlets of the administrative borough farm with so little success that their yields would reduce the average to this extent. Because the figures I obtained have internal consistency and because they were collected at the time of harvest and from the farmers themselves, I am rather confident of their accuracy, but this accuracy diminishes their *comparative* value.

In 1960 Ban Ping's mean yield was 38.0 thang per rai (2,612.5 kg/ha). For Thailand, this yield is extremely good; nevertheless, it is well within the range for glutinous rice. In 1930–31, Zimmerman (1931:146) sampled northern communities whose yields ranged widely from 12 to 45 thang per rai. In 1956, an unusually good year for northern Thailand, provinces growing glutinous rice obtained the following average yields, in thang per rai (see Thailand 1958: table 3):

Chiengrai	34.4
Chiengmai	38.3
Nan	39.7
Phrae	32.7
Lampang	29.2
Lamphun	29.5

Thai government rice breeders recommend six varieties of glutinous rice whose average yield is about 49 thang per rai (Love 1955:40 ff.).

Seeding rates.—Kaufman (1960:43) reports that Bangkhuad farmers, who broadcast sprouted seed onto their beds, use about 0.75 bung per rai, but he does not say whether this figure is the villagers' estimate or his measurement.

Seeding rates expressed in international units would provide a convenient index of technological efficiency and could help in evaluating the criticism that Asian peasants plant too much rice and plant it too closely. Unfortunately, there do not seem to be many published figures on seeding rates. Grist (1959:120) maintains that the "usual rate is about 20 lb. per acre for good land, up to 40 lb. for poorer land," but furnishes few rates to support this generalization. Because of the absence of comparable data, table 31 can only suggest a few vague observations. Ban Ping's seeding rates do not seem to be excessive. The relative infertility of the home irrigated field is apparent once again. It is wrong to assume that broadcasting always uses more seed than transplanting.

Labor productivity.—Ban Ping farmers expend 98.5 man-days per hectare on the Great Field and only 31.8 man-days per hectare at Thunglor; these figures suggest that the tractor reduces labor requirements by about two-thirds. It would be difficult to estimate the corresponding result of mechanization elsewhere, for it is clear that the techniques of agriculture are hardly less important than its tools in determining the amount of labor expended by farmers. In Tonkin, for example, villagers whose tools are the same as those used in Thailand work a great deal harder, for they grow two or even three crops a year and, as table 32 shows, they work twice as hard on each

TABLE 31

Seeding Rates in Kilograms per Hectare

Location	Rate [a]	Source
Ban Ping, home irrigated and semi-irrigated	84 (73.8)	
Ban Ping, distant irrigated	30 (26.6)	
Ban Ping, established broadcast	63 (55.5)	
Perak, multiple nurseries	21 (18)	Grist 1959:119
East Pakistan, broadcast	85 (75)	Grist 1959:114
India, Central Province, broadcast	113 (100)	Grist 1959:115
United States, broadcast	(90–160)	Grist 1959:162

[a] Pound per acre in parentheses.

TABLE 32

Man-Days per Hectare Expended on a Single Transplanted Crop in Thailand and in Indochina

Location	Man-days	Source
Ban Ping, northern Thailand	99	
Nakorn Pathom, central Thailand	102	Thailand 1959:table 45
Cochin China	85	Gourou 1940:360
Tonkin	200	Gourou 1940:297

TABLE 33

Man-Days Expended in Farming a Single Crop in Thailand and in Tonkin
(In percentages)

Task	Ban Ping	Central Thailand	Tonkin
Irrigation	13	[a]	7
Seedbed	5	[a]	4
Tillage	18	23	51
Transplanting	22	35	14
Harvest	42	42	23

[a] Unavailable.

SOURCES: *For central Thailand:* Thailand 1959: table 45. Categories "carefulness" and "miscellaneous" omitted and percentages computed from identifiable categories. *For Tonkin:* Gourou 1940:296. Percentages computed from man-days expended on a single mau (3,600 square meters [Gourou 1956:8]). Postcultivation operations of "cleaning, stirring, and manuring" included in tillage.

of them. Probably, mechanization would cause the largest increases in labor productivity where agriculture is most involuted, but even this is by no means certain unless the tasks obviated by machines are those that use the most labor. The possible extent of relative labor variation for different farming tasks is suggested by table 33. It would also be possible for farmers to invest the labor saved on one task in some other task, and so complicate the prediction of increases in productivity. In Cochin China, for example, animal-plowed broadcast fields require only thirteen man-days per hectare less than the eighty-five man-days expended on a hectare of transplanted land (Gourou 1940:360). In Italy, similarly, "the weeding of broadcast rice requires more work than does the transplanting and weeding of transplanted rice" (Dumont 1935:349).

Glossary of Lue Terms

aw haeng	to take strength, a form of labor exchange
bi ngern	ancient unminted silver money
bun	religious merit, good fortune
cang	to hire
coj	to help
du	energetic, strict, fierce
hern	household property as contrasted with private or individual (*lork*) property in rice or land
het na	rice farming
kamnan	chief headman of an administrative borough
kaw	to make mounds with a harrow
kha-cang	wage
lap	food made of chopped raw meat
lo	cooperative labor
lork	individual or private property, as contrasted with household (*hern*) property in rice or land
maj	title for those who have been Buddhist novices
myang	political unit larger than a village
na	rice fields
na ferng	"straw" fields, developed fields at Thunglor
na pa	"forest" fields, undeveloped fields at Thunglor
pan	to give, a gift
pha	rent
phi	protective spirit, ghost
sio	age-mate, intimate friend born in the same year
tambon	administrative borough
term	to add to—a form of labor exchange
termkan	mutual aid
tyt	to open and level the mounds made by *kaw*'ing
xaw	rice
xaw kin	rice intended for subsistence uses
xaw xaj	rice intended for sale

Units of Measurement

baht — Basic Thai monetary unit. During period of fieldwork worth approximately 5 U.S. cents.
bung, tang, thang — Unit of volume officially equivalent to 20 liters. A bung of unmilled Ban Ping rice weighs approximately 11 kg.
hap — Unit of volume equivalent to two bungs.
rai — Unit of land area officially equivalent to .40 acre (.16 ha; 6.25 rai = 1 ha).
sork — Unit of linear measure, the distance from the tip of the middle finger to the elbow joint. Approximately .5 meter.

Key to Genealogical Information

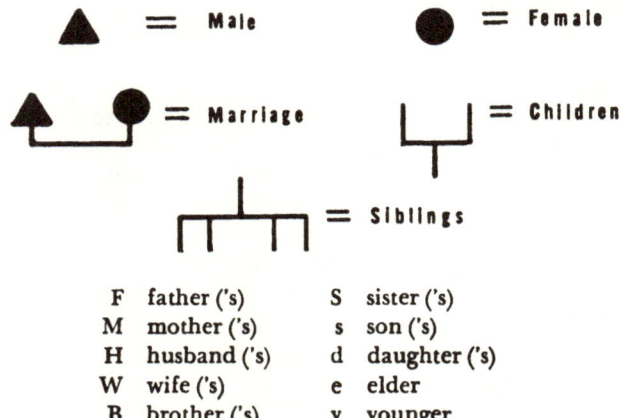

F father ('s)   S sister ('s)
M mother ('s)   s son ('s)
H husband ('s)   d daughter ('s)
W wife ('s)   e elder
B brother ('s)   y younger

Orthography

The usual spelling is retained for common Thai words (e.g., rai, *amphur*) and place-names (e.g., Bangkok, Chiengmai). Otherwise, transliterations are italicized and glosses are enclosed in quotes. The orthography follows Haas (1956:viii–ix) but is modified for typographic convenience and is simplified for ease of reading; it indicates neither tone nor vowel length. A list of transliterations follows.

b   *b*, as in *b*aby
c   voiceless unaspirate palatal stop, rather like *J* in *J*ohn

EXPLANATORY NOTES

ch	voiceless aspirate palatal stop, rather like *Ch* in *Ch*arles
d	*d*, as in *d*ad*d*y
f	*f*, as in *f*un
h	*h*, as in *h*ouse; indicates aspiration of preceding stop
j	*y*, as in *y*ou
k	voiceless unaspirate velar stop, rather like English hi*cc*up, French *c*afé
kh	*k* as in *k*ey
x	voiceless velar fricative, like German a*ch*
l	*l*, as in *l*ook
m	*m*, as in *m*other
n	*n*, as in *n*ice
ng	*ng*, as in si*ng* (but can occur initially)
p	voiceless unaspirate bilabial stop, rather like s*p*ort
ph	*p*, as in *p*in
s	*s*, as in *s*it
t	voiceless unaspirate postdental stop, rather like s*t*aff
th	*t*, as in *t*oe
w	*w*, as in *w*alk or ho*w*
a	*a*, as in f*a*ther
e	*e*, as in th*e*y
i	*i*, as in mach*i*ne
o	*o*, as in h*o*pe
or	low back rounded vowel, rather like *o* in s*o*ng or *aw* in l*aw*
ae	low front vowel, rather like *a* in p*a*t or m*a*t
er	mid-central vowel, rather like *e* in h*e*r or *i* in th*i*rd
u	high back rounded vowel, rather like *oo* in s*oo*n
y	high central unrounded vowel made, says Haas, "by raising the center part of the tongue while keeping the lips in relaxed or protracted position"

References Cited

ADAMS, INEZ
1948 Rice cultivation in Asia. American Anthropologist 50:256–282.
ANDREWS, JAMES M.
1935 Siam, 2nd rural economic survey: 1934–1935. Cambridge: Peabody Museum, Harvard University.
ANONYMOUS
1954 Thaj Lyy thi chiengkham [The Thai Lue of Chiengkham]. Khon Myang [The Northerner] 1:118–127. Chiengmai, Thailand. (In Thai.)
ARCHER, W. J.
1888 Report of a journey in the vice consular district of Chiengmai, Siam. Presented to both houses of Parliament, June 1888. London: H.M.S.O.
AYAL, ELIEZER
1966 Private enterprise and economic progress in Thailand. Journal of Asian Studies 26:5–14.
BARTON, THOMAS FRANK
1960 Growing rice in Thailand. Journal of Geography 59:153–164.
BAUER, P. T., and B. S. YAMEY
1957 The economics of under-developed countries. London: Cambridge University Press.
BERLIN, ISAIAH
1957 The hedgehog and the fox: an essay on Tolstoy's view of history. New York: Mentor Books.
BIRDSELL, JOSEPH B.
1957 On population structure in generalized hunting and collecting populations. Evolution 12:189–205.
BLANCHARD, W., ed.
1958 Thailand: its people, its society, its culture. New Haven: Human Relations Area Files Press.
BLOFELD, JOHN
1960 People of the sun. London: Hutchinson.
BOHANNAN, PAUL
1963 Social anthropology. New York: Holt, Rinehart, and Winston.
BOSERUP, ESTER
1965 The conditions of agricultural growth. London: George Allen and Unwin.
BURKILL, I. H.
1935 A dictionary of the economic products of the Malay Peninsula. London: Crown Agents for the Malay Government. 2 vols.

BURLING, ROBBINS
  1962 Maximization theories and the study of economic anthropology. American Anthropologist 64:802–821.
  1965 Hill farms and padi fields. Englewood Cliffs, N.J.: Prentice-Hall.
CASAGRANDE, JOSEPH B.
  1959 Some observations on the study of intermediate societies. *In* Proceedings of the 1959 annual meeting of the American Ethnological Society. Seattle.
CHIANG, YING-LIANG
  1950 Pai-yi sheng-huo wen–hua [The life and culture of the Pai-yi tribesmen]. Shanghai: Chunghua Book Co. (New Haven: Human Relations Area Files, typescript translation.)
COLBY, B. N.
  1966 Ethnographic semantics: a preliminary survey. Current Anthropology 7:3–32.
CONKLIN, HAROLD C.
  1957 Hanunóo agriculture. Forestry Development Paper no. 12. Rome: Food and Agriculture Organization of the United Nations.
  1962a Comment [on the ethnographic study of cognitive systems, by C. O. Frake]. *In* Anthropology and human behavior. T. Gladwin and W. C. Sturtevant, eds. Washington: Anthropological Society of Washington.
  1962b Lexicographical treatment of folk taxonomies. International Journal of American Linguistics, vol. 28, no. 2. *In* Problems in lexicography. Fred W. Householder and Sol Saporta, eds. Bloomington: Indiana University Research Center in Anthropology, Folklore, and Linguistics. Publication 21.
  1964 Ethnogenealogical method. *In* Explorations in cultural anthropology. Ward H. Goodenough, ed. New York: McGraw-Hill.
DAMRONG, RAJANUBHAB, H. R. H.
  1918/19 Introduction to the chronicle of the state of Chiengrung. No. 3 of Prachum Phongsawadan [Collected chronicles]. Bangkok. (In Thai.)
DASANANDA, SALA
  1960 Interview with Deputy Director-General, Department of Rice, Ministry of Agriculture, Kingdom of Thailand. December 23.
DE LAGUNA, FREDERICA
  1957 Some problems of objectivity in ethnology. Man 57, article 228.
DE SAUSSURE, FERDINAND
  1959 Course in general linguistics. Trans. Wade Basken. New York: Philosophical Library.
deYOUNG, JOHN E.
  1955 Village life in modern Thailand. Berkeley and Los Angeles: University of California Press.
DOBBY, E. H. G.
  1956 Southeast Asia. London: University of London Press.
DODD, WILLIAM CLIFTON
  1923 The Thai race, elder brother of the Chinese. Cedar Rapids: Torch Press.

DUMONT, M. R.
　1935　La culture du riz dans le delta du Tonkin. Paris: Société d'éditions géographiques, maritimes et coloniales.

EGGAN, FRED
　1941　Some aspects of culture change in north Luzon. American Anthropologist 43:11–18.

EMERY, F. E., and O. A. OESER
　1958　Information, decision and action: a study of the psychological determinants of changes in farming techniques. Melbourne: Melbourne University Press.

EPSTEIN, T. SCARLETT
　1962　Economic development and social change in south India. Manchester: Manchester University Press.

ERASMUS, CHARLES J.
　1956　Culture structure and process: the occurrence and disappearance of reciprocal farm labor. Southwestern Journal of Anthropology 12:444–470.
　1961　Man takes control. Minneapolis: University of Minnesota Press.

FALLERS, L. A.
　1961　Are African cultivators to be called "peasants"? Current Anthropology 2:108–110.

FIRTH, RAYMOND
　1951　Elements of social organization. London: Watts and Co.

FIRTH, RAYMOND, and B. S. YAMEY, eds.
　1964　Capital, savings, and credit in peasant societies. Chicago: Aldine.

FISHER, CHARLES A.
　1964　South-East Asia: a social, economic and political geography. London: Methuen.

FORD, CLELLAN S.
　1937　A sample comparative analysis of material culture. *In* Studies in the science of society. George P. Murdock, ed. New Haven: Yale University Press.
　1942　Culture and human behavior. Scientific Monthly 55:546–557.
　1945　A comparative study of human reproduction. New Haven: Yale University Publications in Anthropology, no. 32.

FOSTER, GEORGE M.
　1961　The dyadic contract: a model for the social structure of a Mexican peasant village. American Anthropologist 63:1173–1192.
　1965　Peasant society and the image of limited good. American Anthropologist 67:293–315.

FRAKE, CHARLES O.
　1962　The ethnographic study of cognitive systems. *In* Anthropology and human behavior. T. Gladwin and W. C. Sturtevant, eds. Washington: Anthropological Society of Washington.

FREEMAN, J. D.
　1955　Iban agriculture. Colonial Office Research Studies, no. 18. London: H.M.S.O.

GARFINKEL, HAROLD
　1962　The rational properties of scientific and common sense activities.

In Decisions, values, and groups. Vol. 2. Norman F. Washburne, ed. New York: Pergamon Press.
1964 Studies of the routine grounds of everyday activities. Social Problems 11:225–250.

GEDDES, W. R.
1954 The land Dayaks of Sarawak. Colonial Office Research Studies, no. 14. London: H.M.S.O.

GEERTZ, CLIFFORD
1957 Ritual and social change: a Javanese example. American Anthropologist 59:32–54.
1963 Agricultural involution. Berkeley and Los Angeles: University of California Press.

GEORGESCU-ROEGEN, N.
1964 Economic theory and agrarian economics. *In* Agriculture and economic development. Carl Eicher and Lawrence Witt, eds. New York: McGraw-Hill.

GOLDHAMMER, HERBERT
1954 Fashion and social science. World Politics 6:393–404.

GOODENOUGH, WARD H.
1951 Property, kin, and community on Truk. New Haven: Yale University Publications in Anthropology, no. 46.
1956 Residence rules. Southwestern Journal of Anthropology 12:22–37.
1957 Cultural anthropology and linguistics. Georgetown University Monograph Series on Language and Linguistics, no. 9. Paul Garvin, ed. Washington. Repr. *in* Language in culture and society. Dell Hymes, ed. New York: Harper and Row.
1963 Some applications of Guttman scale analysis to ethnography and culture theory. Southwestern Journal of Anthropology 19:235–250.
1964 Review of Kinship and marriage in a New Guinea village, by H. Ian Hogbin. American Anthropologist 66:185–186.

GOUINEAU, ANDRE-YVETTE
1959 Laotian cookery. *In* Kingdom of Laos. René de Berval, ed. Saigon: France-Asie.

GOUROU, PIERRE
1936 Les paysans du delta Tonkinois. Paris: Ecole Française d'Extrême-Orient.
1940 L'utilization du sol en Indochine française. Institute of Pacific Relations. Trans. S. H. Guest, E. A. Clark, and K. J. Pelzer, 1945.

GRIAULE, MARCEL
1957 Méthode de l'ethnographie. Paris: Presses Universitaires.

GRIST, D. H.
1959 Rice. London: Longmans.

HAAS, MARY R.
1956 The Thai system of writing. American Council of Learned Societies, Publication Series B, no. 5.

HALL, D. G. E.
1955 A history of Southeast Asia. London: Macmillan.

HALPERN, JOEL MARTIN
  1958 Aspects of village life and culture change in Laos. Prepublication report. New York: Council on Economic and Cultural Affairs.
HANKS, L. M., JR.
  1958 Indifferences to modern education in a Thai farming community. Human Organization 17:9-14.
HOCKETT, CHARLES F.
  1942 A system of descriptive phonology. Language 18:3-21.
HOLMBERG, ALAN R.
  1954 Adventures in culture change. *In* Method and prospective in anthropology. Robert F. Spencer, ed. Minneapolis: University of Minnesota Press.
HOPFEN, H. J.
  1960 Farm implements for arid and tropical regions. Agricultural Development Paper no. 67. Rome: Food and Agriculture Organization of the United Nations.
HOWARD, ALAN
  1963 Land, activity systems, and decision-making models in Rotuma. Ethnology 3:407-440.
INGRAM, JAMES C.
  1955 Economic change in Thailand since 1850. Stanford: Stanford University Press.
IZIKOWITZ, K. G.
  1962 Notes about the Tai. Bulletin of the Museum of Far Eastern Antiquities (Stockholm), no. 34.
JANLEKHA, KAMOL ODD
  1955 A study of the economy of a rice growing village in central Thailand. Bangkok: Ministry of Agriculture, Office of the Undersecretary of State, Division of Agricultural Economics.
JOHNSTON, BRUCE F.
  1951 Agricultural productivity and economic development in Japan. American Economic Review 51:566-593.
JONES, JENKIN
  1948 *Commentary on* Rice cultivation in Asia. American Anthropologist 50:256-282.
JUDD, LAURENCE C.
  1964 Dry rice agriculture in northern Thailand. Data Paper no. 52, Southeast Asia Program. Cornell University (Cornell Thailand Project Interim Report no. 7).
KARDINER, ABRAM, with collaboration of RALPH LINTON, CORA DU BOIS, and JAMES WEST
  1945 The psychological frontiers of society. New York: Columbia University Press.
KATONA, GEORGE
  1951 Expectations and decisions in economic behavior. *In* The policy sciences. Daniel Lerner and Harold D. Lasswell, eds. Stanford: Stanford University Press.

KAUFMAN, HOWARD KEVA
  1960 Bangkhuad: a community study in Thailand. Locust Valley, N.Y.: Association for Asian Studies, monograph no. 10.
KINGSHILL, KONRAD
  1960 Ku Daeng—the red tomb: a village study in northern Thailand. Chiengmai, Thailand.
KNOX, ROBERT
  1681 An historical relation of Ceylon. As reprinted in Ceylon Historical Journal 6, no. 1-4 (July 1956-April 1957). Maharagama, Ceylon.
KROEBER, ALFRED L.
  1948 Anthropology. New York: Harcourt Brace.
KUNSTADTER, PETER, ed.
  1967 Southeast Asian tribes, minorities, and nations. Princeton: Princeton University Press.
LEACH, EDMUND
  1954 Political systems of highland Burma. London: Cambridge University Press.
  1960 The frontiers of "Burma." Comparative Studies in Society and History 3:49-68.
  1961 Pul Eliya: a village in Ceylon. London: Cambridge University Press.
LEBAR, FRANK M., G. C. HICKEY, and J. K. MUSGRAVE
  1964 Ethnic groups of mainland Southeast Asia. New Haven: Human Relations Area Files Press.
LEHMAN, F. K.
  1963 The structure of Chin society. Illinois Studies in Anthropology, no. 3. Urbana: University of Illinois Press.
LE MAY, REGINALD R.
  1926 An Asian arcady: the land and peoples of northern Siam. London: Cambridge University Press.
LEONARD, OLEN, and C. P. LOOMIS
  1941 Culture of a contemporary rural community: El Cerrito, New Mexico. Rural Life Studies, no. 1. Washington: Bureau of Agricultural Economics, Department of Agriculture.
LESSER, ALEXANDER
  1939 Problem versus subject matter as directives of research. American Anthropologist 41:574-582.
LEWIS, OSCAR
  1951 Life in a Mexican village: Tepoztlan restudied. Urbana: University of Illinois Press.
LINTON, RALPH
  1939 The Tanala of Madagascar. *In* The individual and his society. Abram Kardiner, ed. New York: Columbia University Press.
LOCKWOOD, WILLIAM W.
  1955 The economic development of Japan. London.
LOEB, EDWIN J. M., and JAN O. M. BROEK
  1947 Social organization and the longhouse in Southeast Asia. American Anthropologist 49:414-425.

REFERENCES CITED

LOUNSBURY, FLOYD G.
- 1953 Field methods and techniques in linguistics. *In* Anthropology today. A. L. Kroeber, ed. Chicago: University of Chicago Press.
- 1956 A semantic analysis of the Pawnee kinship usage. Language 32:158–194.

LOVE, H. H.
- 1955 Report on rice investigations, 1950–1954. Bangkok: Department of Rice, Ministry of Agriculture.

McCARTHY, PHILLIP J.
- 1957 Introduction to statistical reasoning. New York: McGraw-Hill.

McHALE, THOMAS
- 1960 Personal communication.

MATSUO, TAKANE
- 1954 Rice culture in Japan. Tokyo: Ministry of Agriculture and Forestry.

MAUSS, M.
- 1948 Les techniques et la technologie. Journal de Psychologie Normale et Pathologique 41:71–78.

MOERMAN, MICHAEL
- 1964 Western culture and the Thai way of life. Asia 1:30–51. Reprint 171 of the Institute of International Studies, University of California, Berkeley.
- 1965 Ethnic identification in a complex civilization: who are the Lue? American Anthropologist 6:1215–1230. Reprint 214 of the Institute of International Studies, University of California, Berkeley.
- 1966a Ban Ping's temple: the center of a "loosely structured" society. *In* Anthropological studies of Theravada Buddhism. Yale University Southeast Asia Cultural Report, no. 13. Reprint 213 of the Institute of International Studies, University of California, Berkeley.
- 1966b Kinship and commerce in a Thai-Lue village. Ethnology 5:360–364. Reprint 226 of the Institute of International Studies, University of California, Berkeley.
- 1967a A minority and its government: the Thai-Lue of northern Thailand. *In* Southeast Asian tribes, minorities, and nations. Vol. I. Peter Kunstadter, ed. Princeton: Princeton University Press. Reprint 249 of the Institute of International Studies, University of California, Berkeley.
- 1967b Being Lue: uses and abuses of ethnic identification. American Ethnological Society, proceedings of the 1967 spring meeting. Forthcoming.

MURDOCK, G. P., C. S. FORD, A. E. HUDSON, R. KENNEDY, L. W. SIMMONS, and J. W. M. WHITING
- 1950 Outline of cultural materials. New Haven: Human Relations Area Files Press.

MUSCAT, ROBERT J.
- 1966 Development strategy in Thailand. New York: Praeger.

NADEL, S. F.
- 1957 The theory of social structure. Glencoe: Free Press.

NAGAI, ISABURO
  1959 Japonica rice: its breeding and culture. Tokyo: Yokendo.
NASH, MANNING
  1957 Cultural persistences and social structure: the Mesoamerican calendar survivals. Southwestern Journal of Anthropology 13:149–155.
OHKAWA, KAZUSHI, and HENRY ROSOVSKY
  1964 The role of agriculture in modern Japanese economic development. *In* Agriculture and economic development. Carl Eicher and Lawrence Witt, eds. New York: McGraw-Hill.
PAVIE, AUGUSTE
  1901 Mission Pavie Indo-chine: géographie et voyages. Paris: Ernest Leroux.
PELZER, KARL J.
  1945 Pioneer settlement in the Asiatic tropics. New York: American Geographical Society, Special Publication no. 29.
  1958 Land utilization in the humid tropics: agriculture. *In* Proceedings of the Ninth Pacific Science Congress. Bangkok.
PENDLETON, ROBERT L.
  1962 Thailand: aspects of landscape and life. New York: Duell, Sloan and Pearce. An American Geographical Society Handbook.
PFANNER, DAVID E., and JASPER INGERSOLL
  1962 Theravada Buddhism and village economic behavior. Journal of Asian Studies 21:341–361.
PHETSARATH, TIAO MAHA UPAHAT
  1959 The Laotian calendar. *In* Kingdom of Laos. René de Berval, ed. Saigon: France-Asie.
PHILLIPS, HERBERT P.
  1965 Thai peasant personality. Berkeley and Los Angeles: University of California Press.
PICHARN, PHYA VANPROK
  1923 List of common trees, shrubs, etc. in Siam. Bangkok.
PLATENIUS, HANS
  1963 The North-East of Thailand: its problems and potentialities. Bangkok: World Bank Advisory Group Report to the National Economic Development Board.
PRESBYTERIAN BOARD OF PUBLICATIONS
  1884 Siam and Laos as seen by our Western missionaries. Philadelphia.
RAJADHON, PHYA ANUMAN
  1961 The life of the farmer. *In* Life and ritual in old Siam. William J. Gedney, ed. and trans. New Haven: Human Relations Area Files Press.
REDFIELD, ROBERT
  1956 Peasant society and culture. Chicago: University of Chicago Press, Phoenix Books.
RHIND, D.
  1959 The genetics of paddy. *In* Rice, by D. H. Grist. London: Longmans Green.

REFERENCES CITED 221

RIVET, PAUL
 1953 Préface de la première édition. *In* Les pays tropicaux, by Pierre Gourou. Paris: Presses Universitaires.
RUTTAN, V. W., A. SOOTHIPAN, and E. C. VENEGAS
 1966 Changes in rice growing in the Philippines and Thailand. World Crops (March):1–16.
SAENZ-LASCANO-RUIZ
 1950 Contributions à l'étude des riz gluants. Saigon: Archives de l'office indochinois du riz, no. 28.
SANTIWONGSE, YAI SUAPHAN
 1913 An outline of rice cultivation in Siam. Bangkok: Ministry of Agriculture.
SCHULTZ, THEODORE W.
 1964 Transforming traditional agriculture. New Haven: Yale University Press.
SCHUTZ, ALFRED
 1953 Common-sense and scientific interpretation of human action. Philosophy and Phenomenological Research 14:1–37.
SHARP, LAURISTON
 1952 Steel axes for stone age Australians. *In* Human problems in technological change. Edward H. Spicer, ed. New York: Russell Sage Foundation.
SHARP, L., L. HANKS, R. TEXTOR, O. JANLEKHA, et al.
 1953 Siamese rice village. Bangkok: Cornell Research Center.
SRISIWASDI, BUNCHUEY
 1952 Sam-sip chaat thi Chiengraj [The thirty races of Chiengrai]. Bangkok. (In Thai.)
 N.d. Thaj sibsongpanna [The Thai of the Sip Song Panna]; Lyy khon thaj naj pratheed ciin [The Lue: a Thai people in China]. Bangkok. (In Thai.) 2 vols.
SWANSON, GUY E.
 1960 The birth of the gods. Ann Arbor: University of Michigan Press.
TERRA, G. J. A.
 1952–53 Some sociological aspects of agriculture in Southeast Asia. Indonesie 6:297–316, 439–455.
THAILAND, GOVERNMENT OF
 1947 A compilation of the results of experimental work on rice. Phraya Bhojakara and Y. S. Israsena, compilers. Bangkok: Department of Rice. Mimeographed.
 1957 Agriculture in Thailand. Bangkok: Ministry of Agriculture.
 1958 Final rice crop report for Thailand for the 1956 season. Bangkok: Department of Rice.
 1959 Report on economic survey of rice farmers in Nakorn Pathom province during 1955–56 rice season. Bangkok: Office of the Undersecretary, Agricultural Research and Farm Survey Section.
 1961 Agriculture in Thailand. Bangkok: Ministry of Agriculture.
 1965 Annual report on 1962 rice production in Thailand. Bangkok: Department of Rice, Ministry of Agriculture.

WALLACE, ANTHONY F. C., and JOHN ATKINS
1960 The meaning of kinship terms. American Anthropologist 62:58–79.
WHARTON, CLIFTON R., JR.
1965 Research on agricultural development in Southeast Asia. Monograph no. 1 for the Research Program of the Agricultural Development Council. New York: Agricultural Development Council.
WICKIZER, V. D., and M. K. BENNETT
1941 The rice economy of monsoon Asia. Stanford: Stanford University Food Research Institute.
WIJEYEWARDENE, GEHAN
1965 A note on irrigation and agriculture in a north Thailand village. In Felicitation volumes of Southeast Asian studies presented to His Highness Prince Dhaninivat Kromamun Bidyalabh Bridhyakorn. II:255–259. Bangkok: Siam Society.
WISSMANN, HERMAN VON
1943 Süd-Yunnan als Teilraum Südostasiens. Schriften zur Geopolitik, no. 22. Heidelberg: Kurt Vowinckel.
WITTFOGEL, KARL A.
1957 Oriental despotism. New Haven: Yale University Press.
WOLF, ERIC R.
1955 Types of Latin American peasantry: a preliminary discussion. American Anthropologist 57:452–471.
1956 Aspects of group relations in a complex society: Mexico. American Anthropologist 58:1065–1078.
1957 Closed corporate peasant communities in Mesoamerica and central Java. Southwestern Journal of Anthropology 13:1–18.
ZIMMERMAN, CARLE CLARK
1931 Siam rural economic survey, 1930–31. Bangkok: Bangkok Times Press.

Index

Agricultural Development Council, 20-21, 27
Agricultural techniques: Japan and Java compared, 81-83, 180, 186; in Japan, 87, 195
Agriculture. *See* Rice farming
aw haeng, 117

Ban Ping, 4, 5, 8-9
Boserup, Ester, 86-87
Broadcast sowing: timing of, 64, 65, 66; techniques of, 64-65; reseeding, 65, 66-67; knowledge acquired for, 76; yield of, 161-162, 185
Buddhism: as institution, 18; and ecclesiastical information, 77; rites against pests, 77-78, 79, 80; Lent, 130

Carts: for farm tasks, 41, 52, 56, 58, 64, 202; cost of, 56; for trading trips, 57, 58, 75, 134; ownership of, 58, 75; access to, 58, 75-76; hiring of, 58, 76, 157, 173; regional variants of, 75n
Cash: as resource, 80, 86, 98; value assigned to, 105, 126, 141; for labor, 129, 133-134, 141; as input, 146, 153-154, 158-159; costs of farming, 172-174, 202
Categories: anthropological, 23-29, 191; native, 84-87, 141-144, 191
Chiengkham district, 2, 4, 5, 6, 7, 13, 14
Chiengkham town, 2, 5, 6-7
Chiengkhawng, 2, 5, 6, 7n
Chiengmai, 2, 4, 5, 55, 57, 72n, 75
Chiengmuan, 13, 91
Chiengrai, 2, 4, 5, 7
Chinese, occupations of, 8, 49
coj, 116-117
Commercial crops, 68-69, 187, 196
Commercialization, 16, 53, 107, 111, 133, 136, 191-193
"Commodity," 92, 94, 105, 112, 192
Cooperative farming (*lo*), 117, 126
Cornell, 16, 18
Costs and returns, 146, 153-154, 158-159
Credit, 74-75, 80, 86, 181
Cultural change, 187-188
Culture, 22, 185, 192

Cutch production, 104

Debt, 76, 84, 137, 140
Decision making, 26, 142, 189-190, 191
Dependent incompleteness, 20
Distant flood field. *See* Thunglor
Distant irrigated field: location and acreage of, 34-35; irrigation of, 43; farming techniques on, 43-44; acquisition of, 92, 96; rental of, 100; tillage labor on, 119-121; transplanting labor on, 123-124; harvest labor on, 125; reasons for farming, 182-183
"Dividend," 146, 172-174
Domain, 23-29, 190
Double cropping, 84
Drought, 77, 155
Dry plowing, 43, 171
Dry rice farming. *See* Swidden farming

"Eating rice" (*xaw kin*), 35, 47, 49, 69, 98
Economic development: and peasants' attitudes, 20-21, 28, 143-144; and farming operations, 80-87; and labor productivity, 82-83; and capital, 83; and government, 83, 87, 143; and anthropology, 83-84, 86, 87, 142; and native categories, 84-87, 141-144; and middlemen, 140, 144; and resource components, 141-144
Epstein, T. Scarlett, 187
Ethnicity: pride in, 9, 92; and variations in farming techniques, 41, 44, 53, 55, 56; manipulation of, 71, 72
Ethnography, 21-26
"Exchange," 117
Extracommunity relations, 26, 32

Farmers' almanac, 59-60
Farming. *See* Rice farming
Farm management: choice among field types, 142-143, 154-157, 182-183; combining field types, 147-149, 189
"Fellowship," 116
Fertility, 161-163
Fertilizer, 36, 42, 49-50, 81, 187, 188
Firth, Raymond, 142

Fishing, 64, 65, 68, 104
Flooding: at Thunglor, 15, 61, 185; at home flood field, 43, 61; as danger, 60, 77, 80, 155; in 1961, 63
Forest farms (*na pa*), 96, 126n, 142-143, 160, 181, 186
"Fun," 16, 67-68, 124, 181

Geertz, Clifford, 81-82, 83-84, 186
"Gift" (*pan*), 117
Glutinous rice, 11, 19, 68, 81, 195-197
Goodenough, Ward H., 26, 27
Gourou, Pierre, 18
Great Field. *See* Home irrigated field
Green rice, 67, 74, 181

Harrowing, 38-39, 157
Harvesting: at home fields, 41, 68; as critical period, 45-46; timing of tasks of, 46-47, 67; at Thunglor, 67-68; as "fun," 68, 124; labor, 124-126, 166-168, 171
Haw, 8, 55
Hill tribes, 4, 7-8
Home flood field: location and acreage of, 33-35; farming operations on, 43; tractor plowed, 63; acquisition of, 95
Home irrigated field: location and acreage of, 33-35; fertilizing, 36, 49-50, 155; irrigation of, 36-37, 50-53; seeding of, 37-38, 53-54; tillage of, 38-39, 54-55, 118-119, 122; transplanting on, 39-40, 55, 123; weeding of, 40; harvesting of, 41, 55-56, 125; acquisition of, 94-95; rental, 100-103; timing labor demands for, 147-148; reasons for farming, 182
Home rainfall field: location and acreage of, 33-35; farming difficulties on, 42-43; tractor plowed, 63, 66; for peanuts, 69; acquisition of, 95; harvesting labor on, 124
Huejkhawkam, 5, 6, 92

Inheritance: of land, 92-94; of house, 94; and rental, 101-102
Insecticides, 77-79, 80
Institutions, 25, 96-97, 141-142
Inundated rice. *See* Wet rice farming
Involution, 81-83, 186
Irrigation: on home fields, 36-37, 42, 43; tools, 36-37, 50; on distant fields, 43; government interest in, 50, 51-52; local organization of, 50-53; and concrete dam, 51-52; labor expenditure for, 166-168, 170, 201, 202

Janlekha, Kamol Odd, 18

kha-cang, 117
Kinship: in anthropology, 25, 28-29; and commercial relations, 58, 68, 72, 75-76, 113, 118-119, 121, 127-129, 135, 141, 159, 191; importance of, for trade ventures, 97, 106; in Pul Eliya, 106
—in family life: multifamily longhouse, 97-98, 135; solidarity of sibling group, 105-106, 115; relations between generations, 106, 108, 115
—in labor mobilization: irrigation, 52-53; carting, 58; clearing land, 92-93, 106; as labor resource, 98, 127-133, 135, 141; fellowship as reward, 116; *coj*, 117, 121-124, 129, 136; tillage season, 118-121, 135; transplanting, 122-123, 136-137; tillage task, 122-124; cooperative farming (*lo*), 126; harvest, 126, 128, 131-132; Myangkhawp Lue, 137-138
—in land acquisition: clearing, 92-93, 106; inheritance, 93-95; purchase from siblings, 94, 106; gift, 95, 98; as acquisition resource, 96, 99, 106, 114; rental, 101-104, 111-113, 115

Labor: as resource, 92-93, 96, 98, 141-142, 164; as input, 146, 153-154; adjustive devices, 148-150
—division of: by ethnic group, 7-8; by sex, 39-40, 55, 120, 121, 122-123, 126n, 141
—expenditure: decrease, 80; for townsmen, 138-140; at irrigation, 166-168, 170; at harvest, 166-168, 171; on various fields, 170-172; at tillage, 171; at transplanting, 171
—hired: for clearing land, 92-93; professional farm workers, 118, 135, 137; seasonal, 118-120, 125, 126, 137-138; daily, 123, 124, 125, 126
—mobilization: influenced by landholding, 116; and resources in kin, 118-119, 121, 122, 123, 129-132, 133, 135-137, 141, 182; and outsiders, 123-124, 133, 134, 137-141, 182; and task difficulty, 124, 126-128, 141; and resources in cash, 129, 133-134; and plot size, 129-130, 141; in central Thailand, 135
—productivity: and tractor, 80, 168-170, 171-172, 205; and casual farming practices, 80n, 81; in Java, 82; and economic development, 82, 164; in Japan, 83; villagers' view of, 183-184; in Tonkin, 205-206; and mechanization, 205-207
—relations: at home fields, 70-74, 135, 141; at Thunglor, 136, 141

—rewards for: defined, 116-117; decisions between, 117, 128, 141; for tillage, 118-124; to kin, 118-119, 120-123, 124-125, 126; to nonkin, 119, 120, 121, 123-124, 125, 126; by sex, 126
—supply and demand: at various fields, 79; shortage, 81, 86, 136; tillage season, 116, 121-124; harvest season, 116, 124-126; seasonal, 116, 128-129, 140; relation of, to kin, 133
Lampai, 106
Lampang, 2, 14, 55, 57, 75
Land: measurement of, 63, 67, 99-100, 201; ownership of, 84, 85, 105-108; as cause for dispute, 104, 114; as input, 146, 153-154; price of, 154n, 156; fertility of, 155, 156
—acquisition of: availability of, 81, 85-86, 91, 92, 104-105, 114, 116, 140; by clearing, 91; primary and secondary, 92, 114; by inheritance, 93, 94; by claiming, 93, 99; by purchase, 94, 95-96, 105, 142-143; by gift, 95, 112; kinship resources, 96-99, 105-108; by young, 97-98; through outsiders, 98-99; effects of, on family life, 105-108, 115; through cooperation, 106; dependence on townsmen, 108-110, 115; techniques of, 114
—clearing of: at Thunglor, 63, 64, 66, 68, 142-143; Ban Ping's history of, 91-92, 114; cooperation in, 92-93, 97, 98
—registration of: filing claim papers, 93; protection of title, 99-100, 109-110, 114; attitude to government, 110, 115; importance of headman, 110, 115
—rental of: at distant irrigated field, 100; at Thunglor, 100; reasons for, 100; price of, 100-101, 110-111, 115; at home irrigated field, 100-103, 182; within and outside village, 101-104; ethnic factors, 101-104, 110; kinship factors, 101-104, 111-113, 115; size of plot, 101-104, 114; in India, 103; as commercial transaction, 104; as tie to other villages, 110; in central Thailand, 113; in kind, 113-114
Lao, 3, 53
Leach, Edmund, 23, 28
Linguistics, 23-24
lo, 117
Longhouse, 97-98, 106, 114, 135
Lue: population, 3n; houses, 8; dress, 8-9, 72; eating customs, 10, 19; history, 12-16; farming techniques, 41, 44, 53, 55, 56, 80; marriage and residence rules, 92, 107, 130-131; rental to, 101, 110; laborers, 133, 137-138

Maize, 143
Marriage, 107, 130-131
Merit (*bun*), 59, 67, 79, 175
Miao, 8
Middlemen, 109, 139, 140
Myang Khawp, 5, 6, 137-138

Nan, 12, 13
Ngaw, 13, 16
North Thailand: appearance of, 2, 4-5, 75n, 195; rice yields in, 14, 195, 196
Nutritional density, 84-85

Officials. *See* Villagers
Ordinary (hard) rice, 68-69, 195, 196, 197
Oxen: for trade, 14; for plow, 54

pan, 117
Patron-client relations, 71-74, 108-109
Peanuts, 69, 77
Peasant: "peasantness," 17, 19-20, 191, 199; and economic development, 20-21, 28, 143-144; as rational, 27, 69, 153, 189-190; vs. farmer, 143, 181
Pests, 66, 67, 77-79, 157
Phayao, 2, 5, 6, 7, 14, 54, 57, 75
Phong, 13
Plow agriculture: definition of, 36; operations, 38-39, 80n; animals used in, 38, 54, 63; dry plowing, 43, 171; timing of tasks, 44-47, 79; knowledge of, 47-49, 78-79; tillage tasks, 54-55; casualness, 81; tillage labor, 118-124, 171; vs. tractor agriculture, 157-158. *See also* Home irrigated field; Rice farming
"Pointing" at fields, 62-63, 67-68
Pong, 5, 6
Population: raids, 12-13; scarcity, 13; density, 84, 85; in Thailand, 85; pressures, 92, 114, 141-142
"Private" (*lork*) rice, 92, 97, 98, 114, 116, 129, 136, 192
Productive inputs, 84-87
"Productivity," 146, 163-172

Quantitative comparisons, 204-207
Quantitative data, 198-203
Quantitative techniques, 158, 198-207

Rainfall field. *See* Home rainfall field
Rainfall prediction, 60
Rajadhon, Phya Anuman, 18, 47, 54
Reaping, 41, 55
"Reciprocity," 53, 58, 75, 76, 80, 114, 117, 136, 137, 141, 192
Residence rules, 92, 107, 130-131

Rice: and social roles, 10-11, 16; sale and trade of, 14, 16, 68-69, 74, 117-126 *passim*, 174, 187, 196; milling properties, 47, 197; varieties, 53-54, 150, 155, 189; price of, 68-69, 80, 196; quality of, 81, 195-197; maturation date, 148, 197; grain types of, 150, 195-197

Rice farming *(het na)*: importance of, to villagers, 9-11, 17, 96; cycle, 10, 164-165, 167; importance of, to anthropology, 17; kinds of, 17-19, 195; requires rational choice, 18, 60-61; as domain, 21, 24, 190-191; skills, 47-49; knowledge of, 47-49, 76-79; as career, 104, 114, 181; professional farm workers in, 118, 135, 137. *See also* Farm management; Home irrigated field; Plow agriculture; Tractor agriculture; Wet rice farming

Rituals, 59, 77-78, 79, 80

Roads, 5-7, 14, 54, 57, 134

School instruction, 58

Seed: selection, 53-54, 81; culling, 64; criteria, 152-153; ratio to harvest, 175-176

Seeding: techniques on home fields, 37-38; seedbed preparation, 37-38, 40n, 42, 201; techniques on distant fields, 44; timing of, 45-46; dry seed drilling, 53; labor mobilization for, 121; rates per unit of land, 205, 206

"Selling" rice *(xaw xai)*, 34, 47, 65, 98

Semi-irrigated field: location and acreage of, 33-35; agricultural operations on, 42; acquisition of, 95; harvesting labor on, 124-125

Shocking, 41

Siamese, 3. *See also* Tai; Thai

sio, 13, 14, 72

Sip Song Panna, 12, 15, 59

Spirits *(phi)*: for village protection, 8; belief in, 9, 91-92; of dam, 50; of rice, 59

Sticky rice. *See* Glutinous rice

Sugar growing, 104

Swidden farming, 18, 53, 84

Tai, 3, 4

Technology, 16, 26, 27-28, 32, 185

term, 117

Thai, 3n, 4

Thailand: administrative division, 4n; population, 85; history, 143; regional differences, 195. *See also* North Thailand

Therng, 5, 6, 62

Threshing: at home irrigated field, 41; ethnic variations of, 41, 56; techniques, 55-56; at Thunglor, 65

Thunglor: flooding, 15, 61, 185; first farming attempts at, 15, 92; location and acreage of, 34-35, 62; measuring, 62-63, 67-68, 201; clearing, 63, 64, 66, 93, 201; broadcast sowing, 64-65, 68, 201; harvest, 68, 125-126, 132-133; acquisition, 95-96; rental, 100; labor, 136, 149, 171-172; choice, 183; in 1965, 185-186. *See also* Tractor agriculture

Tillage. *See* Home irrigated field; Labor; Plow agriculture

Tillering, 39, 81

Tools, 36-37, 41, 50, 54, 55, 56-58, 62, 205

Tractor agriculture: plowing schedule, 62, 63, 73-74, 79, 80; tasks involved, 62-67, 80n; timing of tasks in, 65-66, 79; and nonvillagers, 67, 69-75, 76, 87, 108-109, 138-140, 191; knowledge of, 76-79; advantages and disadvantages of, 79, 157-158, 171-172, 185, 186; and labor productivity, 79, 168-173; in 1965, 185-186. *See also* Rice farming; Thunglor; Tractors

Tractors: where used, 15, 16, 62-63, 66, 147-148, 185; acceptance of, 59, 62, 80, 87, 186; ownership of, 62, 69-71, 158; and change, 62, 79, 185-193 *passim*; decision to use, 63, 65, 66, 69-70, 157-158, 185, 186, 187; fee for, 63, 70, 74, 76, 140, 173; access to, 69, 70-75

Trading ventures, 14, 57-58, 60, 72, 75, 97, 99, 106, 114

Transplanting: description of, 39-40; sex division of labor, 39-40, 55; as critical period, 45-46; ethnic variation in, 55; labor mobilization for, 122-124, 123n, 136-137; villager's view of benefits of, 148; planting density, 156; relation of, to yield, 157, 161-162; labor expenditure in, 171

Uprooting, 39-40, 122

Villagers: and officials, 10-11, 51-52, 69, 87, 143-144, 188, 199; and townsmen, 15, 50, 67, 69-75, 80, 140, 191; economic base of, 70, 73, 109, 141; knowledge, 71, 76-79, 188-189; and businessmen, 87, 188-189; as entrepreneurs, 143-144

"Wage" *(kha-cang)*, 117

Wage rates, 123, 126, 128

Weeding, 40, 81, 162, 207

Wet rice farming: and diversity of cultures, 17; as central Thai institution, 18; literature on, 18; vs. dry farming, 53. *See also* Rice farming

Winnowing, 41

Yao, 7-8

Yield: in North Thailand, 14, 204; defined, 146; as criterion, 154, 159, 174; dependability of, 155, 157, 163; height, 155-156, 175; when transplanting, 157, 161-162; where broadcasting, 157, 161-162; and maturation type, 159; on various fields, 159-161; and soil fertility, 161-163; villagers' comparative information on, 174-175, 177-178; ratio of seed to, 175-176; in Thailand, 204-205

Yuan: as Tai, 3; in Chiengkham, 7-9; farming techniques, 53, 55, 56; and labor, 110, 123, 133, 138; rental to, 110-111

www.ingramcontent.com/pod-product-compliance
Lightning Source LLC
Chambersburg PA
CBHW021703230426
43668CB00008B/705